T0144856

The Next Horizon

To Conrad, Daniel and Rupert

The Next Horizon

CHRIS BONINGTON

Vertebrate Publishing, Sheffield
www.v-publishing.co.uk

The Next Horizon

Chris Bonington

 **Vertebrate Publishing**
Crescent House, 228 Psalter Lane, Sheffield S11 8UT, United Kingdom
www.v-publishing.co.uk

First published in Great Britain in 1973 by Victor Gollancz.
This paperback edition first published in 2016 by Vertebrate Publishing.

Maps drawn by Wendy Bonington.

Chris Bonington has asserted his rights under the Copyright, Designs and Patents Act 1988 to be identified as the author of this work.

This book is a work of non-fiction based on the life, experiences and recollections of Chris Bonington. In some limited cases the names of people, places, dates and sequences or the detail of events have been changed solely to protect the privacy of others. The author has stated to the publishers that, except in such minor respects not affecting the substantial accuracy of the work, the contents of the book are true.

A CIP catalogue record for this book is available from the British Library.

ISBN 978-1-911342-17-5 (Paperback)
ISBN 978-1-910240-88-5 (eBook)

Every effort has been made to obtain the necessary permissions with reference to copyright material, both illustrative and quoted. We apologise for any omissions in this respect and will be pleased to make the appropriate acknowledgements in any future edition.

Printed and bound by Lightning Source UK Ltd.

Contents

1 Chilean Expedition

The two trucks rattled and bounced over the rough dirt road in a swirl of dust that was instantly whipped away by the blast of the wind. On either side of the road was a forest of dead trees, a graveyard of whitened skeletons with limbs twisted by incessant wind and bleached by sun and weather; a sky filled with a fleet of great sausage-like clouds, brown-grey zeppelins driven in from the Pacific by the constant fury of the Roaring Forties. In the distance, just visible above the petrified forest, were the mountains – jagged dark shapes that seemed dwarfed by the high vault of the sky.

It was the 28th November 1962 and we were on the last leg of our journey to climb the Central Tower of Paine. It didn't matter that we were cold and uncomfortable in the back of the lorry, sandwiched between packing cases and the canvas roof, for we were very nearly at the end of our journey, soon to see the mountain we had to climb. This first glimpse of the objective is one of the most exciting moments of any expedition. Up to that point there is always a feeling of unreality about the entire enterprise. It is difficult to believe that one will ever overcome all the mundane problems of raising money, begging equipment; it is even more difficult to imagine the jump from England to mountains in some distant corner of the earth.

We had spent over three weeks travelling from England, firstly by passenger liner to Valparaiso in Chile, then on an exhilarating flight down the spine of the Andes to Punta Arenas, a small windswept town on the Straits of Magellan, and now we were driving north, across the pampas, towards our objective.

The truck pulled up a small hill and round a shoulder; the ground, grass clad, with only the occasional lonely finger of a dead tree, stretched down into a shallow valley, rising gently on the other side to a low ridge. The pampas was like an Atlantic swell, rolling away into the foothills of the Paine Massif, dusty green, and yet the air was so clear that you could pick out each windswept shrub and protruding spine of rock. And there, some twenty miles away, was the Central Tower of Paine – a slender blade of rock that at this distance seemed dominated by the squat mass of the mountains round it.

It was this peak that had triggered my resolve to abandon a conventional career and make a living around climbing, but at that instant, as we gazed at the distant nobble of rock which was to be the focus of our lives for the next few weeks, I was filled with a simple excitement at the prospect of tackling it.

One of the features of climbing is the intensity of concentration it exacts. In its basic form, if you are poised on a rock wall a hundred feet above the ground, all other thoughts and problems are engulfed by the need for absolute concentration. There is no room for anything other than the problems of staying in contact with the rock and negotiating the next few moves. In this respect, climbing offers an escape, or perhaps it would be better to describe it as a relaxation from everyday worries of human relationships, money or jobs. This relaxation lasts for longer than just those moments when you are actually climbing and life is in jeopardy.

Sitting on a ledge, belaying one's partner, senses are extra acute; the feel of the rock under hand, of the wind and sun, the shape of the hills – all these are perceived with an extra intensity. Absorption in immediate surroundings once again excludes one's everyday life. On an expedition the same withdrawal from everyday affairs takes place, but here the expedition becomes a tiny little world of its own with, in microcosm, between its members, all the tensions and conflict that can take place in the larger world. The all-consuming aim is to climb the mountain of one's choice and this transcends in importance anything that might be happening beyond it.

For the next few weeks nothing mattered to me but this distant tower of rock and the small group of people who were concerned in climbing it.

There were nine of us altogether, seven climbers, two wives (one of them my own), and a three-year-old child. Wendy, Elaine and young Martin were not part of the expedition but inevitably filled part of the story. Barrie Page, the leader of the expedition, was a geologist and had visited the Paine Group two years before as a member of a scientific expedition. With him had been two other members of our group, Derek Walker and Vic Bray. They had made a map of the area and carried out a geological survey, but they had been enthralled by the Towers of Paine: three magnificent granite spires, set in the midst of some of the most exciting rock scenery in South America. The smallest, the Northern Tower, had been climbed by an Italian expedition in 1958, but the Central and Southern Towers were unclimbed. The Central Tower was especially attractive, forming a perfect rock spire, sheer on every side. They didn't have the equipment to tackle it but resolved to return. Barrie had invited Don Whillans and myself. I had at first refused because of my new job with Unilever, but had then realised that I could not resist the opportunity. The sixth member of the team was John Streetley, who had had a mercurial climbing career in the mid-fifties while studying at Cambridge, and had then returned to his native Trinidad to build up a successful business. He was going to join us later in the expedition. Ian Clough, with whom I had climbed the North Wall of the Eiger that summer, had joined us at the last minute, giving up a place he had at a teachers' training college, and paying his own fare out.

Our little convoy came to a halt at a police check-post – it was like a small

Customs point, with a hut by the road and a red and white drop-bar barring our way. There were two carabineros in neat grey uniforms with pistols at their sides. They seemed almost to expect us. The chief, lean, tough-looking and very tanned, asked Barrie something in Spanish. He got out some papers; the carabinero looked at them but didn't seem satisfied and started to grill Barrie. The other carabinero, a great slob of a man who reminded me of pictures I had seen of Hermann Goering, just looked bored.

At first the rest of us had taken no notice, thinking that our passage through the checkpoint would be a routine matter, but we could quickly sense Barrie's growing excitement and the hostility of the carabineros. We gathered round, tensed and anxious.

'What's up, Barrie?' asked Don.

'Oh, just a bit of bureaucracy,' said Barrie, and kept arguing.

'Seems to be more than that to me,' said Don. 'Why won't the buggers let us through? We've got permission to climb the Tower, haven't we?'

'Of course we have,' said Barrie.

'Well haven't you got it with you in writing?'

'We don't need it. We've got blanket permission to go into the Paine Massif,' said Barrie. 'They're just being awkward.'

'Well they should bloody well know, shouldn't they? Either you need permission or you don't.'

There was something about Barrie's manner – he was a born salesman, effervescent, fast talking and very difficult to pin down – that was the very opposite to Don, who likes everything spelt out in black and white. The argument developed into a three-cornered battle between Barrie, Don and the carabineros, with very little communication between any of them. The post was at the Estancia Castillo, a big ranch managed, as many of the estancias are, by an Englishman. He eventually came to our rescue and talked us through the police post, calming our ragged nerves with a very English afternoon tea in his home. Set in the great empty space of the pampas, Mr Saunders' house was what I imagine an English country house of forty years ago must have been like, with its array of servants, tea in a silver service and big soft armchairs nestling on a thick pile carpet. Our own appearance, modern-day climbers, must have seemed a little incongruous. We were still agitated by the brush with the police, the possibility that having come so close we could be stopped from reaching the Tower. We had already heard that an Italian climbing expedition was coming out later in the season. Don read Machiavellian plots into what had just happened.

'The Italians could be behind this,' he said. 'Are you sure you asked for permission to climb the Tower, Barrie?'

'Of course I did; it was all tied up in the general application. I was talking to the authorities in Santiago about it.'

'Yeah, but what about having it down in black and white. Cut out the waffle, and let's see your application.'

'What on earth's the point? I haven't got it here anyway.'

'Well, there you are, if you haven't got permission in black and white I reckon those Itis are behind this. They'll try to stop us any way they can; I've seen it before.'

One obvious problem was the ambiguity of the title of our expedition. When Barrie, Vic and Derek had been to the area before, they had called themselves the South Patagonia Survey Expedition. To maximise on any goodwill gained by this earlier expedition, Barrie had named ours 'The South Patagonia Survey Expedition II 1962/3'. Don, therefore, had grounds for his suspicion that Barrie could have failed to make a specific application to climb the Central Tower.

And the argument went on and on; it had developed into a witchhunt against Barrie with, I suspect, very little justice; but we all wanted a scapegoat to ease our fears. The Saunders just looked bewildered and seemed quite relieved when we continued our journey.

Another twenty miles over open grassland, with the massif of the Paine getting ever bigger on the horizon, and we reached Estancia Cerro Guido. This was run by another British family, the Neilsons. By European standards it was huge, with 100,000 head of sheep and covering 300 square miles. Both the Estancias, and indeed the bulk of Chilean Patagonia, were owned by a single company that had originally been under British control but had been turned over to the Chileans. The Chilean Government had then forced the British to sell off some of its lands, but it remained a landowner of immense power. Most of their farms were still managed by Britons, who lived at a high standard of living with practically no security. Their pay was not particularly high, yet they received their keep and a lavish entertainment allowance so that they could look after guests sent down by the company. In this way they were professional hosts as well as sheep farmers.

Theo Neilson was a tall, distinguished-looking man, with an air of sadness, almost defeat, about him. His wife, Marie, bubbled with vitality and obviously loved plenty of people around. They gave us a wonderfully warm welcome, put us up for the night, and that evening we had a magnificent dinner; yet it seemed strange to be sitting around a formal dinner table, being waited on by uniformed waitresses, here in the middle of the pampas. I felt guilty about my impatience with the long-drawn-out meal and conversation; an impatience caused partly by the fact that I am shy about talking in a big group. But more than this was a longing to be beneath the open sky, close to the grass and earth, without the need to make polite conversation to one's next-door neighbour.

But the next morning we set out on the final leg of our journey to the base of the Paine. The rough dirt track curled through undulating hills, past little rock outcrops and the skeletons of dead trees. Pink flamingo rose laboriously from a small lake as our truck rattled past. Big woolly sheep browsed on the short coarse grass, and horses, temporarily free, gambolled over the pampas. I had a feeling of release and excited anticipation in the clear morning air, glimpsing, at each bend in the road, the mountain we had come so far to climb. As we drew closer, the spire of the Central Tower seemed as slender as ever, the rock compact, without any sign of weakness. I just prayed that Barrie was right and that there was a way up the other side.

The site of our base camp was near a small estancia nestling immediately below the mountains. It reminded me of a Scottish hill-farm, with its little two-storied stone-built house, corrugated iron buildings and wooden sheep-pens. It seemed to blend into the landscape, becoming an integral part of this wild and lonely country. Our own camp was in a coppice of stunted trees and scrub, sheltered from the wind by a couple of low hummocks. As we unpacked boxes of gear and food, all the tension of the previous day was replaced with the excited anticipation of the climb to come. We had chosen Barrie as a scape-goat for our own uncertainty when it had seemed that we might be prevented from attempting the climb, but with the uncertainty removed these doubts were put aside. As leader of the expedition, Barrie was in an invidious position anyway, since Don, Ian and myself knew each other well and had considerably more climbing experience than he had. However, because of the compact size of the expedition, this barely mattered. A party of six on a comparatively small mountain can afford to come to decisions in a democratic way, allowing leaders to emerge through the natural process of personality and experience. Through the course of the expedition, decisions were reached through discussion with comparatively little argument.

For the rest of that day we were immersed in the process of unpacking, and that evening were invited to a barbecue by Juan Radic, the owner of the neighbouring estancia. It was a magical experience, in complete contrast to the formal dinner party we had had the previous evening. It was held in a sheltered arbour of trees at the side of the house. Cows' horns were nailed to the trunks; chairs were formed from tree stumps and in the centre of the glade was a smouldering wood fire, over which a spitted lamb, opened out on a frame, was turned from time to time. The aroma of the lamb mingled with the wood smoke, the scent of the trees and of the earth.

Juan Radic was a big man, now going to fat with the hint of a pot belly. He was of Jugoslav stock and had started the farm from scratch, but now he was able to spend most of his time in Punta Arenas, leaving the day-to-day running of the farm to his brother, Pedro. One felt he was more a businessman than a farmer, but Pedro was everything that one imagined a gaucho to be: tall, lean and hard, with a face battered by the winds; strong yet lonely, with a strange tinge of melancholy. He could have stepped straight out of a cowboy movie, with his scarlet shirt, black baggy breeches and sombrero, and bristling black moustachio. That night it was Pedro who tended the meal, basting the sizzling meat with a sauce made from mint and garlic, passing round the skin sack of wine which we squeezed to send a fine jet into the backs of our throats. There were no glasses, no knives or forks. The only concessions to civilisation were some chipped plates and a big bowl of salad: the only available vegetable in that part of Patagonia, a form of coarse, pleasingly bitter-tasting lettuce.

All the newcomers were initiated into Patagonian life by trying to squirt some wine down their throats from the wine sack – a knack which took some acquiring. Pedro then sprinkled a few mysterious drops over each of our heads and made the sign of the cross. And then the feast began. We tore the meat from the carcase with our fingers, sat in the cool dark, warm-lit by the smouldering fire, and gorged ourselves on succulent tender meat; squirted wine down open throats. Next morning in my diary I wrote:

> The real thing about the night was the feel of it – the atmosphere. Eating because you want to eat, tearing the meat, held in greasy hands, with your teeth. Drinking when you want to, talking naturally, because you have something to say; listening because you are interested. This was a real enjoyment that went to the depth of my being.

And next morning we had splitting hangovers, but we set out all the same for the Central Tower of Paine. The Towers were hidden from our base camp by the rounded bulk of the Paine Chico. To reach them we should have to follow a long valley to the back of the Towers, where Barrie assured us we should find a comparatively easy slope, leading up to the col between the Central and Northern Towers. It was about twelve miles to the foot of the Tower and we would have to carry up all the food, climbing gear and tentage we were going to need. This, obviously, was going to take several days. The weather was perfect and apparently had been so for the past fortnight.

'That could be the whole season's good weather gone,' Don remarked dourly; but to me, on my first visit, it seemed difficult to believe that it could ever get really bad. We were all talking of climbing the Tower in the next few days.

That morning we plodded slowly up the grass slopes that led up the side of a gorge leading out of the valley we were going to follow. It was stupefyingly hot without a breath of wind; flies buzzed round us, attracted by the sweat trickling down our faces, and every few yards we stopped for a rest, unfit, boozed-up from the night before. From the top of the rise, the valley was laid out before us, steep scree slopes leading down to dense scrub-like forest. There were no traces of paths or of anyone ever having been there before, though to our knowledge three expeditions had been this way.

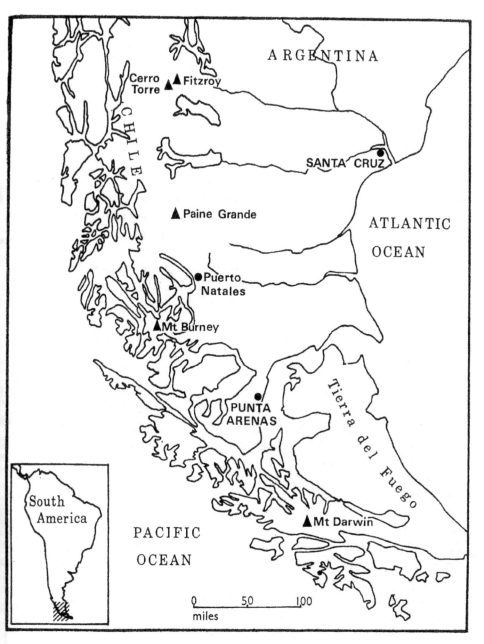

Patagonia

We stumbled and hacked out a route to the base of the glacier which guarded the eastern flanks of the Towers. From this angle the Central Tower seemed invincible, a magnificent monolith, presenting a sheer face of about 3,000 feet – a face that today might be possible, but which in 1962, with the gear we had available, was out of the question. We dumped our loads and plodded back towards base camp. On the way we discussed tactics. We were still two days' carry from the foot of the Tower and were obviously going to have to ferry a large quantity of gear to its foot, but we were keen to take advantage of the good weather and start climbing as soon as possible. We therefore agreed that Don and Barrie should go out in front, establishing our second camp on the glacier immediately below the Tower and then push up to the Tower itself, while two of us ferried gear from Camp I to the glacier and the other two stayed at base camp. That night in my diary I wrote:

> Obviously I should like to have gone on the recce party, but I feel that Don could be better qualified in a way. He has a good eye for a route and anyway I want to try to hold myself back a bit. I want to be out in front, I love finding the route and making it, but at this stage it is more important to establish our camps and get up all the equipment we shall be needing.

We agreed that Ian Clough and I should toss for moving up to the first camp to do the carry up to the glacier; I lost the toss and therefore was to stay behind at base camp with Vic Bray, to ferry loads up to Camp I. In the next few days I was afire to be out in front, dreamt of what Don and Barrie might be doing on the Tower itself, even imagining that they might have climbed it, with me still back at base – and yet it was a pleasant, easy rhythm, each day plodding up the 'grind' – the long slope leading into the Ascencio Valley – and each day finding it a little easier. Vic was a good companion; he was older than the rest of us, being in his thirties. He was not a brilliant climber, but had spent some years with the Royal Air Force in Mountain Rescue, and was a good steady goer. A confirmed bachelor, he was self-contained and yet most considerate of other people, always ready to lend a hand even if it was thoroughly inconvenient to himself at the time. During this period Wendy was still staying with the Neilsons and I only saw her for one short visit. She was bursting with vitality, and yet her greatest love of all was frustrated. As a child she had been devoted to horses, spending her entire time in the local stables. Here in Patagonia horses were still the principal means of transport, but she hadn't been able to ride, and in fact never did.

The weather stayed fine for a further three days, just enough to enable Don and Barrie to reach the 'Notch', the steep col between the two Towers. 'It'll go all right,' Don told us. 'There's a crack line practically all the way up, with only one gap on a slab at about quarter height.'

They were keen to go down for a rest, and at last it was to be my turn to go out in front with Ian Clough. Wendy had now moved from the Neilsons, and the two girls were staying in the Estancia Paine, the agreement being that they should look after the house for the Radic brothers and do the cooking. The rest of the team were opposed to their staying at Base Camp, and they had only come out on the understanding that they were to stay at one of the estancias.

Young Martin, the Pages' three-year-old child, was the principal problem. He was a pleasant enough child, but none of us, at this stage, had any children and as a result we were completely intolerant of his natural need for attention and his spirit of inquiry. Even Wendy now admits that she had no concept of the trials that Elaine must have gone through, trying to keep Martin from under the feet of a crowd of resentful climbers, and at the same time amused and out of mischief. My own loyalty was constantly split between Wendy and my enjoyment of having her with me, and my need to feel part of the expedition. Looking back, it all seems incredibly petty, but at the time it was very real, in the little, slightly neurotic, world of the expedition. Most expeditions find a scapegoat and in our case it now became three-year-old Martin – in some ways this was fortunate, since he remained happily unaware of our feelings, though undoubtedly they must have affected Elaine. She is a down-to-earth, practical person, who one felt would be more at home running a suburban house to a nine-to-five routine than trying to cope with the involved politics of a climbing expedition and the problems of looking after a three-year-old in the middle of the wilds.

But the focus of our small world remained the Tower. On the 4th December, Don and Barrie had reached the col between the Central and North Towers and Don had deemed the climb feasible. They had returned to the glacier and the following day, since the weather had deteriorated, had returned to our camp in the Ascencio Valley. Meanwhile, Ian and I moved up for our turn to go out in front. The way to the west of the Towers led through dense scrub forest and then up through a chaos of boulders on to the lateral moraine of the glacier. At the head of the glacier towered the huge walls of the Fortress and Shield, two magnificent peaks that were still unclimbed. On our left was a long scree and boulder slope, leading up to the foot of the Central and Northern Towers, that stood like Norman keeps on the top of a giant earth mound. That afternoon Ian and I carried tentage and supplies up to the site of a camp a few hundred feet below the foot of the Tower, and left the gear on some platforms built by a former expedition to the North Tower.

The following morning we set out to make our first attempt on the Central Tower. Up to this point the weather had been unbelievably mild, with plenty of sunshine and practically no wind. But now, as we picked our way over broken scree slopes, a few snowflakes scudded down and the wind began to stab at our faces. Broken ledges led across the foot of the North Tower and

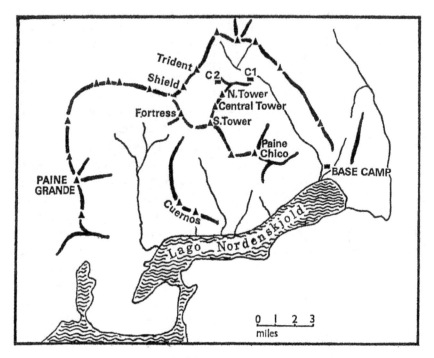

The Paine area

then a gully blocked with great rocks swept up between the smooth, sheer walls of the two Towers towards the col.

Its crest was like a wind tunnel that seemed to concentrate all the fury of the gale blowing across the Patagonian ice cap. Below, we had some protection, but now we were battered by its full fury. Even so, I could not help looking, enthralled, around me. Immediately in front, through a split in the rock that might have been the castellated wall of a crusader's castle, I could see down to the jumbled rocks of the East Paine Glacier, across to the shapeless mound of the Paine Chico, and beyond to the pampas, its lakes set like jewels of copper sulphate, blue, slate grey, brilliant green, on an undulating mantle of rough, grey-green tweed, that stretched to the far horizon.

On either side, the walls of the Tower reared above, brown and yellow granite, solid, unyielding to the pounding gales; and behind us, the driving hammering wind that raced past the massive, square-cut walls of the Fortress and over the smooth white shawl of the ice cap.

For an instant I felt a heady exhilaration to be here in the arms of the elements, far from other people, from the rest of the expedition; but as soon as we started to sort out gear for the climb, my pleasure was doused by the numbing cold and driving wind. A pedestal of rock about a hundred feet high leaned against the Tower – a clean-cut crack up its centre invited us – but to reach it we had to climb a short step immediately above the col. I set out, belayed by Ian, but immediately wind tugged at my body, hands were numb, and resolve drained out of me. Having climbed the initial step, I hammered a peg into the crack behind it and abseiled off – at least we had climbed the first twelve feet of the Central Tower.

We turned tail and fled back to our campsite, chased by the wind. There seemed no point in staying there, eating food we had so wearisomely carried up, and so we collapsed the tent and plodded back to the floor of the glacier, but even as we went down I began to wonder if I had made the right decision. That night in my diary I wrote:

> If tomorrow is good we shall have wasted half a day in coming back up again, and a lot of energy. Having taken a decision, I have the terrible habit of reviewing it and re-reviewing it – often deciding that I had taken the wrong decision after all. As in this decision, there are so often equally important factors on both sides. The thing I must realise, and then practise, is that a positive decision, once taken and then pursued, is more right than dithering from one thing to another.

As it turned out, our decision was right, for the next morning it was blowing and raining even harder than it had been the previous day, and so we returned to Base Camp.

Our attempt to climb the Central Tower of Paine now slowly degenerated into a struggle with the weather, in which the Tower itself took a second place. A temporary improvement in the weather tempted Ian Clough and me back up to our highest camp on the 13th December. We pitched a Blacks' mountain tent, built a dry stone wall round it, and prepared to sit out the storm, still convinced that somehow we must remain in easy reach of the foot of the Tower so that we could seize the first available opportunity to snatch a few hours' climbing if the wind dropped, rather than waste the good weather in plodding up to the camp site. That night the wind just strummed across the tent, and we both slept long and deep. The following morning snow scudded down and the wind seemed to be rising, but I determined to sit it out. Ian was a fine companion for this type of long wait; quiet, easy-going, and always ready to do more than his share of the day-to-day drudgery of cooking and washing up. On the boat trip out I had been irritated by his almost naive enthusiasm for everything new, but now, cooped up in a tent about 2,000 feet above the rest of the team, I felt his real worth.

During the day, the weather steadily deteriorated. It was rather like having one's tent pitched across the tracks in a railway tunnel. The air would be quite still, and then, in the distance, would come the roar of the wind, tearing through the Towers above us and down the slope until it hit the tent with a solid force, bellying out the thin cotton, stretching the seams until it seemed impossible that it could resist the remorseless force. And then, with equal suddenness, the wind would vanish and we were left, lying limp and helpless in our sleeping bags. That night we got very little sleep, and it seemed impossble that the tent could stand up to this kind of punishment for very much longer. The following morning, relieved at having survived the night, we packed up, collapsed the tent and fled down to the glacier.

But as we walked down, the wind dropped, blue sky appeared, the sun peered out from behind a cloud. Had I made a mistake? Should we go back? Could I suggest it to Ian? But he, mind made up, was heading down. I followed in agony from indecision. The others were obviously surprised to see us. The wind had barely reached the glacier. Don immediately made his decision.

'Barrie and I might as well go up,' he commented, and they started to pack their rucksacks. We were now very low on rations and fuel, so Ian and I, with heavy hearts, agreed to go down and get some more supplies. But that night I wrote in my diary:

> I felt a great wave of lost opportunity as I watched them prepare to go up. If only we had waited there a bit longer, if only we had had more determination. What are my motives on an expedition? There is an awful lot of desire for personal glory. I want to be out in front. I want to be taking the lead. Is it an inferiority complex that makes me need the assurance of my success? I wish I could control it – cut it out. To have a major part in climbing the Central Tower, and then to reach the top in the first party, means a tremendous amount to me. I know it shouldn't, but it does.

I was longing to be back on the mountain, and yet, as we came down the last slopes of the hillside above the estancia we bumped, by chance, into Wendy and suddenly all the doubts vanished in my pleasure at being with her once again; until later that night, when a sky studded with stars in black velvet reminded me again of the mountain – how I longed to be at grips with it, feeling the brown granite, hammering in pitons, immersing myself in all the rich simplicity of climbing. Even in Wendy's arms, gorged with love-making, the driving urge to climb was greater – an urge caused partly from my love of the actual process of climbing, partly from my competitive drive to be out in front.

But we had something more tangible to worry about, for John Streetley, the seventh member of our expedition, had arrived at Base Camp that day, and armed with the scantiest information about our whereabouts, had set out to find us. Ian and I should have met him on our way down, but somehow we had missed him – easy enough in the dense scrub of the Ascencio Valley.

'He might well have gone up the wrong valley,' I commented. 'He can't come to any harm, anyway: he knows how to look after himself.'

The next morning we set out for the mountain, laden with stores for the rest of the team, confident that we should find John at our camp on the glacier. The weather had turned bad once again and so all my own secret worries about having gone down had been proved pointless. The wind was now reaching down even to the glacier, chasing over the boulders, blowing clouds of dust that penetrated every chink of clothing. Don and Barrie had been forced back down the mountain, their tent blown over in the middle of the night. They had even had to collapse the tents on the glacier, and I could see them at work under a huge boulder, trying to dig out a cave.

As I scrambled up to the boulder I hoped desperately that John Streetley would be there. I suddenly felt guilty about taking it for granted that he had found the others, but yes, there he was, just behind Don. I formed some kind of attempt at a humorous question about his wanderings, but as I groped, saw that I had been mistaken – it was Vic Bray.

'Where's John? Has he arrived?' I asked.

I was greeted with blank looks. A great wave of guilt overwhelmed me. He had now been out for two nights, with a third coming on, and I had only wandered back up to see the others. I could visualise him lying in the boulder field with his foot trapped by a fallen rock.

'Why, when did he arrive?' asked Don.

'Afternoon before last. He just asked the girls where we were, and pushed on up.'

'He could be bloody anywhere,' commented Don. 'He's probably just wandering around, looking for us. Anyway, I suppose we should have a look for him. He might be in the other valley.'

We divided into two parties and searched either side of the valley on the way down to Camp I. We had succeeded in selling the story of the expedition to the *Daily Express*, and I was the official correspondent. I took this very seriously, as it was my first assignment with a proper newspaper. The *Daily Express* had bought the story of my ascent with Ian of the North Wall of the Eiger, but they had used one of their own writers and had sensationalised the entire business. I had hoped to be able to redress this in the reports I sent back telling our story on the Central Tower of Paine, but now, faced with the possibility of a disaster, I dreaded my obligation to have to report it.

Full of doubt and worry I worked my way down, across the boulders of the glacier, and then through the dense scrub of the lower part of the valley. Don was just in front of me, and as we approached the dump of supplies which made up Camp I, he let out a shout. As I arrived, I saw that the tarpaulin covering the dump had been made into a bivvy shelter, and there was John's head, impish and grinning, sticking out from under it! Suddenly, in our relief, we were all shouting and joking. He had wandered up into the wrong valley, had bivouacked up there and had then returned to the dump, and next day was planning to walk round to the western valley, where we were ensconced.

That night we stayed at Camp I, crowded under the tarpaulin, and the next morning discussed what we should do.

'I reckon we're due for a rest at Base Camp,' said Don. 'But I think we should try to keep a pair up on the glacier to take advantage of the weather if it does improve.'

'Well, I'm keen to have a go at the Tower,' said John. 'I don't mind going up.'

Everyone else remained silent.

'How about you or Ian?' suggested Don. 'You've just been festering at Base Camp.'

Impulsively I agreed, and almost immediately regretted it – split between my desire to climb and hunger for the flesh-pots of Base Camp and Wendy. The mountains were once again clad in cloud, and even here, in the woods, the wind was hunting in the trees. With regret I watched the others heading down the valley, and started with John back through the dripping woods to the glacier. We could barely stand upright in the wind. There was no question of pitching a tent and we spent the rest of the day digging away at the cave under the boulder in an attempt to make a weathertight shelter for the night.

As so often, once committed, the very wildness of conditions became attractive. There was a satisfaction in hauling and pulling rocks to make walls for our shelter – it was back to the fun of building shelters as a child, and, as it turned out, our shelter was not very much more effective than the rickety lairs I had built many years ago. The fine, swirling glacier dust covered everything in a grey film; but no matter: we were in the mountains, twelve miles from the nearest human being.

John was a good companion. Small and stocky like Whillans, he had a similar personality in many ways – a quick dry wit, forceful, immensely strong, more relaxed than Whillans – easier to get on with, perhaps through success or a more comfortable upbringing. His family originated in Trinidad and he had had a traditional education at public school and Cambridge. At university he had starred as an athlete and sportsman, getting blues for boxing and running. He took to climbing casually, showing a natural genius for it, making a few brilliant ascents, and then returned to the Americas where he built up a successful business. At a time when Joe Brown and Don Whillans held sway over British climbing, he was the only person to put up a new route of comparable difficulty to theirs – on Clogwyn du'r Arddu, finest and most well known of all the Welsh cliffs.

He had a self-sufficiency and lightning wit that made it difficult to feel you ever really got to know him, but as a companion, on that basis, he made pleasant and easy company.

That night we cooked a magnificent meal, lightly garnished with glacier dust, and settled down for the night. I began to dream I was lying in a waterfall and then, slowly, reality merged with my dream-world, and I woke in the pitch dark to hear the sound of running water, to feel cold rivulets running down inside my sleeping bag. I fumbled for the torch; couldn't find it; woke Streetley to share my discomfort – he had a lighter. Eventually we got a candle going, and saw that the cave on which we had worked so hard the previous day was neatly channelling water down its sloping roof and over all the flat spots on the floor. We spent the rest of the night curled into niches which were out of range of the prying streams.

There was an element of the ludicrous in our struggles with the elements: here were seven experienced mountaineers, defeated time and time again, not by the technical difficulty of a steep mountain but by a mixture of wind and rain. Perhaps if we had shown greater stoicism in the face of discomfort, we could have achieved more, but somehow I doubt it. There is a sapping power to the force of continuous wind that can only be borne for a limited time.

But we were still determined to stay in range of the Tower, and the following morning started trying to construct a new shelter, this time a hut with dry stone walls roofed with the tarpaulin. By the end of the day we had a hovel with barely sufficient headroom to sit up. The tarpaulin roof thrashed over us in the wind, slowly tearing itself to bits on the rocky walls. Before the first night was out holes had appeared in it and every time a gust hit us it threatened to take off. I dozed intermittently through the night, planning my retreat to the dubious shelter of the boulder, and wondering if we should ever be able to get to grips with Big Ned. We had vested in our objective a definite personality, regarding him with a mixture of hostility, yet at times affection; we had the same kind of relationship with the Central Tower that a primitive tribe might have with an implacable forest god, who could destroy them at any moment, yet who was also responsible for their wellbeing.

But that morning the god was kind, and the sky cleared; though serried streamers of cloud marching across it, high over the Central Tower, were a sure sign that more bad weather was on its way. We resolved, anyway, to go up to Camp III and at least sort it out and stock it with some more food. As we plodded up the long boulder slopes, the clouds came scudding in, round the walls of the Fortress. The air was full of fine racing snowflakes. But I wanted to press on, up to the Notch, in spite of the weather. I was convinced that we needed to try to climb in these bad conditions to make any progress at all, so that when, at last, the weather did improve, we should be sufficiently high on the Tower to make an immediate summit bid.

Camp III proved to be a depressing place. Half-eaten food was floating in pools of water on the floor of the collapsed tent; everything was wet and soggy. We put up the tent and had a brew. I suggested rather tentatively that we went up and had a try at climbing, and John, keen to get to grips with the mountain, was agreeable.

By the time we reached the Notch, a full gale was howling through it, hammering our senses and making every movement a painful effort. It was strange looking down through the Notch to see gently rolling pampas, bathed in sunlight. Down there it was warm and dry; the others were probably lying in the sun; Wendy, perhaps, was painting, while here on the Notch, life and our own efforts seemed very puny against the force of the elements. But once I was in harness, and at the foot of the crack, submerged in concentration, all was forgotten.

Clip in étrier, step up, look round for a place for the next peg, hammer it in. Hell, my gloves are in the way; take them off; my hands are quite warm. Concentration – nothing in the world except the rock, all brown and rich, and the crack. Holds now; feel them; can I pull up on them? Yes. Where should I put my foot? Over there – use an étrier to help; I stick my foot out, but the étrier is swinging in the wind at 90 degrees to me. Cock my foot up above my head and field the étrier; step up. Then an awkward hand jam; it hurts like hell, but I'm up a bit more. Time for another peg; the crack is opening up inside, so that only half an inch of rock is in contact with the peg; but it holds my weight. And so, up and up and up, timeless, oblivious of cold and wind, of Streetley stamping with cold down below. At last I pull on to a ledge. To me, it had seemed only a few minutes, but it had been one and a half hours and I had completed only eighty feet of climbing.

'Do you want to come up, John?' I shouted.

'I'm bloody frozen down here. I don't think I could move if I tried,' he replied.

'Okay, I'll come down. Can you tie those ladders to the rope?'

We had brought out some electron caving ladders and these seemed ideal for the steep bottom step. Today we should have used jumar clamps to climb the rope, but in 1962 these aids were almost unknown. It was nearly dark by the time we had rigged the ladder, and I had returned to the Notch. We were tired and cold, yet we felt jubilant at our tiny success. We had at least climbed a single pitch on Big Ned after four weeks' struggle with the weather.

But the weather was winning. That night we tried to sleep at Camp III, and spent most of it watching the seams of the tent stretch and contract as they were battered by the wind. In the morning we fled downhill, and pushed straight back to Base. For the time being, the weather had won. Our tents would not stand up to the wind, and even the boulder camp on the glacier was untenable. There seemed nothing for it but to wait for a spell of fine weather at Base Camp. And anyway, it was the 20th December, only a week to Christmas.

2   Christmas in Patagonia

Christmas in Patagonia meant roast mutton, quantities of booze and a friendly visit by the Neilsons from Cerro Guido. We had been at Base Camp for over a week and the big saucer-like clouds that cruised over the Paine Massif were a sure sign that it was windy as ever in the mountains. The team sank into a restless inertia. Don, John Streetley and I made a foray to attempt to climb the Cuernos, an attractive peak about eight miles down Lake Nordenskjold, the huge glacier-fed lake that lay alongside the Paine range. A rainy bivouac in the woods cooled our ardour, however, and we returned to Base Camp.

It was a restless, disturbing period for me. Wendy and I had planned to wander up through the Americas after the expedition, spending the money I had made from climbing the North Wall of the Eiger. It had seemed an attractive scheme, but now my basic caution and need for stability began to affect me. I longed for solid roots, was worried about getting stuck into a new career and writing the book which had been commissioned just before I left England. I decided, therefore, to go back with the others rather than spend another six months travelling. Wendy was bitterly disappointed, for in many ways she is more adventurous than I. She is the product of a home that had always been unstable financially, yet had remained a close-knit unit. Her father, Leslie, is an amazing man with a free-ranging intelligence, spirit of inquiry and basic strength, that has enabled him to emerge through a series of personal crises that would have overwhelmed a lesser person. Like mine, his father pulled out when he was still young, leaving his mother to bring up four children in Birkenhead. He left school at the age of sixteen to join the art department of Newnes, where he showed special promise as a cartoonist. He would probably have followed a steadily developing career in the magazine world, but then, at the age of eighteen, he was caught by evangelism. This eventually led him into the Baptist ministry. But he had ideas that were years ahead of their time, especially for his parishioners in Buckinghamshire. He tried to apply a psychological interpretation to their problems; I should imagine his sermons went straight over their heads, for he has a philosophical bent, constantly inquiring about the nature of his own belief and that of others, trying to get to the roots of a problem, rather than skating over the surface in the way that I suspect most of his churchgoers would have preferred. Eventually, he fell out with his parishioners and fellow churchmen. Disillusioned, shaken in his beliefs, he left the church and faced the problem of making a new career with practically no qualifications. He started working as a medical artist and then progressed to illustrating children's books and magazines.

He had married shortly before going into the church and had two children, Neville and Wendy. Money had always been short, with disaster looming just around the corner, but Les somehow managed to give the two children a good education and a stable home life. Wendy went to Brighton High School and then on to Art College, where she stayed for only three years, just getting her intermediate certificate before leaving to earn some immediate money, like her father, as a freelance illustrator.

In many ways she had a lonely childhood, isolated by lack of money, which made her different from most other children at school. This gave her a superficial shyness, yet hidden beneath it was a real strength that enabled her to do without the conventional props of economic security.

I, on the other hand, had had a childhood that was relatively secure financially, but very much less stable emotionally. My parents' marriage had broken up before I was a year old and my mother had been left, without any help from my father, to bring me up at a time when jobs were hard to get and salaries for women painfully low. Fortunately, as an advertising copywriter, she managed to achieve a reasonable earning capacity and compared to Wendy's family we were positively wealthy. But the fact remained, she was very much on her own in a thrusting, unstable profession. Because she had to go out to work I was brought up, until the age of five, by my grandmother. Then, on the outbreak of war in 1939, with the scare of bombing, I was sent to boarding school. I was there till 1942, when I was brought back to London and lived alternately with my mother and my grandmother. They were strange, lonely years, for my mother had few friends and there were none of the conventional family contacts with other family groups. I had plenty of love but at times there was a tussle for possession between my mother and grandmother. I suspect this left me with the feeling of insecurity and a need for family existence that made service life very attractive, and tempted me to prolong my National Service into a regular commitment. When I became disillusioned with the army, I had needed another big organisation to jump into and had secured a management traineeship with Unilever. It was largely meeting Wendy, and her contempt for traditional security, that gave me the courage to abandon a conventional career and plunge into the unknown; but a conflict between my desire for security and love of freedom remained. In addition, I don't think I was ready for wandering in the sense that Wendy was. I had little perception or awareness outside the narrow field of climbing; my entire ambition and concentration was focused on the Central Tower of Paine and my own part in the expedition, to the exclusion of almost everything else. My senses were alive to the feel of the wind and sun, the empty beauty of the pampas, the architecture of the mountains, the mystery of dark pools and tangled glades in the forest below the Paine. But it got no further than my immediate senses. I absorbed the beauty and atmosphere of the place but was lacking in curiosity; I learnt little of the life of Pedro or the gauchos who worked on the estancia. I was too tied up in the climb and my own problems to be able to gain much from a sightseeing adventure through the Americas.

It was a hard time for Wendy. She was so close to everything she had dreamt of doing, yet was unable to fulfil her dreams. The expedition was a man's world; so was the estancia, and she had become an unwilling appendage. If Elaine had not had a child with her, the two girls could probably have gone off exploring on their own, becoming independent of the expedition, but in the circumstances this could not be.

Just after Christmas the situation changed once again. We were told that Juan Radic, the owner of the estancia, was bringing his wife and family up from Punta Arenas, which meant that the girls had to move from the farmhouse. Much later, I learnt from Derek Walker that this was only an excuse; in fact Juan and Pedro had become tired of having someone else's small child running riot in the house, and did not really appreciate the girls' housekeeping. Meals were seldom on time and they weren't served the vast quantities of food to which they were accustomed. Another irritant must have been the presence of Barrie and me when we were resting at Base Camp. I always felt uncomfortable invading the privacy of their house, but naturally wanted to sleep with Wendy.

There was considerable opposition to the girls staying at Base Camp from the very start. This was largely because it had been understood back in England that Barrie had made arrangements for them to stay in an estancia for the entire trip, and therefore the others, quite naturally, had a feeling of being misled. Not having women or wives of their own with them, one could hardly blame them for resenting the ones who had. The communal mess tent had a feeling of a London Club in its male exclusivity, and I could hardly blame them for wanting to retain it. Wendy and I set up camp in a little two-man tent about a hundred yards from the other tents. I was torn between two emotions: one part of me wanting to immerse myself in the expedition, to be part of the tribe, and the other part enjoying my love for Wendy. At the time I wrote:

> An expedition is very much a living, single unit. I find it myself in many ways, and I think Wendy feels it. An awful lot of you goes into the expedition and the mountain you climb. I hope to God it does not mean that I am just not passionate because the depth of my love for her is total and complete, and yet I feel I can't give her everything; somehow, at times my sexual passion seems to be drained, I think – I hope – by the efforts of the expedition, my own channelling of enthusiasm.

This was when I was tired after our return from the Cuernos, and worried about my relationship with the rest of the expedition because of the girls' presence in Base Camp, yet in the constant pendulum of emotion that I have always been prey to, the next day, refreshed, I wrote:

> We woke up to hear rain pattering on the tent and a distant roar of wind. Although the sun spread a dappled pattern of leaves on the roof of the tent, I felt that the weather had changed once again. It had, and got progressively worse during day.
>
> But Wendy and I spent a delightful morning, in fact a whole delightful day, just loving each other with a great, warm, fresh, light-hearted love. It's strange, all the aspects of love that you plumb; light-hearted, bubbling, idiotic love that is all coloured and playful; deep love that goes right into your emotions; doubtful love, when you just want to be loved, but can't imagine anyone loving you.
>
> I think that on this trip we've gone through a big range of loving, and of doubts about the present and future, but never doubts of our own love for each other. I know that every day that goes by, my own love, and the confidence that I have in that love, gets stronger and yet each day I feel that I have reached an absolute optimum of loving.

We had known each other for less than a year, had been married for only six months, and were still in that tentative, finding-out stage of a relationship. In spite of the pressures caused by my own split loyalties, the general feeling of resentment against the girls, and Wendy's sense of lost opportunity, we had some wonderful times together during that fortnight, as we wandered down by the slate-grey waters of Lake Nordenskjold, making love in the soft grass of the pampas, confident that no one would pass our way, and overlooked only by a condor, soaring high above our impassioned limbs.

In face of the continuous bad weather the team seemed to have lost much of its single-minded push to lay siege to the Central Tower. Don was planning to make another attempt on the Cuernos with Derek Walker, though I was surprised that he was prepared to miss a chance of fine weather on the Central Tower. The rest of us were planning to return to the foot of the Tower yet again, to try to build a storm-proof camp where we could wait out the weather. But there was little sense of urgency, or even real unity, in the team at this stage – and then something happened to shake the team out of its fast-growing apathy.

We had known all along that an Italian expedition was on its way to climb in our area, but somehow, until they actually arrived, we never took the threat seriously. On the 28th December, the day that Don and Derek were due to set out on their mini-expedition, we heard that they had reached the Estancia Guido, and the following day they pitched camp about half a mile from ourselves. Derek and Don immediately cancelled their plans, and that afternoon we went over to size up our potential rivals. They were an impressive-looking bunch, slightly older than we were, very neat in matching sweaters and breeches that gave them an almost military air. They gave an impression of disciplined single-mindedness, very different from one that any stranger would have gained from our own motley group.

They greeted us with wary courtesy, and a spate of introductions followed. There were seven of them altogether; their leader, Gian Carlo Frigieri, was grey-haired and could have been in his late forties; a non-playing captain, I suspected. Their star was undoubtedly Amando Aste, dark-haired, rather sullen, who obviously resented our presence in the mountains they had come to climb. He had a reputation for hard solo climbing in the Dolomites, with many well-known routes to his credit. It was undoubtedly a strong team – on average experience probably a good deal stronger than ours.

Unfortunately, they could speak little English, and we no Italian. Barrie produced a postcard of the Towers and pointed to the Central Tower.

'This is our Tower. We have climbed high on it with much fixed rope in place.' He pointed to a spot considerably higher than our real high point, a puny eighty feet above the col. They did not seem very impressed; Amando Aste scowled even more fiercely and muttered something in Italian.

Barrie tried once again. 'South Tower very good, just as steep as Central.' It looked good in the photograph, if anything more slender than the Central Tower, but it had been taken face on and did not show that the Tower comprised a long, comparatively easy-angled knife-edge ridge. The Italians were not impressed; they had obviously seen photographs of both Towers from more revealing angles.

Before leaving we invited them round for a drink that night and then returned to our camp for a council of war. As we talked, I could sense the growing unity of purpose caused by this threat of competition.

'Those buggers'll go for the Central Tower,' said Don.

'You never know,' said Barrie. 'I think I talked them out of it. They can't possibly use our fixed ropes, and we've got the only line up the Tower.'

'I shouldn't be so sure of that,' I said. 'All they've got to do is climb one of the cracks on the side of the pedestal, and they could come out above the ladder. If they get into that central dièdre, we could never get round them.'

'Well, we'll get them well wined up tonight, and persuade them that there's a good route round the back of the Tower,' said Barrie.

'You're not going to shift them by giving them a bit of booze,' said Don. 'In one way, you can't blame them anyway; calling ourselves the South

Patagonia Survey Expedition! How the hell did they know we were going to be a climbing expedition? If you haven't got proper permission for us to climb the Tower, Barrie, they might well have us moved off altogether. I reckon that's what they're up to now.'

'In that case let's move up to the foot of the Tower,' I suggested. 'I can't see a policeman walking all the way up there. Anyway, unless we find a way of living immediately below the Tower in this bad weather, we're going to waste the first windless day in getting back up there. How about pulling Camp II back into the woods, just below the glacier, and sitting it out there?'

'I think that's still too low,' said Don. 'What we could do with is some kind of hut where Camp III is, just below the Tower. You could then keep a pair in it the whole time, and they could just nip out as soon as the weather got fine, and be on the Tower in a couple of hours.'

'It would be a hell of a job getting materials up, though, wouldn't it?' said Derek.

'I don't know,' said Don. 'All you need is a solid framework, and you could make the walls out of tarpaulin.'

'There's a lot of timber in Juan's wine store,' said Vic. 'I'm sure he'd let us use it. It would be ideal for the frame. We cut it to size down here and then carry the whole lot up.'

Don and Vic went off to find materials for the box. Thus was born an important new concept in expedition tentage, which was to enable us to beat the high winds of Patagonia on this trip, and which, eight years later, in a more sophisticated form, was to play a vital part in our ascent of the South Face of Annapurna.

The presence of the Italians had acted as a catalyst, giving us a stronger sense of purpose and unity than we had had for some time. That night, as we prepared the communal tent for our reception, there was an atmosphere of almost childish gaiety. Wendy, wearing a pullover of brightly coloured patches, looked positively seductive, curled up on one of the camp beds.

'We'll have to leave you here on your own to receive the Italians,' suggested Derek. 'You might be able to turn their thoughts to other things.'

Meanwhile, Don and John Streetley were fooling around, Don climbing on John's shoulders, dressed in a long cagoule, to resemble a misshapen seven-foot giant. We were all excited, talking louder than normal, getting a kick out of the potential threat of the situation. It was the feeling of people about to go to war – a little apprehensive, yet excited at the same time.

And then the Italians arrived. There were more handshakes, a pretence at bonhomie, but the conversation soon lagged – apart from anything else, we spoke too little of each other's language.

I found myself sitting next to an Italian called Nusdeo. We talked in broken French, our only mutual language, and quickly exhausted the normal conversational gambits of what each had climbed, and whether we had any mutual climbing acquaintances. He had been on the North Wall of the Eiger only a few days before Ian and me, making the first true Italian ascent. And then the conversation lulled. Because I couldn't think of anything else to say, I asked if they intended to tackle the South Tower. He looked embarrassed, muttered something about being obliged to go for the Central, for this was the objective their club had sent them to tackle. There was a strained silence in the room, and the Italians left soon after.

As they trooped out of the tent there was an even stronger sense of unity and determination in our group.

Don summed up everyone's feelings when he said, 'If those buggers think they're going to push me around, they've got another thing coming to them.'

I don't know what the Italians made of us. They must have noticed the huge pile of empty beer bottles outside the tent. We had been in the area for a month, and had obviously made very little progress; at this stage, they had no concept of how savage the weather could be – that the principal problem of climbing in Patagonia was mere survival in the high winds rather than technical difficulty. We were a good deal younger than they, and seemed less well-organised. I suspect we had much the same appearance as Britain did to the Germans in 1940 – disorganised, few in numbers, and fairly contemptible.

'We've got to have it out with them,' said Don, 'and find out just what they're planning to do. If we're not careful, they'll be shinning up our fixed ropes.'

'How about formulating some simple questions with a "yes" or "no" answer?' I suggested. 'We can then go over to see them tomorrow and nail them down to some kind of commitment.'

'That sounds all right,' agreed Don. 'What we want to know is – are they going for the Central Tower or not. If so, do they intend to use our col? And if they do, are they thinking of using our fixed ropes? If they do, some bugger's going to get a bloody nose.'

Next morning, Don, Barrie and I went over to the Italian camp. Barrie acted as spokesman, asking the questions we had formulated the previous night. Their leader repeated Nusdeo's assertion that they had to tackle the Central Tower, since this was what their club had financed them to climb. He also complained bitterly that they had no idea that an expedition called the South Patagonia Survey Expedition could possibly have designs on difficult rock peaks.

Barrie ignored this complaint and went on to the next question. 'Well then, are you going from the Col Bich?' This was the col between the North and Central Towers. It also gave the only obvious route up the Tower. The answer was 'yes' once again.

'But we are already established on the Col Bich with fixed ropes going up one crack line. You don't intend to use our fixed rope, do you?'

They showed every sign of indignation that we should even make such a suggestion. Taldo, a big tough character, who was the most friendly and outgoing of the Italians, was very positive, smashing his fist into his hand to emphasise his assertions that they wanted an Italian route, a solely Italian route, up the Central Tower, totally separate from any 'voie Britannique'. There was no sign of Aste; and Aiazzi, his climbing partner, just sat it out in the corner, his face expressionless.

We returned to our camp and Don, Vic, John Streetley and Ian Clough, the practical men of the expedition, began building the prefabricated hut – our secret weapon to beat the Tower. Don Whillans and Vic Bray were the craftsmen, cutting the timbers to the right length and marking out the tarpaulins. At the end of the day, they had completed the hut, tacking the framework together and fitting over it the tarpaulin shell. Even the hinged door was complete, with its written inscription, HOTEL BRITANNICO — MEMBERS ONLY. Each component was then numbered and the hut was dismantled, ready to be carried to the foot of the Central Tower.

It was New Year's Eve, and that night the bachelors welcomed it in with a hard drinking session. The feeling of unity in the group, engendered by the presence of the Italians, was still not sufficient to overcome their resentment of the girls' presence, and they preferred to celebrate in masculine seclusion. As a result, I slipped away early, and was asleep well before the arrival of 1963. I woke early to the sound of rain pattering on the tent.

The weather was as bad as ever, but I was anxious to get the prefabricated hut established as soon as possible so that we could take full benefit from the first break in the weather. There was a risk that the Italians, reaching the col and forcing the crack line to the side of the pedestal which we had climbed, would establish their route in the big groove that was the main feature of this facet of the Tower and, seemingly, the only way up it.

Capturing the enthusiasm of the rest of the team was no easy matter. The Base tent was surrounded by the debris of the night before, and they all had splitting hangovers.

'What's the point of going up in this kind of weather?' said Derek. 'The Italians aren't going to do anything on a day like this. Remember, they don't even know the way up through the forest yet.'

'But we've got to keep our advantage,' I replied. 'God knows, it's little enough. They've only got to push one pitch up from the col and they'll be out in front. Short of having a dobbing match halfway up the Tower, we'd never get past them. We must get a pair established below the Tower as soon as possible.'

'I agree with Chris,' said Don. 'Now that we've got the box made we want to get it into position quickly.'

'In that case, how about getting our camp on the glacier pulled back into the woods today? That will give us a secure intermediate camp. We can then carry the box up tomorrow and erect it at the site of Camp III,' I suggested.

'Sounds all right,' said Don.

And that settled it; with Don on my side, the rest soon agreed to abandon the comfort of Base Camp, and return to the front line.

It was nine o'clock in the morning before we were ready to set out. The dismantled hut weighed, with all its timber beams and heavy tarpaulin, about 250 pounds, but divided amongst the seven of us, the loads were a reasonable weight, though some of the timbers were awkwardly long. We left camp surreptitiously, anxious to avoid being seen by the Italians with our secret weapon. Progress up the Ascencio Valley was slow; the rest were suffering from severe hangovers, and the seven-foot-long timbers kept getting caught in the branches of trees and undergrowth. Once out of the forest and on the glacier, it was even worse. The wind whipped across the snow, treating the timbers of the box as sails. It was difficult, anyway, to keep one's footing on the snow-covered boulders of the moraine, and in the wind we were blown about like a helpless flotilla of dinghies, capsizing in hidden snowdrifts and foundering amongst the jumble of hidden rocks. It was three o'clock before we reached the camp on the glacier. The cave we had excavated under the boulder was full of snow and the gear and food were buried beneath it, a mess of unwashed pans and broken food boxes.

'You left the place in a hell of a mess,' I told Barrie. 'Couldn't you have washed up and sorted the place out before coming down?'

'You'd have left it in no better state,' he replied. 'It's all very well to talk, but it was all we could do to keep the tent up, the wind was so bad.'

'So bloody what! You could still have done a bit of tidying up. We're not on a Boy Scouts' picnic, you know.'

But almost as my temper flared, I felt ashamed of my lack of control. It was an anger born from the cold driving wind, and my resentment of the invidious position in which I had been placed in relation to the other members of the expedition because of Wendy's presence in base camp. In the micro-world of an expedition the pettiest details, like an unwashed pan or an irritating mannerism, are blown up out of all proportion.

But there was no time for anger now. We were battered and half-frozen by the winds, and only had a few hours of daylight to retreat to the woods and put up a new camp. We grabbed tents, cooking stoves and a few dirty pots and pans, and fled back down the glacier to the woods. In these conditions, the mere act of living, trying to stay dry in a waterlogged tent, lighting a fire from wet wood, took up all our energies. During the entire period we had been in the vicinity of the Central Tower of Paine, we had had only about two hours of technical climbing; the rest of the time had been taken up in our losing struggle with the weather.

When we woke in the morning, everything was muffled and quiet. We were near the height of the southern summer, and yet the scene outside the tent could have graced a classic Christmas card, with every branch weighed down by snow. We were so exhausted from the previous day that it was eleven o'clock before everyone had emerged from their sleeping bags and breakfast was cooked.

'I think we should try to get the hut up today,' said Don.

'Christ, have a heart,' said Derek. 'I'm shattered, and I think we all are. Can't we leave it until tomorrow? The Italians won't get in front of us in this.'

'Okay. Fair enough, but we must get it up tomorrow.'

'We're going to need some more food as well,' I suggested. 'Someone had better go back for some.'

'Well, what about you and Barrie?' said Don. 'You've got your women waiting down there for you.'

And so it was agreed. Barrie and I set out through the forest, all silent, rather mysterious and very beautiful under its mantle of snow. We heard the sound of distant talking.

'Could be the Italians,' said Barrie.

'We'd better avoid them,' I suggested. 'The less they know about our movements the better.'

And we slunk through the trees like a pair of partisans; I must confess, I've always had a fondness for playing at soldiers and, on the whole, found the Italian threat thoroughly stimulating.

We returned the following day with big loads of food, to arrive just after the others had returned from putting up the box. They were all jubilant. It had been a savage day, blowing hard and snowing in gusts, but in spite of this they had lugged the timbers up to the site of Camp III, and had erected the hut in position. That night I felt a tremendous feeling of affectionate loyalty to the others. We seemed, at last, to be on the way to beating the elements. The camp in the woods was well sheltered and storm-proof, and, with a bit of luck, the hut would stand up to anything the wind could do round the foot of the Towers.

'We've put it up, so you and Barrie might as well go and sleep in it tomorrow,' said Don.

'That's all right by me,' I replied, and let myself drift off into contented sleep. Next morning I woke to the sound of the wind howling through the tops of the trees and the patter of snow on the roof of the tent. I stayed in my sleeping bag, reading, delaying the moment of decision when I should have to leave the comfort of the camp in the woods for our vigil high on the flanks of the Paine.

Don shook me out of my lethargy. 'Well then, are you going up the hill today?'

It was two o'clock in the afternoon, and we'd barely have time to reach the hut before dusk. The weather seemed to be clearing, with patches of blue being torn in the high flying cloud; and then the clouds themselves began to disintegrate into broken gossamer that merged pearly grey with the brilliant blue of the sky. The covering of snow that had made the going so difficult two days before had now been blasted away by the wind to fill the dip between the moraine ridge and the slope leading up to the Towers. Following the crest of the ridge we were able to reach the site of our former Camp II quite easily, but in a matter of minutes the weather changed yet again. As we collected a few extra tins of food from the dump we had left in the cave, there was a roar of wind. It raced down the slopes of the Paine, its front defined by a crest of swirling powder snow, and hit us with a solid force, hurling us to the ground. All I could do was cling to a rock, fearful lest I should be blown away – load and all. Our progress became little more than a crawl between gusts, as wave upon wave of wind rolled down and engulfed us in its demonic fury. I was tempted to turn back, but kept going on two scores: partly out of anxiety for the state of the hut, wondering whether anything might have worked loose in the wind, but more, I suspect, from a fear of appearing to be weak in the eyes of the others.

The hut was still standing, a solid haven against the fury of the wind. It was about seven feet long, five feet broad and four feet high; squat, ugly, yet completely functional – the only habitation that we could have carried up from the valley and which would stand up to the winds.

We spent three nights in the hut and each day tried to make progress on the Tower. I was convinced that we had to climb in the bad weather and high winds, even if it only meant making token progress, so that the moment the weather did improve we should be poised to make a bid for the summit. It was easy to formulate such a plan in the comfort of Base Camp, but the reality of wind-battered rock and ice vanquished resolution. It was all we could do the first day to struggle up to the foot of the Tower and improve the line of ropes we had left on our previous visit. The following day it had started to snow, but hoping that this might be accompanied by a drop in the strength of the wind, I persuaded Barrie to come out once again. The rocks were covered by a white blanket; what had been a walk the previous day was turned into a precarious climb; ropes were concealed and, once discovered, were coated in ice. It was as bad as climbing the North Wall of the Eiger in a winter's blizzard. We reached the Notch, to find the rocks ice-plastered and ropes frozen in wire-like tangles. My resolve faltered, faced by the sheer immensity of discomfort and cold, and the snow that plastered the rocks, penetrated clothing, froze hands. So often, climbing becomes a battle between resolution and self-indulgence. How far can one force one's body on in face of such discomfort? My emotions said 'fight on', but common sense counselled retreat. After all, we could only climb a few feet beyond the high point on a day like this, and with a good 2,000 feet to go, it became pointless when balanced with the risk and suffering we would undergo for so tiny a gain. We turned back, and as we went down the clouds began to scatter, the wind dropped and the sun began to warm us. Should we turn back and have another go at making progress? I looked at Barrie, wondered if I dared suggest it, but then abandoned the idea. The best part of the day was gone and we were established in retreat.

Don Whillans and Ian Clough were waiting for us at the hut. It was their turn to stand sentry, and it looked as if the weather might at last show us some favour. We pressed on down to Base Camp for a rest – I, torn between the pleasure of seeing Wendy and the longing to be back on the mountain, obsessed by the fear that Don and Ian might snatch a couple of days' fine weather to climb it while I was resting.

They did have one fine day – enough to make the first real progress after six weeks on the Tower. This was the first sunny, windless day we had experienced since the first few days after our arrival. The snow vanished in a matter of hours; the rock was warm to the touch and it was as pleasant as climbing in the Llanberis Pass on a hot summer's day. They quickly scaled the wire ladder that John and I had left just before Christmas, and then reached the top of the pedestal which leaned against the main mass of the Tower. Their way was now barred by a region of smooth, steep slabs, leading into the centre of the face where a great, open corner swept up into its upper reaches. This seemed to be the only obvious line.

Don spent the entire day working his way across the smooth, blank slabs. There were few holds for hands or feet; hardly any cracks to hammer in a piton for running belays. A slip could very easily have been fatal. He reached the foot of the great corner just as dusk was falling. He was tempted to spend the night there and carry on next day, but they had barely adequate bivouac kit, and a line of high-flying clouds was building up over the ice cap – a sure sign that the weather was reverting to normal. Next morning the wind was hammering once again on the walls of the Whillans Box.

The Italians had used the one fine day to carry a tent up to a ledge a few hundred feet above our Box, close under the base of the Tower. But they soon learnt, the hard way, that no tent can stand up to the fury of a Patagonian gale. It was blown down during the night, and the following morning, discomfited, they retreated to the woods.

A few days went by. John Streetley and I had another sojourn at the hut, tried to force a route beyond Don Whillans' high point, but were beaten by the cold and wind. You could only climb rock as steep and hard as this in perfect conditions. We too retreated to the woods, pursued by the fury of the wind, which, even in the shelter of the tree trunks, threatened to destroy our tents. We were now running short of food, but no one was keen to go down to Base to collect more, for fear that the weather might improve while he was away, and the Tower be climbed in his absence.

'How about tossing for who should go down?' I suggested.

'I don't know. If two go down, every bugger might as well go down,' said Don. 'This weather isn't going to improve for a few days.'

Eventually Derek and Ian decided to continue the siege at the hut, hoping for a further good day, but the rest of us abandoned the camp in the woods, and headed back for the flesh-pots of the estancia. That night we had a drinking session. Don and I happened to go out for a pee at the same time. We stood looking up at high cloud, scudding across the moonlit sky. We looked at each other.

'I don't think we've miscalculated,' he said.

'You know, Don, we've avoided each other up to now – I think we'd best get together.'

'Aye, I've been thinking on the same lines. We'd better do the next spell on the hill together.'

I had a tremendous feeling of relief after this conversation. During the expedition Don and I had sensed a definite strain in our relationship. This had stemmed, in large part, from the previous summer, which we had spent together with our wives in the Alps. The main objective had been the North Wall of the Eiger. We had made one attempt together, had become involved in the rescue of another British climber after his companion had been killed at the top of the Second ice-field, and had then gone off to Austria.

We had pitched our tents next door to each other at the camp site in Innsbruck, and then led almost completely separate existences, except when we came together to climb. Once on the mountain, we climbed superbly well together, but in the valley we had too little in common, were too different in temperament. I respected him, couldn't help liking him, but our backgrounds and attitudes to life were too different for us to achieve any kind of intimacy. Don is shrewd, very calculating, makes up his mind after careful thought and then sticks to his decision to the point of stubbornness. On the other hand, I tend to be impulsive, very often plunge into a commitment on an emotional impulse, and then feel forced to change my mind after more mature reflection.

At the end of the summer the weather had, at last, shown signs of improvement, but Don had agreed to give a lecture in England at the beginning of September. In his position I should probably have cancelled the lecture, but Don had settled in his own mind that the climbing holiday was over, and that, as far as he was concerned, was that! The girls were to hitch-hike back, while Don and I took his motorbike, planning to complete one last climb, the North Wall of the Badile. We then drove back to Chamonix; the weather was still perfect and I, therefore, decided on impulse to stay on, and snatch another climb. Ian Clough was also without a partner, and so we went up to climb the

Walker Spur of the Grandes Jorasses, realised how well we were going together and dashed off to the North Wall of the Eiger. We completed it in near-perfect conditions. It represented a superb climax to a long summer, both in terms of climbing experience – for I don't think I have ever been so much in tune with the mountains, moving so well, or being so very fit – and also as the means of launching out into a new career. The successful ascent had brought a commission to write a book, lectures and newspaper articles. It had also shown the risks involved in selling a story to the popular press, when one's own words can be taken out of context, and sensationalised.

Don had written me a very bitter letter, accusing me, with some justice, of having cheapened the entire climb by what I had said afterwards. Inevitably, I think there was some bitterness as well. Don had always, at that time, seemed to have missed the boat. In his partnership with Joe Brown he had been overshadowed, and it had been Joe, not he, who had been invited to go to Kangchenjunga. He had been on two Himalayan expeditions at a later stage, but these had lacked the aura of romance and importance that surrounded the third-highest summit of the world. Through no fault of his own, the first expedition, to Masherbrum, had failed. On the second, to Trivor, he had worked so hard in the early stages he fell sick at the time of the summit assault, and therefore had to stand down.

I think my opportunism and material success inevitably acted as a barb to a relationship that was fragile anyway. At last, under the stress of circumstances, and the sheer scale of the problem that the Paine presented, our differences seemed unimportant. Climbing together on the Central Tower of Paine we should undoubtedly be faster and more effective than if we split up and climbed with any other member of the team.

And so, that night, on the 13th January, we agreed to climb together.

All we needed now was a fine day.

3 The Central Tower of Paine

We returned to the camp in the woods the following day, as Derek and Ian came down from the hut after spending two more days sitting out the bad weather. The wind was still gusting hard, but after another two days had dragged by it showed signs of dropping.

'We might as well move up to the hut,' said Don. 'No point hanging around here.'

'If you and Chris climb together, John and I can come up in support,' said Barrie.

And so it was settled. We walked up that afternoon. For the first time in weeks there was hardly a breath of wind. The clouds had vanished and the sun blazed down as we sweated our way up the long moraine slope leading to the hut. As we pitched a second tent beside the hut, we heard a rattle of stones from below us. Two Italians were also coming up. They passed without saying anything, and plodded up to the site of their camp, about 500 feet above us.

'We'll have to be bloody careful they don't get out in front of us,' I suggested, always suspicious of the intentions of others. 'Let's make a really early start in the morning.'

'I don't think we've got too much to worry about,' said Barrie. 'They can't know just how far we have got up the Tower.'

'All the same, I'd rather be on the safe side. I'll try to wake up about four o'clock.'

It was a perfect night. The contrast to what we had experienced in the last six weeks was so great that it was difficult to believe that these were the same mountains. It was still and silent, and the sky was a clear blue that slowly darkened to the deepest of violets. To the west, high above the snow-clustered cone of the Paine Grande, was a band of cloud that slowly changed colour from grey to a rich yellow-brown, merged into orange and, as the blue sky deepened, turned to crimson, cut by the massive black silhouette of the Fortress. It had a feel of peace and beauty that belittled our own internal rivalries and our race with the Italians. None of us said much that night; our sense of unity was cemented by the sheer grandeur of our surroundings. As the cloud slowly lost its fluorescence to merge with the dark of the sky, we climbed into sleeping bags and settled down to the tense wait that comes before any big climb.

The sense of exultation, though, gave way to a mixture of excited anticipation and some fear at the thought of the morrow's venture. What will happen if the weather breaks while we are on the upper reaches of the Tower? Can we possibly get back in high winds? Will I, personally, be up to the difficult climbing we shall undoubtedly have to face?

> I poke my head out of the tent; the stars glitter, cold, silent, windless. I look at my watch, 2.50; wait patiently for what seems an hour, and I look again at 3.00; John Streetley tosses at my side.
> 'Are you awake, John?'
> 'Yes.'
> 'I reckon we should start cooking.'
> 'I don't know. It's bloody early yet.'
> 'Okay, we'll give it half an hour.'

The time drags slowly past, and on the dot of 3.30 I crawl out of the tent to wake the others. Big Ned, dark and solid against the sky, stands patiently waiting. In the months of skirmishing at his feet we have given him a live personality. 'Big Ned's won again. He's in a bloody awful mood today.'

The others wake quickly, a hurried breakfast and we're off, plodding through the quiet half-light of the dawn. Tiptoe past the Italians – we don't want to wake them – then up the fixed ropes in the gully, hand over hand, feeling the weight of the packs on our backs. The Italians have been to the Notch; no sign of any progress on the Tower, but a great pile of gear that looks newer and better than ours.

'Shall we chuck it down the other side?' I suggested jokingly.

'No need. We'll beat them by fair means,' said Don. 'They can't get in front of us now.'

And up the fixed ropes. Compared to today's climbing techniques we were in the dark ages. Our fixed rope was made from ordinary hemp; we had no jumar clamps or other aids to climb the rope but had to pull up hand over hand. There were no modern hard steel pitons, harnesses or expansion bolts. As a result, our adventure was, perhaps, the richer.

Don went first, and I followed. We climbed the ropes one at a time, belaying each other with our climbing rope. It was just as well. As Don pulled up the blank slab just below our high point, the rope parted in his hands. It had had a tremendous battering from the wind, and the fibres of hemp must have simply disintegrated. That he stayed in contact with the rock was a miracle. Most people would have heeled back from sheer shock, but he somehow kept his balance on the steep slab, managed to remain standing on a couple of sloping rugosities, didn't drop his end of the rope, and then calmly joined the two ends in a knot. He was about eighty feet above me and I, not expecting a crisis, had been happily dreaming of the climb ahead. If he had fallen, he would have gone down 160 feet before I felt the impact, and I doubt if I could have held him. It was a remarkable escape – an indication of Don's uncanny power of survival.

I followed up the rope, more shaken I think than he was, and looked up at the new ground ahead. An open groove led up to a square-cut roof overhang. Above this the groove soared out of sight round the corner. But there were crack lines for our pitons. It might be hard, but it was possible.

This was the climax to weeks of frustration. The rock was warm and dry to the touch, rough-textured, solid, satisfying. I climbed the crack leading up to the square-cut overhang with the aid of pitons. I could hear vague shouts below, but ignored them. All that mattered was the rock a few inches in front of my nose.

But at the foot of the Tower, events were dramatic. Derek Walker and Vic Bray had spent the night at the camp in the woods and had left before dawn with the aim of getting a grandstand seat. They passed the Italian camp at about seven in the morning, a time when we were already near the top of the fixed ropes on the Tower. The two Italians, Nusdeo and Aste, were just emerging from their tent. They, obviously, had no sense of urgency and, at this stage, I suspect they had no idea that we had made so much progress on the Tower. Derek called out to them, and pointed upwards. He could just see us, two tiny dots on the sunlit rock of the Tower, below the big groove.

'Look, there they are,' he called out.

They looked, were obviously appalled by what they saw, and started to pack their rucksacks. At that moment the rest of the Italian party arrived, and immediately went into a huddle. There was obvious disagreement about the best course of action, but after a few minutes of fierce discussion they grabbed a load of gear and set out up the hill in pursuit of us. In the heat of the moment, they had forgotten their claims that they wanted a purely Italian route, and immediately started climbing our fixed ropes.

The climb was developing into a bizarre race, with Don and me in the lead. There was always a risk, however, that if we took a wrong line, and were forced to retreat, they could profit from the mistake and get ahead of us on the right line. We had intended to leave a line of fixed ropes behind us to safeguard our retreat, in the event of bad weather and high winds, but in the face of this threat of competition, Barrie Page and John Streetley pulled up the ropes behind them.

Meanwhile, out in front, I was climbing, happily oblivious of the drama down below. A couple of pitons hammered into the roof of the overhang above me, and I reached over the top. I have always preferred free climbing to artificial climbing; this, and the traditional British aversion to an excessive use of pitons, has always made me use as few as possible. At this point I overplayed my purism, trying to reach up over the overhang and pull up on a rounded ledge; my feet, standing in étriers, but jammed at an angle against the rock to give me a little more height, suddenly swung free, and the next instant I found myself hanging upside down, fifteen feet below the overhang.

I wasn't hurt – just angry at having made a mistake. I was so tied up with the climbing that I don't think I was even shocked by the fall. I swung back on to the rock, put in an extra piton, and pulled up. I spent over two hours on this 150 foot pitch; it was the best piece of climbing I have ever done: steep, sustained, on magnificently firm rock. On either side, the granite dropped away, smooth and sheer, and we seemed to be on the only possible line up this part of the Tower.

A shout from below. Barrie and John had realised that they would only slow us up if they tried to follow in our steps, and therefore, very unselfishly, they elected to go back down. Meanwhile, the Italians were just coming into sight on the slab leading up to the long groove. But somehow their presence seemed to matter no longer. It was insignificant, compared to the scale of the rock around us – the immensity of the Patagonian ice cap stretching out to the west. We could hear the cries far below, but they were thin and reedy, lost in the clear sky above.

And we were a close-knit pair, united just for a few hours by our mutual efficiency and common drive to reach the top. We said hardly anything to each other; there was no need for words; each knew what the other had to do. Our differences in background, personality and outlook on life were temporarily submerged by the scale and gripping absorption of the problem in hand.

I had reached the end of my pitch, tired, nerves extended, yet elated. Don followed up. Gave me the accolade:

'That was 'ard.'

He carried on up the next pitch, a square-cut corner as steep and high as the famous Cenotaph Corner in North Wales. He bridged up it with beautiful confidence, legs straddled on the walls in continuous, deliberate movement. Above, the angle dropped back and we began to climb more swiftly. Pitch followed pitch, and we were on the shoulder that was a major landmark from below.

'It doesn't look too bad from here,' said Don.

'Yes, but what about the time? We can't have more than a couple of hours of daylight, and it looks a hell of a way to the top. I think we'll have to do a lot of traversing.'

'We'll just have to go a bit faster. We should be able to get back here by dark. We'll leave our bivvy gear and travel light.'

We dumped the gear and set off over broken rocks towards the crest of the ridge. The angle was now much easier, but there were other problems. Every crack was gummed with ice, and there was snow on all the ledges. Don led a particularly frightening pitch, balancing up iced rocks. He used no pitons for protection and climbed with amazing speed. When I followed, he was out of sight and the rope was at an awkward angle. Had I slipped, I should have spun across the slab to come crashing into a rocky corner at its side.

I crawled fearfully up the iced cracks, full of wonder at how Don had managed to lead them in such fast style. Our way was now barred by a smooth rock tower; an abseil down the side, a scramble over a snow slope, and we were back on the ridge, with yet another tower in front. The light was beginning to fade. Don even dumped his camera to give him greater freedom of movement. It was steep, awkward climbing, but we were now barely aware of it, our sense of urgency was so great. We were in a race, not against each other but against the fast-falling dusk: the sense of euphoria and single-minded concentration that grips the long-distance runner at the end of a race must be very similar to what we now felt.

Another rock tower barred our way. Surely it must be the top. I pulled over the crest but there before me was yet another. Don went into the lead, balanced across a short, steep wall, stepped up round the corner and let out a shout. He was on the top.

I followed, and found him sitting on a block-like summit the size of a small table. The sun, a red orb, was dropping into the snow-white mantle of the Patagonian ice cap; a huge glacier like a grey speckled puff adder curled down from the cap to an ice-dotted lake, now fast fading in lengthening shadows. At last we could see all round us, the ephemeral reward for weeks of struggle: the Cuernos' sharp beaks down to the left, the Fortress and Shield, solid, seemingly impregnable, to the right, and in front, across another glacier, the Paine Grande, an ice-encrusted pyramid.

It was difficult to believe that the winds that had held us at bay for seven weeks could ever have existed, the feel of silent peace was so great, and yet our own memories were not so short. In the moment of elation there was still the worry of how we were to get down, the threat of what could happen to us, should the weather break.

We hammered into the summit block a Cassin Piton, just to show the Italians that we had been there, and then, I'm not sure whose idea it was, shouted in unison, 'Big Ned is Dead!'

As we shouted I knew a second of superstitious dread. Were we tempting the fates in decreeing the death of the personality we had built these last few weeks? But there was no time for delay; the light was fast fading and we had a long way to get back to our bivouac gear on the shoulder. We left the summit, having spent a mere ten minutes on it, scrambled and abseiled back down towards the shoulder, reaching it in the gathering dusk.

We had been on the go for fifteen hours, without anything to eat or drink. It was now that we realised that when Barrie and John had turned back, they had all the food and the gas stove with them. They had even called up to ask if we wanted anything passed up to us, but at that point, all we could think of was the summit, and we shouted 'No.'

We were parched with thirst; there was plenty of snow, but without a stove it was useless. We went through our sacs.

'I've got a can of sardines and two Mars Bars,' I said.

'Fat lot of good that is. I can't find my matches. I'm dying for a bloody smoke.'

Don made another search and found them. He was content for the night, thirst and all. It was a perfect, cloudless night, the sky clear and black, glittering with stars. Thirst and hunger seemed unimportant, to be savoured as a prelude to the food and drink we should have at our victory feast.

The snows of the ice cap were cherry pink in the light of the early sun, as we coiled ropes and packed our rucksacks. We were on the way down, full of victory, but part of me called out for caution. There was still 1,000 feet of sheer rock between us and solid ground. Fix the abseil rope, check the anchor, slide down, full of fear and caution. Will it pull free at the bottom? Thank God, it does; fix the next abseil, and so we go down.

Two rope-lengths from the shoulder, we meet the Italians. They spent the night in the groove, crouched on tiny ledges. First, there's Aste and Aiazzi. They glower at us, but then, on the next ledge, is big friendly Taldo. He grins happily, shakes hands and says in broken English, 'It is good you getting to the top. This is your route. We should not be here.' In fact the Italians reached the summit at 5 p.m. that afternoon, the same time as Ian Clough and Derek Walker arrived (twenty-two hours after us) at the top of the North Tower.

We laugh and smile – we can afford to now – and carry on down. It's the very last rope length. Derek, Ian and Vic are waiting for us at the Notch.

'We've got some booze for you to celebrate with,' shouts Derek, waving a bottle.

Don throws down the doubled ropes. They don't quite reach the bottom. We slide down all the same, stopping on a square-cut block about fifteen feet from the base of the Pillar. Don starts pulling down the doubled rope – all 300 feet of it. It comes down in a tangle, its end jamming in a crack just below us.

The end in sight, raked by thirst and fatigue, it seemed too much trouble to untangle so much rope to descend that last little step. A piece of hemp rope was lying on top of the block – it was the same that had broken when Don pulled on it on the way up. We picked it up, gave it a tug.

'Should be all right if we go carefully,' said Don.

He tied it to a piton and started to slide down it – oh, so slow and cautious. He was down, and it was my turn.

I eased my way down the rope, transmitting as much of my weight as possible through my feet on to the wall. I came to the place where our 300-foot rope had jammed in the crack, paused to free it, and in that pause – or perhaps as a result of the tug I gave to the other rope – I put too much strain on the hemp rope. It parted and suddenly I was somersaulting backwards.

A lightning thought: 'I'll hit the snow at the bottom.' I did, but didn't stop and rolled on down.

'God, I've had it.' Scrabbling with my hands, rolling over and over, frantic, clawing at the rock. And I came to a halt on the brink of a 500-foot drop. I was trembling violently, panting with pain and horror. The others sat around, giving me time to simmer down; someone handed me a water bottle. I became aware of my limbs, noticed the agonising pain in my ankle and was convinced it was broken. I took my boot off and tried to wiggle my toes.

'Looks firm enough to me,' said Don encouragingly. I rested for an hour or so, and then we set off down; for me, there was no more exhilaration, just slow, painful movement and the realisation of how close I had been to death. But even that was engulfed by the reality of a pain-filled present. It took us two hours to get back to the hut.

I was on the point of breakdown from fatigue and shock, yet still felt compelled to write a report, for the *Daily Express*, of the successful climb and my near-accident. Once I had finished the report and had given it to John Streetley to take down, Don remarked, 'You'd better do the cooking, Chris. I'm no good at it.'

It could have been a piece of fine psychology – and certainly worked out that way – but I suspect it was Don's laziness. He really did hate having to cook. Anyway, I started cooking a magnificent spaghetti and Don did his best to cheer me up.

'Tonight it'll be agony; once the shock wears off. I had five days on my own on Masherbrum with a sprained ankle. It was bloody awful trying to get out of the tent for a shit. I ended up just sticking my arse out of the door. I reckon you'll have to stay up here till the swelling goes down.'

'Perhaps one of the others might feel like staying up here too,' I said hopefully.

'I very much doubt it. They'll all want to get down to Base. What's the point anyway? We can leave you plenty of food.'

Having had his spaghetti, Don pushed on down to Base Camp, leaving me to doze in the tent. Later on that afternoon, Derek Walker and Ian Clough, just down from the North Tower, came to the hut. I was relieved when they decided to spend the night there, and resolved, come what may, to stagger down with them the next day.

It should have taken less than an hour to reach the camp in the woods; it took me four hours of unmitigated agony. There was no question of getting all the way down to Base Camp, but the others were keen to get back to comparative civilisation – to gallons of white wine, fresh roast mutton and all the other fruits of our victory.

'I've got to get a bit more film up here,' said Vic. 'I might as well stay up here with you and we can go down together tomorrow, if you're fit.'

I suspect he made this excuse to salve my pride. He had a rare sensitivity and kindness in his make-up. I was deeply grateful for his company that night. Next morning the swelling had lessened and I felt sufficiently rested to tackle the long plod back to Base Camp. I tried to ignore the pain and, as a carrot to keep me going, fixed on a vision of Wendy coming to meet me.

At last, on the long grass slope leading down to the valley, I saw her. I had kept a tight hold of myself up to this point, but now, in her arms, we both let ourselves go. The others had tried to underplay my narrow escape, but she had heard them talk about it amongst themselves. Somehow, this had made it worse. We clung close to each other in the hot grass; Wendy cried in agonised relief, and my tears mingled with hers. And then slowly we walked down, past the skeletons of dead trees, back to Base Camp.

My ankle was badly sprained – perhaps broken – and I obviously needed to get an X-ray. I resigned myself, therefore, to going to Punta Arenas, while the rest of the team began to think of a further objective. The weather seemed to have settled into a good spell, and they therefore decided to make an attempt on the South Tower of Paine.

Meanwhile, we cadged a lift into Cerro Guido, and then got the bus down to Punta Arenas. The town has a feeling of empty neglect; it is a place of greys and browns, of swirling dust and corrugated iron roofs. The general atmosphere reflected my own mood, for I longed to be back in the Paine, at grips with the South Tower, could imagine the others climbing under the hot sun, could almost feel the rough texture of the granite under my hands. The moments of joy and excitement of climbing the Central Tower were past and finished. The present was a swollen ankle, a sparse hotel bedroom and a drab hospital. I was X-rayed one evening and they discovered a hairline fracture on my ankle bone. I was put in plaster for a week, and had to eke out the time around Punta Arenas. Wendy and I spent much of the time in bed, playing interminable games of Scrabble, which Wendy invariably won. I have always been an appalling loser and ended up in a fit of temper, hurling the Scrabble set out of the first-floor window. Fortunately, the board didn't hit anyone walking in the road below.

My gloom was temporarily lifted when we met Eric Shipton, who was passing through Punta Arenas after one of his many exploratory trips in South Patagonia. I had never met him before, but he had been one of my heroes in the early 1950s when I had started climbing, and his book *Upon that Mountain* had been my bible. His appearance certainly lived up to my early dreams. He was in his late fifties, with a mane of silvery hair, balding in front to reveal a high forehead, and sweeping back behind quite large but neat ears. But his commanding feature was his eyes – a brilliant blue, that forever seemed searching some distant horizon from underneath a pair of bushy grey eyebrows.

There was an asceticism in his mouth, which was pursed, almost prim, and yet somehow this was softened by a manner that was distant, yet had a gentle warmth about it. He was a person that I felt one would never be able to claim to know well, yet at the same time could be a delightful companion in any venture. He gave the impression of a man at peace with himself – who had discovered the lifestyle that he wanted to adopt, and who would just go on quietly following it. With three companions, he had been investigating Mount Burney, to discover whether it was an active volcano. Characteristically, the weather had been continuously bad, and in the month they had spent in the vicinity of the mountain, they never actually saw its top, or enough even to work out a reasonable route to the summit. Shipton is not a man to remain idle, and they therefore circumnavigated the mountain, carrying all their gear on their backs and remaining on the move for seventeen days, in appalling weather.

Their daily ration was porridge for breakfast, a bit of chocolate and cheese for lunch, and a concentrated meat bar for supper. They had forgotten to take any salt, and I shall never forget Shipton's look of quiet satisfaction when he remarked: 'You know, we hardly noticed its absence at all. I think we might well leave it behind on our next trip.' The remainder of his team did not seem quite so enthusiastic at the prospect of saltless porridge.

I couldn't help comparing our two ventures. We had spent two months in one area, laying siege to a supremely difficult mountain. Without this persistence, we should never have attained the summit, for we had to lie in wait near at hand to snatch the odd fine day. Shipton, on the other hand, had covered a couple of hundred miles of exciting, unknown country, in the same period. He hadn't reached the top of any mountain, had barely tackled anything harder than scrambling, but through weeks of grinding effort and discomfort, he had come into closer contact with the romance of wild country than we did. Our climb also had its mysteries, had certainly stretched us to the limit, had very nearly killed me, but the mystery was one of technical problems. We knew the way to the foot of the mountain – Derek and Barrie had already been there – the sense of discovery was in looking up at a stretch of rock and saying, 'Yes, I think there is a route up there', and then tackling it, using our skill and experience to confirm our prior judgement. In a way, it was just an extension of attempting a new route on a crag in Britain. The scale was bigger, the weather much worse, the risks greater, but the principle remained the same.

The mountain traveller is looking for something different – he wants to see what is beyond a mountain range, and having reached the watershed, and looked down the other side, he is driven on to the next horizon. Facets of individual mountains, even the summits, cease to have such importance. He is interested in a mountain range as a whole.

Shipton was on his way down to Tierra del Fuego to explore the Darwin Range. It was obvious that I would not be able to climb again in the next few weeks, so I resigned myself to taking on the role of the tourist and wandering across Southern Chile and the Argentine with Wendy, to meet the rest of the expedition in Buenos Aires on their way back.

I now kick myself for my lack of curiosity, but I was too tied up with climbing, wanted too much to be on the South Tower. Even so, once we had made the decision, had our rucksacks packed and a flight booked to Puerto Montt in Southern Chile, I couldn't help catching Wendy's excitement, for this was her voyage of discovery. We were well laden, being equipped for almost any eventuality, with a heavy mountain tent borrowed from John Earle (one of Shipton's party), Wendy's guitar, a box of oil paints and easel, a huge rucksack, a suitcase with our respectable clothes, and various string bags full of bits of food, cooking pots and other items.

From Puerto Montt we followed the tourist trail through the Chilean Lakes, beneath the volcano Osorno, to Bariloche. Sometimes we stayed in cheap hotels, sometimes we camped. Soon I was able to forget the Paine, stop envying the others on the South Tower, in the idyllic present of our wanderings.

We spent three weeks on our own travels, wandering through the lake country, catching steamers and local buses. For a couple of days we camped on a volcanic shelf that jutted into the clear, limpid waters of Lake Llanquihue, cooking over a wood fire, drinking cheap local wine and swimming nude, unworried at being overlooked. Then on to Bariloche, and up to San Martin Los Andes, where we stayed with an old friend of Eric Shipton who ran a little guest house. We went riding through scrubby hills, sunbathed below the blazing sun, and just absorbed the country around us. It was all over too soon – time to return to Buenos Aires to meet the others. In those weeks of happy-go-lucky wandering, the Paine had already receded from my mind, and I had ceased fretting about the superb climbing I might be missing.

As it turned out, I had missed little. They had been forced to turn back from the South Tower after making a lightweight push up its South Ridge, hoping that this would give the easiest route. But they found it to be a great whaleback of a knife-edge ridge, with serried gendarmes, each of which would have taken a long time to surmount. At the same time, the Italians had tackled it from the north, which was steeper, and displayed difficulties of a more concentrated nature. In addition, perhaps, they were more forceful, having been beaten in the race for the Central Tower. They reached the summit, and our team then turned their attention to the Cuernos, the other attractive unclimbed peak quite near our Base Camp, but failed on this as well.

I must confess, I could not help feeling relieved that I had missed nothing. It made the retrospective enjoyment of our own little holiday that much greater. I was looking forward to our return to England, to finding a place to live, with a new career – of what, I wasn't sure – to carve out.

4   Woodland

'Where shall we live? How about Wales? Or the Lakes? Or perhaps even the Peak District?' This was a freedom I had never known before and which, I suppose, comparatively few people ever know. Where I lived had always been conditioned by my work, first for the army, and then for Unilever.

But now I was a freelance – in what, at this stage, I wasn't at all sure. We got back to England at the end of March. Our possessions consisted of a few clothes, plenty of books, Wendy's guitar and paints and my climbing gear. I had spent most of the money I had made from climbing the North Wall of the Eiger on taking Wendy with me to South America. I now had an advance of £500 for the book I had been commissioned to write by Livia Gollancz of Victor Gollancz. But most of this went on our first essential, a vehicle to get around in. We bought a brand-new Minivan – the first vehicle I had ever owned.

The immediate future was quite clear: I had my book to write and in the autumn I had some lectures. Beyond that I wasn't at all sure, and, in fact, downright frightened. People had a habit of asking, 'How long can you keep up this climbing business?'

'Oh, well into my forties,' I'd reply.

'Yes, but what are you going to do then?' they'd ask.

I'd put on a brave front and reply, 'Well, I'm going into the communications game – to learn how to write and talk about climbing. If I can do that successfully, I'll be able to make a real career of it.' They'd look sceptical, and I'd felt little conviction in what I had explained.

But in the present, there was a book to write – my first venture in the communications game – and I put off starting it time and again, frightened of the sheer scale of the project, of all those words I should have to spew forth. At that stage my total writing experience consisted of four articles in mountaineering club journals; and so I chased after easy alternatives, and there were no shortage of these.

Immediately on our return I was involved in making a commentary to Vic Bray's film of the Central Tower. Don and I had taken no film at all on our push for the summit, and Vic had been down in the valley; we were therefore desperately short of climbing footage, and so the BBC hinted that perhaps we might try to 'find' some film of the summit assault – good, close-up material of pitons being bashed in, hands going on to holds, and so on. Time was short, money shorter, and so we decided to shoot the necessary sequences near Don's home.

'I know just the place,' he said.

Our 'Potted Paine' was in a quarry high above a Yorkshire valley, near the village of Heptonstall. Below us, the chimneys of the mills jutted like granite needles out of the smog. The rock itself was steep enough, though it was stained black by centuries of pollution and the texture was coarser than that of granite. Most embarrassing were the initials and messages carved into the rock. Vic had his work cut out to avoid filming either the factories in the background or the graffiti on the quarry wall – even so, there crept into the corner of one of the sequences used in the film to depict our summit assault, a rough-hewn heart inscribed 'Kate loves John'.

To bolster our lack of film still further, the BBC built a ten-foot-high replica of the Tower, round which I had to peer as I made my commentary direct to camera. It was the first time I had ever been in front of a TV camera, and I was so nervous I could barely keep the quaver out of my voice as I read the script from the autocue.

While I was in London I met a long-lost cousin who was something – I'm not sure what – in television. He was quite a bit older than myself, very sophisticated, and had all kinds of important connections. My appetite for filming had been whetted, and I mentioned to him a scheme that was in my mind.

'How about making a film on the North Wall of the Eiger – a documentary of a complete ascent?'

My cousin knew just the man to finance such a venture, a man who had various television interests in the former Commonwealth. I went to a sumptuous office off Sloane Street, and was immediately in a strange world – it seemed almost straight out of a TV spy thriller. I was very much at sea as we talked of a £50,000 budget, production companies, and so on. But I went ahead and invited various climbing friends to join the bonanza – Whillans, Clough, Patey, MacInnes and several others. We were all going to spend the summer below the Eiger, playing at film stars. It seemed too good to be true – it was. I was handed over to an assistant, who handed me on to someone else, and from buoyant enthusiasm they became more and more cautious, until eventually the entire scheme fizzled out. This was a period of enjoying an ephemeral little glitter, of being a minor celebrity – something that had never happened to me before. I was eager to snatch at every opportunity to get myself established as a writer, film-maker, what-have-you, in an effort to find a clearly defined career.

Making a living around climbing was nothing new, even in 1962. Frank Smythe had done it successfully before the war, through his writing, photography and lecturing. Edward Whymper could, perhaps, be described as the first climbing journalist, though of course his income was primarily based on his profession as proprietor of a wood-engraving firm. In the post-war period, Alf Gregory and some of the other Everest climbers had made a fair amount of money by lecturing, but there was still a strong feeling of amateurism in the sport. I was often asked at lectures, 'Are you using the fee to finance your next expedition?' as if there were almost something slightly nasty about using the fee as part of one's income.

We had still not decided where to live. Wendy, at this stage, was uncommitted to any one area, provided that it was deep in the country. We had had six months together in a furnished room in Hampstead before going to Patagonia, and that was enough for her of London living. I felt the same, and obviously wanted to live in a mountain area. Originally, we had planned to settle in Wales, with the hope that I could get into the University College of North Wales at Bangor, but this seemed no longer necessary.

I was attracted to the Lake District, partly perhaps because I had done comparatively little climbing there, but also because it has a quality of beauty lacking in Wales. Snowdonia has a grandeur that is difficult to match anywhere south of the Border, but it is a beauty that is somehow alien to man. The farms and cottages suggest harsh austerity, unsoftened by hedgerows or gardens. Somehow, they don't seem to belong. The Lakes, on the other hand, are altogether softer, and more varied in their appeal. Each valley has its own special character. Man has succeeded in becoming an integral part of the country, with the cottages and houses blending into the hills as if they were an essential part of the landscape. There are more trees in the valleys, hedgerows intermingle with stone walls, and even on the open fell, there is a lighter, warmer quality.

And so we settled for the Lakes, loaded our brand-new Minivan with our few possessions – sleeping bags, Wendy's guitar and paints, my climbing gear – and drove north. We were under the happy illusion that we should be able to find a charming country cottage for about £1 per week. We were soon disillusioned. The summer season was nearly upon us and holiday cottages were at a premium. Even a two-roomed cottage could cost as much as £10 per week.

We stayed with friends in Keswick and started hunting. After a week, we had looked at a dozen cottages, had chased after several long-odds tips, had even applied for a council house in Mungrisdale, though, not surprisingly, failed to get it.

We were beginning to give up hope of finding something that we could afford, and were even thinking of looking for a cottage in the Peak District, when we called in at the Royal Oak, in Ambleside, one Sunday lunchtime to have a drink. I began talking to the barman, and it emerged that he was a climber. After working through the normal climbing gossip of mutual friends, we mentioned that we were looking for somewhere to live.

'If you're really desperate, I know a place near here,' he said. 'I stayed in it myself last winter. It's a single room over a garage on a farm. It's pretty rough, but at least it's a roof over your heads.'

This was to be the first time I had met Mick Burke, and it was to be another two years before we met again. At this stage, he was just one of the lads who had chucked up regular jobs to live in the hills with the minimum of work and the maximum of climbing. He came from Wigan, had started as an insurance clerk, but had quickly tired of a routine nine-to-five job, and had spent the previous year around Ambleside, doing a bit of labouring, or working the bar in the Royal Oak when he felt in need of a rest.

We left without further delay, and drove to Loughrigg Farm to see if the room was still vacant. The farmer warned us – 'It's a bit rough, you know.'

It was. An outdoor staircase led up from the farmyard to a small balcony. A peeling wooden door opened into a fair-sized room, lit by a couple of windows. The walls were of bare plaster, brown with dirt, and traced with a network of cracks. The floor was covered with rotting linoleum, which had long lost its colour, and the room was furnished with a few pieces of battered furniture that had probably been rescued from a refuse dump. The nearest water was from a tap in the yard and the sanitary facilities were limited to an earth closet, most primitive and smelly of all toilets, placed at the back of a pigsty. Set in the backstreets of a city it would have been unbelievably sordid, but here, in the heart of some of the most beautiful country either of us had ever lived in, it didn't seem to matter.

Loughrigg is on the southern edge of the Lake District, nestling amongst the broken foothills that spill down from the Langdale Pikes. From the balcony outside the door we could gaze across the farmyard, over the spring green grass of a field, dotted with clusters of Scots pine and larch, to the still waters of Loughrigg Tarn. A scattering of elm, still bare of leaves, ringed the lake, and beyond it, breaking up the fields and part-concealing other farm houses, grey-barked spinneys' arms intertwined, merged with the darkling green of spruce forest. This, in turn, mingled with the open fell leading up to the Langdale Pikes, picked out by the waning snows.

We lived in Loughrigg for three months, and were able to watch the explosion of colour, of every shade of green, that takes place each spring in this part of the Lake District. I did comparatively little climbing, in part surfeited by our expedition to Patagonia. I was still working on my project to film the North Wall of the Eiger. When that fell through, I thought up a more modest scheme, with the hardy Scot, Hamish MacInnes, to make a low-budget film of the North Wall of the Matterhorn. This was to fill the summer of 1963.

In the meantime, we continued a desultory search for a more comfortable home, and eventually stumbled on one through the good offices of Heaton Cooper, the Lakeland artist. We had never met the Heaton Coopers, but a mutual friend had told them about us. They called on our garret one afternoon when we were out, and left a note inviting us round for coffee.

Several other people were there, and soon the conversation turned to finding somewhere for the Boningtons to live. Fenwick Patterson, another artist, who had abandoned the rat-race and settled in Coniston, thought he knew where we might find a furnished house. In a few days this led us to Woodland – to me, and happily to the vast majority of Lakeland visitors, an unknown corner of the Lake District. It is down in the south-west corner of the Lakes, between Coniston and Broughton-in-Furness. The road runs beneath Coniston Old Man, barely wide enough to take two cars, between a mixture of dry stone walls and hedgerows. You pass Torver, and on either side is the open fell – in no way mountainous, but with mysterious little hills clad in bracken – and then, round a bend, past a farm, you come to the signpost to Woodland, down a steep little tree-clad hill. It's off the road, an oasis of green in the midst of the russet browns of bracken-clad hills. A newly-grown fir forest jostles with coppices of fine old deciduous trees, a few houses and farms spread on either side of the lane; you reach a signpost marked Woodland Hall, a makeshift cattlegrid, a rough, potholed drive; continue through a wood of young birch, past an artificial lake, full of weed, willows brushing the surface of the water: everything is overgrown, wild, attractive, up to the Hall itself.

We're after the Lodge. It's owned by the Dicksons, seed farmers from Essex, who have made their money from market gardening, and have now succumbed to the romance of the Lakes. They have bought the Hall, its attendant farm, and the Lodge, a cluster of buildings clinging just below the crest of a low ridge that bounds Woodland on its western flank. The Lodge is T-shaped, with the base of the T dug into the bank. In the front are two rooms on either side of the hall, and all look out on to Blow Knot Fell, a hump of hill that has an endearing beauty which grows on you as you look at it through the seasons; through the deep browns of autumn to spring, to the light, glistening green of the new sprouting bracken that dulls so very fast as the bracken grows, and which, even at full maturity, when it is a drab grey-green, ripples in the wind to make the hill seem live, capable of responding to the love it evokes.

And Woodland did evoke love – Wendy's and my love for each other, and our love for the place itself. It was a backwater, hidden away from tourists, standing back from the bigger hills of the Lakes and looking across at them. The northern horizon is dominated by Coniston Old Man, framed in trees from the cottage, a graceful, near-symmetrical cone, unbalanced by the sweep of the ridge that embraces Low Water and hides Dow Crag in its grasp. From the top of the ridge, just below the houses, you can look across a marshy valley to another ridge, lower, field-clad, which guards the secret little valley of Broughton Mills. Beyond it, slightly higher, a third wave-like ridge, breaking here and there with rocky surf, guards the Duddon Valley. And then you look down the valley to the Duddon estuary – brown sands and mud flats only covered at high tide. At night there's an angry glow at the end of the estuary from Millom Ironworks – ugly perhaps from close up, but from a distance, strangely beautiful.

But we hadn't yet been accepted as tenants. We walk up to the door of the big house where we meet Ivor and Beeny Dickson – the Pattersons have warned them of our arrival. Ivor is a big, rather sleepy man who has learned to stay silent and allow the constant flow of his wife's talk to continue, unheeded, past him; and Beeny, as we came to know her, is small, birdlike, with endless energy and a great capacity to be interested in the affairs of others. She had been planning to rent the Lodge as a holiday let, but on the promise of at least a year's stay, to include the winter, she agreed to let us have it for £3 a week, fully furnished. We had been paying £5 a week for a single room in London.

And so we moved into Woodland Lodge. It had become increasingly impor-tant to find a firm base, for we were fairly certain that Wendy was pregnant. We had already had one false alarm on the boat back from South America, when she had missed a period. This had seemed appalling in the limbo we were in at that time, with no knowledge of where we were going to live, or what I was going to do. Wendy certainly did not want a child at this stage; she wanted a few more years of freedom, to develop her own work as an artist and, more to the point, to see something of the world. I, on the other hand, had mixed emo-tions. When I viewed the prospect of parenthood logically, it appalled me, but whenever I was drunk a deep-rooted desire to procreate took hold of me.

We were both superbly ignorant of the complexities of pregnancy, but Wendy took a series of ultra-hot baths and went in for violent exercise, on the off chance that this might cause a natural miscarriage. To our vast relief, she had her next period just after getting back to England, and in celebrating our narrow escape, using the laxest of lax rhythm methods, she conceived in earnest.

Now that we were established in the Lake District, parenthood became an easier idea to accept. We were quickly resigned, and then excited, at the pros-pect. Wendy was due to give birth around Christmas, 1963, and we decided that she should come out to the Alps for the summer, while we made our film on the Matterhorn. I succeeded in getting a small advance, and our film stock, from the BBC. Meanwhile, Hamish got everything else organised. I had known Hamish, off and on, over a period of ten years. On my first trip to Scotland, at the age of seventeen, I had met him and had been taken up a series of winter climbs. At this stage I had never climbed on snow and ice, and I was employed as a portable belay. We made the first winter ascent of *Raven's Gully* (described in *I Chose to Climb*), and a couple of other routes.

Our paths had then split, mine into the army, while Hamish, always the lone individualist, had temporarily emigrated to New Zealand; had set out to climb

Everest with another hard Scot, John Cunningham, and had then returned to Britain.

In 1957 we had climbed together again in equally bizarre circumstances. It was to be my first Alpine season, and Hamish had talked me into making an attempt on the North Wall of the Eiger. Fortunately for me, we did not get very far up the Wall before I found an excuse for retreat. It was a matter of out of the frying-pan into the fire, for he then persuaded me to try the other great North Wall of the Alps – the North Wall of the Grandes Jorasses. This attempt also ended in fiasco, when Hamish fell into a crevasse in the pitch dark.

The following year we climbed together once again, and ended up by making the first British ascent of the South-west Pillar of the Dru. This was the first time that I had met Don Whillans. Our present project was very different from these early adventures – then, we had been climbing for fun, now we were trying to make a film. In a way, this was to be my introduction to the problems associated with making a living out of the mountains.

Wendy and I drove out to the Alps in our Minivan, stopping at Chamonix on the way. The weather was perfect, and I was sorely tempted to snatch a climb before starting work in Zermatt – we were due to meet Hamish the following day – but my sense of duty won, and I thrust the temptation aside. Hamish was waiting for us in Zermatt and had already done some superb ground work. He had enlisted the support of the head of the local tourist office and, as a result, we had unrestricted free-access to all the téléphériques, subsidised accommodation in a chalet in the village, and a special concession for hut fees.

We had everything – but the weather. It broke a few days after we reached Zermatt, and never really improved throughout the summer. Hamish filmed goats, cows, tourists and the familiar local life of Zermatt. Ian Clough arrived to take part as one of the 'stars' – I being the other – and we all sat and ate and drank through the long, wet summer.

The only climb I did was an ascent of the Matterhorn by the Hornli Ridge, climbing solo with Hamish, jostling with the long queue which trailed its way to the top of the most famous mountain peak in Europe. On a good day up to 300 people have been to the summit – the majority of them tourists, who are hustled to the top by the local guides, and then raced down to enable the guide to get some rest before taking up the next pair. That summer the fee for an ascent of the Matterhorn was £14, and so in theory the guide could make a fair amount by shuttling clients from the Hornli Hut to the summit, getting back to the hut at midday, having an afternoon rest, meeting the next client and setting out at two o'clock the following morning. The amount he made, though, depended entirely on the weather, and during 1963 the guides must have had a lean time, for even the Hornli Ridge was out of condition for most of the summer.

The profession of guiding has changed a great deal in the last fifty years. In the old days, the local guide was very much the leader of the party, invested with the respect of his clients who, in their turn, were experienced mountaineers. In recent years, however, particularly since the war, the vast majority of climbers have ventured into the hills without guides. A few outstanding mountaineers, such as Walter Bonatti, Gaston Rébuffat, René Desmaison and Michel Darbellay, the Swiss climber who made the first solo ascent of the North Wall of the Eiger, have managed to preserve a select clientele of wealthy amateurs, who are also competent mountaineers, but the vast majority of guides are now dependent on the casual tourist, who would like to be taken to the top of a well-known mountain – Mont Blanc from Chamonix, the Matterhorn from Zermatt. As a result, both the status and ability of guides have declined. A man who spends most of his mountaineering career hauling clients up the Hornli Ridge of the Matterhorn, can gain only limited experience, and this must inevitably diminish the level of his prowess on the hills.

That summer saw the start of my real interest in photography. Up to this time I had always taken a camera with me on my climbs, but had been little more than a holiday snap shooter. Hamish was very interested in photography, and had his own firm ideas on the ideal camera – a massive, old, folding 2¼-inch square Zeiss Ikon which, inevitably, he had picked up at bargain price in a sale. Fired by his enthusiasm, I sank all our savings in a second-hand Hasselblad, which Hamish assured me was a fantastic bargain. It couldn't have been more unsuitable for climbing. It is the Rolls-Royce of 2¼-inch square cameras – a single lens reflex camera, shaped like an oblong box, with interchangeable lenses and backs, to enable one to shoot different types of film without having to finish the spool.

It was bulky, heavy, and even the lens alone was worth about £100. In the hands of someone as unmechanical as myself, it was doomed to a hammering. But for the rest of that summer in Zermatt, I wandered round the foothills above the village taking chocolate-box pictures of mountains framed by trees, or reflected in little lakes. In doing so, I became more visually aware.

By early September, all the climbers had packed up and gone home, the snow was creeping down towards the valley, and an early winter seemed to have arrived. We returned to England.

A wasted summer? In a way, yes; but I had learned a great deal. Wendy, now six months pregnant, was beginning to bulge, and we could feel the movement of her babe in the womb. We were both becoming increasingly excited by our looming parenthood. In the past, I had always had a feeling of anti-climax at returning to England – there had been nothing there for me – but now, with Wendy, the prospect of returning to our little lodge at Woodland was immensely attractive. We were tired of the ordered prettiness of Switzerland. On the way back we stopped for only a day in London, and then hammered towards the Lakes. In the next two years I was to learn the way to Woodland all too well, as I drove, tired, rather depressed after frenetic lecture tours. But I came to know the landmarks of the return, and always felt a rising excitement as I got closer and closer.

The home stretch started at Leven's Bridge, at the turning off the A6, on to the Barrow and Ulverston Road, round the southern part of the Lake District. The next marker was Newby Bridge, at the foot of Windermere – wooded hills, rocks breaking through – and then the dye works at Backbarrow. The road narrows and winds through the works itself – everything stained blue – and then on the right an old iron works which must be one of the oldest, and certainly the most decrepit, in England, with rusty machinery that blends into the landscape. I'm getting excited now, in spite of tiredness; swing round the bends, up the long straight, across the head of the Cartmell Estuary, take a short cut on to the Broughton Road, up narrow lanes, round blind corners, and then back to the main road – now narrower, like the upper reaches of a great river – up to Broughton Fell, swing right on the moorland road to Woodland – we're nearly home – I feel a warm love of the place – could almost stop the car to get out and feel the turf at the side of the road. The fells are bracken-covered and the road winds across, unfettered by walls or hedge, over a final rise, and there's Woodland beneath – the Hall and Lodge a squat, grey mass of buildings, clinging to the crest of a low ridge; beyond, in rolling waves, the hills of the Southern Lake District. This isn't grand, awe-inspiring country, but neither is it pretty. There is a secret intimacy about its little valleys, tree-clad, winding their way into craggy fells.

We race down the hill, the engine, raucous, noisy, past the corrugated iron bungalow where we bought all our eggs, and then up the winding tree-covered drive to the Lodge.

The Lodge wasn't a handsome house; the kitchen was incredibly damp, the rooms were box-like, with ceilings that were too high for their small size, and the sheets on our bed always felt a bit damp – but it didn't matter, for the setting of the place was perfect. We both came to love the changing colours and tones of the bracken-clad hill opposite.

Back at Woodland, it was time for me to start writing my book – but there were also lectures to give, for we had now spent the advance, and were flat broke. Through the autumn and winter I made frequent forays to the south, lecturing about the Eiger until I knew the lecture parrot-fashion. It was lonely, depressing work, for I frequently spent several days, even weeks, away from home, living from my van, staying at a different place each night.

I felt very vulnerable, uncertain of the future, aware that my only asset was an ascent of the North Wall of the Eiger. My activities of the summer heightened these worries, for we had really failed in my first creative venture – we had not produced a film for the BBC. I had little idea of film technique, and my dreams of directing Hamish, who was the cameraman, had proved abortive – Hamish is eminently undirectable. He knew a lot more about filming than I, anyway, and knew exactly what he wanted to do.

We were becoming entrenched at Woodland, building up a circle of friends who, like us, had withdrawn from the conventional career game. There was Tony Greenbank, tall, lank, immensely enthusiastic about every scheme and project. He was my age, had been a librarian, but had always had an ambition to write. It was much harder for him to get started than it had been for me, for he was just an average climber, who got a great deal of enjoyment from his sport, but was in no way a celebrity.

He abandoned his job as a librarian and went to Eskdale Outward Bound School as an instructor, with the intention of using it as a tool to get established as a freelance writer. He was already married, which made his step still bolder. He soon became unpopular with some of his fellow instructors, who resented the fact that he was making money on the side by contributing articles to regional papers such as the *Yorkshire Evening Post*. It was this constantly recurring resentment of professionalism, and particularly of contributing to the media, and hence to the popularisation of climbing, that I had encountered. I suspect that there was often an element of jealousy in it – that you were making money out of something that was just a pastime for the majority. In Tony's case, his fellow instructors' resentment could hardly be based on grounds of professionalism, since they were also making a living out of climbing; I suspect it was a combination of straight jealousy, aligned with resentment of someone publicising their own private world.

Tony took a correspondence course in writing, and then resolved to give up his job at the Outward Bound School and work full-time as a freelance writer once he had reached a self-imposed target of annual earnings. It said much for his determination and sheer hard work that he reached this target in two years, whilst working at a job that was both physically exacting and time-consuming. He then bought a caravan in his native Yorkshire Dales, had his first child there, and somehow still managed to churn out his work. When I first met him in 1963, he had progressed to a small cottage at Arnside, near Kirkby Lonsdale, on the fringe of the Lake District.

Another aspirant writer we came to know was David Johnstone. Very different from Tony, he was small and slight, with a shock of dark hair and delicate features. He was an adept at judo. While Tony had few intellectual pretensions and was essentially a popular writer, David wanted to be a serious writer, and had already written several plays and a novel, sadly, all rejected.

He was the son of the local optician in Ulverston, had been sent to Rossall, a public school near Blackpool, and on leaving it had decided to devote his life to writing. For a time he had survived in London, writing during the day and busking with his violin in the evening – this was before the time when it became fashionable for hippies to pick up a living folk-singing in the passages of Underground stations.

He met his wife-to-be, Caroline, a big voluptuous girl, while flitting on the outskirts of the deb scene, and once they had married they took off to Northern Italy, where for a time they lived an idyllic life under the hot sun, with David writing and Caroline earning a little money by teaching English. Eventually, they were forced to return to England, and when we came to Woodland were living in a caravan near Coniston. Shortly after we arrived we were offered a farmhouse high on a hillside near the foot of the Duddon Valley. We were content with Woodland and so told David about it, and he moved in with his newborn child. They furnished the house from the pickings of a single auction sale, for the magnificent sum of £25. He needed much greater courage than I. He had no publicity to help him, was trying to establish himself as a serious playwright, and fought in the face of repeated rejection by publishers and theatres. He had to earn a living somehow, and so took a job in forestry – back-breaking, hard work, for a minimal wage. He lost this job when the foreman found him asleep in a ditch; and then, after a period on the dole, he found work in the tannery at Millom, hauling maggot-ridden hides and plunging them in the steaming curing-baths. There was no question of writing any longer – just one of brutish survival, of being penniless, desperately tired every night, and somehow trying to maintain a prickly pride in the face of seeming defeat.

Things at last improved when he managed to get the job of Duddon road-man. The pay was £10 a week, barely enough for food and rent, but he was comparatively free, could start the day when he wanted, and wander the roads with his broom and shovel, thinking his own thoughts.

On a fine day I often tempted him from the path of duty, and we would go off climbing on Wallabarrow Crag, nestling amongst trees in the bed of the Duddon, or disport ourselves on the Duddon School of Bouldering – a little array of crags I had discovered near the road.

And so 1963 slipped into 1964. The changing year was marked by the arrival of Conrad, our first child. He was born in the early hours of New Year's Eve, 1963. I had wanted to be with Wendy at the birth, but had been confronted by the solid conservatism of a small local maternity home.

'No one's ever asked for anything like that,' said the iron-willed matron. 'We haven't got the facilities, and anyway you've got to think of the feelings of the midwife.'

I wasn't going to stop there, and phoned the chief gynaecologist of the area.

'My dear chap, I've nothing at all against the husband being with his wife for the birth – it's a personal matter and, I must say, as far as I'm concerned, I think it's best to let the wife get on with it on her own. I've four kids, and I've never been with her – but that's purely a matter of choice. I'd be delighted for you to be with your wife throughout, but I'm afraid we just haven't got the facilities and, in her interests, I've got to say "No".

I didn't have a leg to stand on; they allowed me to stay with Wendy during her initial contractions, but as soon as she went into the second phase she was wheeled into the delivery room and they tried to show me the door. I was probably unnecessarily stubborn, but I insisted on staying at the home. Wendy had a long and painful delivery, perhaps aggravated by the tension caused by the reliance she had placed in having me with her. She spent long hours awake through the night, a lot of the time on her own, unattended, while I spent the same long hours sitting upstairs waiting, helpless – it was all so unnecessary, since she needed me and I could have helped her and the midwife, but we were confronted by the solid prejudice of tradition.

In the later stages I could hear her crying out in pain, gasping and groaning. Had I been with her it would not have been frightening, since I would have been working with her, reassuring her and helping her in what small way I could; but sitting in an empty, cold little room, I could only imagine the worst. I became convinced that Wendy was dying, and, for about the first time in my life, actually knelt down and prayed, from my own absolute helplessness. At the same time I felt a tinge of shame, that I was only doing this as an emotional last resort, for I cannot claim to be a Christian and, if anything, am agnostic. There seems much that we cannot explain in purely physical and scientific terms; there might well be some kind of spiritual force, but it seems sheer wishful thinking to believe that this force is particularly concerned with mankind's wellbeing – there is so much suffering in the world, so much ill done in the name of good, so much crime that does seem to pay. But that night, faced with the fear of losing Wendy, I was snatching at straws and went through an emotional hell, until at long last, at five o'clock in the morning, her raking gasps ceased and were replaced by the persistent raucous cry of a newborn child.

I was allowed down to see her, pale, exhausted, but wonderfully tranquil, and our tiny babe, freshly washed and incredibly ugly. After bandying a lot of names about, we settled on Conrad.

Once she returned to Woodland, life went on very much as before. We got around a lot, carrying the baby in his pram-top in the back of the van, on occasion leaving him in the van when we went to a pub. I had my lectures through the winter, and Wendy accompanied me to some of them. I also skirmished with the book and, as winter changed to spring, snatched every fine day to go climbing.

In many ways it was an idyllic life. Work pressures were few, since I only had the book to write and had not yet succeeded in getting established as a photojournalist. Once the lecture season was over, I had long periods at home. In the evenings we played canasta, and at weekends, when friends arrived, endless games of Risk, a splendid game of world conquest. Wendy learned to drive and then became interested in folk singing. She already played the guitar and had a pure, haunting voice with an extraordinary emotionalism in it. After practising for some time, she screwed up her

courage to sing at a folk-song club in Keswick, run by Paul Ross, a well-known Lakeland climber, with whom I had made the first British ascent of the South-West Pillar of the Dru back in 1958.

Those years of 1963 to 1965 were, in some ways, a limbo period. I had reached a peak in my Alpine career, with the ascent of the North Wall of the Eiger, and was now casting round to try to find the next step forward in my life. As far as climbing went, I had reached a plateau. I had attained a high level of competence in general mountaineering, but to push beyond this level needed a greater degree of organisation and a greater awareness of technical developments, especially those taking place on the West Coast of America in the Yosemite National Park.

That summer of 1964, I hoped to achieve the same level of satisfaction and excitement that Ian Clough and I had achieved in 1962, but I was destined to be disappointed.

5 Alpine Summer

May 1964. I had barely got halfway through my book and was already six months over deadline, but the Alpine season was pressing close and, after the previous year's fiasco, my dreams turned increasingly to getting some good climbing. But what to climb – and with whom? Because of the pressures exerted by my commitment to the book, and my own lack of organisation, I had left everything up in the air.

Then I had a phone call from Tom Patey. 'Would you like to come to the Alps with Joe and me? We've got some good new routes lined up; if you're interested in coming I'll let you know where they are.'

'But who'd I be climbing with? A party of three's no good.'

'I've just the right man. His name is Robin Ford; I climbed with him last week in the Cairngorms.'

'I've never heard of him.'

'That's because he hasn't done much on the English scene, but he's got what it takes to make a great alpinist – you'll have your job cut out to keep up with him. Anyway, have you got anyone better in mind?'

I hadn't; and so it was settled that I should climb with Tom Patey and Joe Brown that summer. I had only climbed with Joe once before, back in 1962. I was still working in London at the time, had come up to North Wales to climb with Don Roscoe, one of the original Rock and Ice members. When I had arrived he told me that he was unavoidably engaged but that Joe, who was working at White Hall, the Derbyshire outdoor activities centre, was up for the weekend and looking for a partner. I had never met him and was intrigued at the thought of climbing with the living legend of British mountaineering.

Joe was keen to finish a new route he had started the previous weekend on Castell Cidwm, a steep little crag on the south side of Snowdon above Llyn Cwellyn. We walked up to the crag, Joe was agreeable but not talkative; I was slightly on edge. I thought I was climbing well at the time, had made early ascents of many of Joe's routes, and had often liked to think that I was in the same class as he, as a rock-climber. I have always been intensely competitive and could not resist wondering how my climbing would compare with his.

'Do you want to have a go first?' said Joe 'I had to turn back last week; you might have a bit more luck. You'll need a lot of chockstones.'

This was in the pre-nut era, when, to protect themselves, climbers still relied on what the rock offered – rock spikes for slings (often only nylon line with a breaking strain of a bare 1,000 lb.) or chockstones jammed in cracks. Joe was probably one of the earliest, and certainly one of the most sophisticated exponents of the inserted chockstone – you carried a pocketful of stones with you and jammed them in the crack. It was a fiddling, intriguing business, demanding a fair level of skill.

The year 1962 was when someone – I'm not sure who – had the idea of stringing bolt-nuts of different sizes on to a sling and using these in place of chockstones. Since then, these nuts have been refined into a series of shapes, tailor-made for their purpose. In many ways, I suspect that this was a retrograde step, for it enabled the climber to gain protection from running belays in places where protection would have been impossible with inserted chockstones or the traditional flake runner. One of the attractions, indeed reasons, for climbing, is the element of risk involved, of pitting one's own judgement against the mountain, with a fall as the price of a mistake. In its purest sense, the solo climber is getting the most out of the sport since he is staking his life on his judgement. Without companions or rope, he has a good chance of being killed in a fall. The majority of us, however, prefer to hedge our bets, climbing with a companion, using a rope and then contriving running belays to reduce the distance we fall if we do come off. The problem is in deciding just how far we should reduce this risk before losing a vital element in the sport.

There has always been a tradition in British rock climbing that has renounced the use of pitons. Since the war, with rising standards of difficulty, and with the progressive encroachment on to every available piece of rock in the country, pitons have become increasingly used when no other means of protection or of natural ascent have offered themselves; but there has always been a stigma attached to their use, and credit has gone to the man who has succeeded in repeating a route with less such aid than his predecessors. The development of the nut and metal wedge has not been accompanied by any such stigma, even though its resemblance to a piton is very close. Both pitons and nuts are metallic foreign bodies that are being slotted into cracks. The obvious difference is that pitons are driven in by a hammer, while the nut, in theory, is only hand-inserted. It is all too easy, however, to apply a few taps of a hammer to the nut to lodge it more securely. Does this turn it into a piton? I wonder. On the other hand, a piton can, on occasion, be hand-inserted. Does this make it a nut?

The development of the nut was a gradual, insidious process which, as a result, roused little controversy and today, in 1972, it is difficult to imagine any kind of effective rejection of nuts proving practical; but back in the early 1960s they could have been rejected in exactly the same way that the pitons had been and still are. If an ethic or rule had been established that any foreign body, metal or plastic wedge, jammed or placed in a crack, should be regarded as cheating, the sport might have maintained a higher level of adventure or risk, and at the same time, I suspect, would have reached the same level of technical difficulty in the routes being pioneered. The difference would have been that fewer climbers could have repeated the hardest routes, simply because the risks involved, and therefore the self-confidence required, would have been greater. I must confess, though, that I use as many nuts as anyone and certainly depend on them to maintain my own climbing standard.

But I have digressed. Joe and I are standing below Castel Cdwm. The rock juts steeply above, in a series of bristling overhangs, cut by a broken crack. If I had been with anyone but Brown, I think I would have suggested we went somewhere else, but I wasn't going to back down in his company. I collected my pocketful of stones, jammed a hand in the crack and pulled upwards – at least there were holds, but it was all overhanging. I began to tire. Ten feet up, the angle lay back to what, from below, had seemed a slab, but once on it I found I was off balance and I couldn't find any holds.

'Where did you go from here?' I shouted down.

'Up the slab,' came the reply. 'You can get some good inserted chocks in the crack above.'

But how the hell to get to the crack above! Suddenly, the cliff seemed to grow above me as my arms progressively weakened. I hammered in a peg.

'What do you think you're doing?' came from below. 'I got above there last time without a peg.'

I dangled on it; my arms felt like stretched spaghetti. The climb was undoubtedly impossible.

'You'd better have a go,' I conceded.

Back down, I took over Joe's rope, and spent the rest of the day watching him at work. It was an impressive sight. He was very methodical and completely relaxed. He drifted up the holdless slab, then at full, elongated arm's reach, placed a tiny stone in the crack above, threaded a sling behind it and sat in the sling. And so he slowly worked his way up the climb.

When I followed him, I got up the pitch quite quickly, cursed myself for turning back, for surely I also could have inserted all those chockstones. It's just a matter of patience – or is it? It was beyond my conception before the start of the climb that chockstones could be used so ingeniously. It was also beyond my ability to relax sufficiently in a lead position to keep going.

On that first acquaintance I had found Joe easy-going, friendly, yet somehow withdrawn. There is something inscrutable about both his features and his personality. He once admitted to me: 'I don't think anyone really knows me – not even my wife, Valerie.'

He was very different from Don Whillans, and you could see why they had fallen apart. Joe and Don between them had made a revolution in British rock-climbing, putting up a series of routes, most of which held a legendary aura of being impossible for any but a breed of supermen of much the same shape and size as Don and Joe – in other words, fairly short and prodigiously strong. They were probably equally good as climbers; Don was attracted by obvious, very direct, usually vicious lines up crags that were often very poorly protected. Joe tended to go for more devious lines, less obvious, but neverthe-less superb routes. In sheer volume of new routes, Joe climbed by far the larg-est number. This was partly because Don began to lose interest in British rock-climbing, preferring the sterner and fresher environment of the Alps, and then the Himalaya. Although Joe has always admitted that he prefers light-hearted rock-climbing to greater mountaineering, his record is impres-sive. In 1955 he went out to Kangchenjunga with the comparatively lightweight party led by Charles Evans, and went to the summit. The following year he joined Tom Patey, Ian McNaught-Davis and John Hartog, on an expedition to the Mustagh Tower, and also reached the summit. This must rank as one of the outstanding mountaineering achievements of the fifties, for the Mustagh Tower is 23,860 feet, and one of the steepest and most shapely mountains in the world. Climbing it with a party of four, and all four getting to the top, was a magnificent achievement. Don, on the other hand, while being a superb mountaineer, seemed to have an unlucky streak. He had been on two Himalayan expeditions by 1962 (one to Masherbrum and the other to Trivor) but on neither reached the summit, and his expedition to Gaurishankar, in the autumn of 1964, was equally unsuccessful. This disparity in success, the fact that Joe was hailed as Britain's greatest-ever rock-climber, the fact that he, and not Don, had been invited to Kangchenjunga, had undoubtedly eroded their relationship, and they had ceased to climb together.

I knew Tom Patey much better than I knew Joe. We had had a superb, happy-go-lucky climbing holiday together in Scotland, in the summer of 1960. Tom told the story of our adventures in a climbing journal shortly afterwards, and it is now published in a collected volume of his works, *One Man's Mountains*. He had a rich and complex personality, with a bewildering variety of talents. He was undoubtedly one of the outstanding British mountaineers of the post-war period, with a host of new routes in Scotland and the Alps to his credit. He was also a brilliant Himalayan performer, having reached the summit of Rakaposhi as well as that of the Mustagh Tower. He was no technician, wasn't even a brilliant rock-climber, but on mixed ground of heather, earth, rock, snow or ice, I have never seen an equal. He moved with an easy speed and confidence over this type of ground, as happy unroped as roped. He had an easy contempt for style and elegance, whether in climbing, appearance or general way of life. There was little grace in his movements as a climber; he just swarmed up a rock face, inelegantly perhaps, but in complete control. His general appearance showed equally little regard for fashion or style.

Off the crag he'd dress in an old ready-to-wear suit, obviously quickly purchased from a multiple tailor, and always crumpled. On business, or a formal occasion, he'd wear a tie that had been purchased with equally little regard for fashion, but at the first opportunity he'd pull it off, stuff it in a pocket and open the neck of his shirt. He didn't look an athlete, smoked heavily, constantly took drops for his hay-fever, and had limbs that seemed to have been hung on to his body with as little regard as the clothes that covered them. His face was that of a man who had seen life – the perfect Raymond Chandler tired-and-battered-private-eye face – grey, creased, hard worn, yet somehow compassionate.

But Tom was more than a mountaineer. He had a boundless, impish imagination and a superb command of the English language. He had that very special ability to satirise lightly without hurting his victim unduly. He was also a good musician and carried his accordion with him wherever he went. He could play anything on it from hearty German marching songs to Highland jigs and reels, but his most unique ability was as a song writer. He composed a series of songs about climbers and climbing which were a form of musical cartoon. His favourite riposte, whenever anyone grumbled at being the target of his pen was:

> The highest compliment that anyone can pay you is to make you the subject of satire. It's better to be written about under any circumstances than to be ignored.

You could always guarantee that a holiday, or even a short weekend, with Tom would be full of surprises – that it would develop into a magical mystery tour of pubs, people and mountains. That summer in 1960 we had climbed fifteen new routes, all discovered by Tom who had an encyclopaedic knowledge of the Highlands. We had started several impromptu ceilidhs, and had met a whole series of bizarre personalities, whom, I am sure, I should never have got to know without him around.

I was full of great expectations and a few misgivings, therefore, when Tom suggested we climb together that summer of 1964. We could be sure of plenty of new routes to climb, for Tom had prepared a dossier of unclimbed lines in the Alps, but they would be routes of his choice.

We drove out to the Alps in his battered Skoda – it was a replica of its owner, unfashionable, untidy, but very rugged. At an early stage of the journey Tom surrendered the wheel and retired to the back seat to play his accordion as we rolled down through France on our way to Chamonix. This was the first time I had met my own climbing partner, Robin Ford. He was in his early twenties and at this stage had done most of his climbing in Britain; almost immediately it became evident that we had little in common. There was too big a gap in age and experience. He would have been better off climbing with someone of the same range of experience, rather than plunging in with quite a high-powered team which had already discovered a great deal about the mountains.

Soon, it also became evident that Tom's approach to alpine climbing was very different from mine. I liked big, exciting objectives, but once having decided on an objective, preferred to plan out the attempt very carefully, leaving as little as possible to chance. Tom, on the other hand, regarded the trip as a light-hearted holiday, enjoyed drinking and singing, in the Bar Nationale and at the campsite, into the early hours of the morning, and then would rush up the hill at the last possible moment to snatch a new route, relying on his flair and speed to get up the climb in the day, and back down to Chamonix for another carousal. He was not interested in the multi-day epic, or the highly technical rock-climb. He was a superb mixed alpinist with a genius both for picking out a good line up a mountain and the ability to climb it, only putting on a rope when the difficulties became acute.

We completed two new routes in this style: one up the South-West Ridge of the Aiguille de Leschaux, a beautiful and very isolated peak at the head of the Leschaux Glacier, and the other on the North Face of the Pointe Migot, a subsidiary of the Chamonix Aiguilles. They were both tributes to Tom's genius for smelling out new routes. He had a big black book full of photographs, often purloined from books and journals loaned to him by friends, in which possible new routes were marked. This was quite an achievement, even in 1964, for almost all the obvious lines in the Chamonix area had long been climbed.

We talked to Lionel Terray, the famous French climber, about our plans for new routes, but he dismissed our ambition with the comment, 'The virgin climbs around here are like dried-up old spinsters. They are not worth taking.'

There was a lot of truth in this, for all the major ridges and walls had been climbed, but an essential facet of climbing is the desire to seek out new ground. This was particularly strong in Tom, and he was happier searching his way up a comparatively undistinguished rock wall, tucked away at the back of a subsidiary glacier, than following a well-worn trail up a climb of much greater quality. I was less satisfied, however, for these new routes we were doing were Tom's routes, not mine. In addition, Joe and Tom were a faster pair than Robin and I. As a result, we were simply following them up the climbs without any of the satisfaction and thrill of picking out the route for ourselves.

On the North Face of the Pointe Migot, Robin and I made a firm bid to get out in front. We had been drinking and singing late into the night in the Bar Nationale, and had caught the first téléphérique up to Plan d'Aiguilles, the halfway station on the way to the Aiguille du Midi. We left the ugly shell of the téléphérique station, and started up the path that led to the Glacier de Blaitière.

The Pointe Migot is little more than a nobble on the ridge that sweeps north from the Aiguille du Plan, towards the Chamonix valley. At its end is the shapely tower of the Aiguille du Peigne, which boasts several classic rock-climbs, on which British climbers habitually sharpen their teeth before venturing on to harder things. Beyond the Peigne is the Aiguille des Pelerins, another granite tower, and hidden behind that is the Pointe Migot, whose North Face, black and virgin, drops down into the head of the Glacier de Blaitière. The North Face of the Migot was a coy, and undoubtedly plain old spinster whom no one had yet bothered to court. Only someone with Patey's appetite for untouched ground would have sought her out.

But that morning our team were in anything but good shape. Patey was muttering about his hay-fever and Joe, recovering from a hangover, was sick halfway up the Glacier de Blaitière. I had retreated to bed early and consequently was feeling moderately fit. I chivvied Robin out into the front, so that we should at least have a chance of taking the lead.

The pace quickened. Patey and Brown obviously guessed what we were up to and tried to reduce our lead. We scrambled up jumbled ice below the Pelerins, and up the gully that led up towards the North Face of the Fou. On our left, the frozen cascade of the hanging glacier on the North Face of the Plan loomed over us. It was a grim place, full of lurking threats of stone-fall. The North Wall of the Pointe Migot was very steep, broken at about half height by a sloping shelf that ran up diagonally from right to left. A system of cracks seemed to lead up towards it.

'Come on, Robin,' I said, sufficiently quietly for the others not to hear. 'If we can get roped up first and into those cracks, Tom and Joe'll never get in front.'

I spurted towards the foot of the cracks and pulled ahead of Robin who was less used to this competitive climbing. The trouble was, he had the rope. We were still fifty yards in front of the other pair. Robin reached me; I grabbed the rope and started to uncoil it – the damned thing was in a tangle. I cursed. Tom was only twenty yards away. I tossed the rope on the ground – should come free – 'You untangle it while I run out the first pitch,' I said.

It was a grotty crack, quite steep, filled with ice. I started up it, climbing fast, ran out twenty feet and the rope tugged from behind. I looked back to see Robin struggling with what looked like a tangled skein of knitting. Patey and Brown were now with him, already roped up. Patey started up the cracks. He reached me.

'I'm glad to see you've a sense of urgency,' he said complacently. 'Very commendable in a place like this. I'm sure you won't object if Joe and I climb past you while you sort out your little troubles.'

'Not at all,' I replied.

By the time Robin had sorted out our rope, Tom and Joe were on the next pitch. I had resigned myself to following them up yet another climb.

The North Face of Pointe Migot

We climbed two more pitches, and the groove we were following divided, one branch going off to the left and the other going straight up. Tom was belayed at the dividing point and Joe was leading up the left-hand groove.

There was just a possibility that they had taken the wrong branch. The groove going straight up was steeper, but it looked as if it might lead directly up to the foot of the gangway in the middle of the face.

'I'll just have a look up here,' I told Tom. 'It'd save a bit of time if Joe's going up a blind alley.'

As soon as Robin reached me I started up the groove. It was filled with ice at the back which pushed me out of balance, but there were sufficient holds for three strenuous pulls and the angle eased off; the groove ran easily straight up to the gangway. We'd won. We were out in front once again. I ran out the rope and called Robin to come out. There was an interminable delay as he fiddled around with his belay. I glanced over to the right and could see Joe belayed at the top of his groove. Tom had already joined him and was now swinging across towards me, using tension on the rope.

'What the bloody hell are you doing down there?' I shouted to Robin. 'Get a bloody move on.'

No reply, but at least he was climbing now. The rope trickled through my fingers. Patey had nearly reached me, a couple more ape-line swings, and he was in the groove just below me. He didn't wait, but climbed straight past, giving me an easy grin. I managed the weakest of weak smiles, and yelled down to Robin to hurry up. But by the time he reached the stance Tom had got to the top of his pitch, and Joe was already on his way across. We had lost Round Two.

The bottom of the gangway was guarded by a small snowfield. Tom launched on to this, kicking into the snow with his boots. He hadn't bothered to put on his crampons – no time in the competitive climbing game. He got about half-way up, and suddenly there was a sloosh, and he came shooting down the steep snow. It was only a few inches thick, lying on hard ice.

Tom fell about thirty feet, but was held by the rope. He obviously hadn't hurt himself, and I couldn't resist letting out a cheer – but how was I to profit from their misfortune? Robin was leading up towards Joe, and was going much too slowly to give us any chance of passing them before they sorted themselves out.

Tom returned to the fray, climbed the snow more cautiously, reached the rock gangway and followed it up to a point where it steepened. I resigned myself to following, and concentrated on enjoying the climbing. This was excellent, being steep and tricky, with the minimum of protection. The whole climb had taken us only four hours, and just after lunchtime we pulled over the top to stand on the summit.

The climb had been fun, the competition had added spice to what was a mediocre route, and we were back in Chamonix that evening. I felt dissatisfied, however, and wanted something bigger and more challenging. Above all, I wanted greater control of the initiative. There was little satisfaction in being on a new route if it was not your own concept and you were just following another pair up it. But that summer I was destined to be disappointed, partly because the weather remained unsettled, but mainly, I suspect, because I was not clear on what I wanted to achieve – either in climbing or in my own life. Tom and Joe were now due to go home, and so I teamed up with two Americans, Jim McCarthy and Dick Williams, in an attempt to make a new direct route up the North Wall of the Civetta, a 5,000-foot limestone wall in the Dolomites. Jim McCarthy had conceived the idea. He had just finished Law School in New York, and was the most outstanding climber on the East Coast of America. Strangely, our paths had already crossed back in 1958, on Jim's first visit to the Alps, when we had met on the lower rocks of the East Face of the Grand Capucin. My companion, Ronnie Wathen, and I had completed the route, but unfortunately Jim had been forced to retreat after his partner had dropped their rucksack.

Jim had come over to Europe with a formidable array of the newly developed American hardware – the chrome molybdenum pitons that had enabled a small group of Californian climbers to conquer the huge granite walls of Yosemite. A few of them had already made their marks on Europe. In 1962, Royal Robbins and Garry Hemming had made a direct start to the West Face of the Dru, up a series of superb crack-lines in the lower part of that face, and the following year, Tom Frost, another Yosemite pioneer, had made the first ascent of the South Face of the Fou, with John Harlin, Hemming and a Scot, Stewart Fulton. Jim wanted to apply the same Yosemite style of climbing to the North Face of the Civetta. He was aware, however, that his team was on the weak side. He had climbed in Yosemite himself, but his companion, Dick Williams, had never been farther afield than the New Yorkers' local crag, the Shawangunks. These are a 200-foot high line of outcrops in upstate New York – the American equivalent of a glorified Shepherd's Crag, or Three Cliffs of Llanberis.

I met Jim one night in the Bar Nationale, and he immediately asked me to find another companion and join him. I had been making plans with Brian Robertson, a young Scots climber, full of big ambitions. He was a leading light in a group of Edinburgh climbers who called themselves the Squirrels, after a famous Italian climbing group called the Cortina Squirrels. Brian was rather like a squirrel, short, strongly built, with a squirrel-like persistence. He was a great enthusiast, becoming near-incoherent in his enthusiasm for whatever happened to be his latest project. He happily agreed to join us, and the next day we all piled into Jim's newly purchased Volkswagen Varient, and were whisked over to the small town that nestles below the North Wall of the Civetta. McCarthy is a great fixer; he already had introductions to one of the senior guides and great pioneers in the area. We spent the night in his barn, and next day, thanks to his good office, had our mound of baggage, ironware and food whisked up to the hut on the little service téléphérique, whilst we wandered up, unladen, through woods fragrant with flowers and the hot resin of pine trees. We stayed in a newly built hut, immediately opposite the face. The more I looked at the wall, the less happy I felt. The line that Jim had chosen was to the right of the Phillip Flamm route, straight up a huge, blank, overhanging wall of grey and yellow rock. There were cracks all right – indeed, the scale was so vast they were probably chimneys – but it all seemed awfully steep. I had not undertaken such a big artificial route before and felt unsure of my own ability and, never having climbed with Jim, felt little confidence in him either.

I insisted on doing a training climb first, and the next morning we all set out to complete the North Face of the Torre Val Grande, a classic route on the far left of the Walls of the Civetta. Brian and I quickly pulled away from the two Americans as we scrambled up the broken gully that led to the start of the real climbing. It was an enjoyable fun-climb, with a thrutchy roof overhang which we swung up in étriers, and then a few good pitches of free climbing. We got back to the hut that evening to find the rest of the team at a low ebb in morale. Dick had never climbed on the loose rock that guards the approaches to most Dolomite climbs. He was unaccustomed to fast soloing, and eventually they had turned back before even reaching the foot of the climb proper.

This boded ill for our plans on the new direttissima on the Main Wall of the Civetta. Dick wasn't keen to commit himself to such a major undertaking, and nor were we. That afternoon, however, we had passed the tent of another British climber, Denny Morehouse. I didn't know him personally, but had heard a lot about him. He had spent a lot of time in the Dolomites, mainly climbing with continental climbers, and had an impressive array of hard routes to his credit.

Sitting in the mouth of his battered tent, he looked a bit like the mad professor in an early surrealist German film. He wore heavy horn-rimmed spectacles, one lens of which was starred, presumably from a falling stone; his gear was in tatters and he had been living for the previous fortnight on a diet of pasta and plain bread.

I suggested inviting Denny, and Jim agreed. We brought him up to the hut, gave him a good meal, and the next day planned to carry all the gear up the face to the start of the difficulties.

The moment we started working together, things went wrong. Big wall climbing demands a high level of teamwork, rope management and awareness of the job in hand. We didn't have a clue. Jim understood the new American methods; was accustomed to the high level of discipline adopted on the walls of the Yosemite; we were blissfully unaware of these techniques. Soon the rope was tangled into an inextricable mess. Denny, out in front, dislodged a boulder the size of a table, and it narrowly missed Jim. I dropped a peg-hammer; a few stones whined down from above and we all retreated for the night to the hut, full of doubts about each other. We were going to set out for the face at three in the morning. I felt half-hearted as I organised my gear, snuggling into my sleeping bag as a haven of safety, dreading the moment of commitment when we set out for a climb that I don't think any of us felt up to. I dropped off into an uneasy sleep, to be woken all too soon by the jangle of the alarm. No one moved – and then Jim jumped down from the bunk, looked out of the window and called: 'The goddamned cloud has come in – you can hardly see the bottom of the face.'

I suspect we were all secretly relieved. I rolled over and immediately dropped into a deep sleep. By morning the cloud had begun to break up, and by midday it had turned into a good day, but the delay had done the trick. With hardly a word said, we abandoned the attempt. Jim and I climbed the Andrich Fae route, a classic free rock-climb to the left of our proposed line, and then we all set off for Chamonix, I anxious to get back to the main scene of action, to snatch at least one good new route before the end of the season.

But our return to Chamonix coincided with the arrival of bad weather. Our little group, that had never coalesced into a team, broke up. Jim and Dick went down to the Calanques, Brian went home, and I stuck it out in Chamonix, just hoping for one good route to make the summer seem worthwhile.

Three weeks went by; three weeks spent hanging around Chamonix, living in other people's tents, listening to the sound of rain drumming on the roof and eking out my beer money in the Bar Nationale, until near the end of the season, I became involved in a BBC documentary on the North Wall of the Eiger. Amongst my plans for that summer had been an attempt on making a new Direct Route up the North Wall of the Eiger. This was the current last great problem of 1964, and already several leading Continental climbers had tried and failed on it. John Harlin, an American climber, was leading contender, and had already made a couple of attempts. My own plans were little more than pipe-dreams – I had neither sufficient equipment nor the right companions for such an undertaking.

I trekked over to Grindelwald to meet the BBC team at the start of September. I should have liked to have talked about my original ascent of the original route on the Eiger North Wall – a climb full of good and exciting memories. The producer wanted something that was more immediate in its appeal, and I allowed myself to be talked into showing all the gear I should have used on an attempt on the Eiger Direct, as if I were about to go on the route. Having abandoned all thoughts of attempting it that summer, I felt cheapened. It emphasised my own vulnerability and made me doubt my own integrity. At the end of the interviews I returned to Chamonix, washed out and depressed.

But the weather was, at last, looking up, as all too often it does in early September –there wasn't a cloud in the sky, and the Chamonix Aiguilles were clear of snow. At last, here was the chance to recoup a wasted Alpine season – one great, exacting route and I could go home happy, my confidence restored. And yet, perhaps, in those weeks of waiting and worry, I had lost sight of the very reasons why we should climb – had lost the sheer spontaneous joy that climbing should entail.

I met up with Mick Burke in the campsite. He, also, was without a companion and we agreed to tackle the South Face of the Fou, a route that still awaited a second ascent, and had the reputation of being exceedingly difficult. I had a few American pegs, sold to me by Jim McCarthy; there weren't nearly enough, and I suspect we could have got ourselves into a precarious situation if we had ever launched ourselves on the climb. Anyway, Mick and I went into Chamonix to get some bivouac food before setting off for the hut that evening.

It was in the supermarket, between the dried-soup shelves and the refrigerated cabinet holding dairy foods, that I suddenly realised that I had drained myself of all my drive and ebullience – I felt an irresistible longing for home, to hold Wendy close to me, to see and play with Conrad. I had already half-filled a basket with bivouac food; I stood there in an agony of indecision, and then just dumped the basket on the ground and walked out of the shop. I found Mick at the campsite, packing his rucksack.

'Y're ready then?' he said. 'There's only ten minutes before the last train to Montenvers, you know.'

'I'm sorry, Mick, I'm not going. I think I've been out here too long. I feel bloody stale, and wouldn't be any use on the climb anyway.'

Mick took it wonderfully stoically, without any recriminations. Having made up my mind, I had the homing instinct of a carrier pigeon. I caught a train for Paris that evening, spent most of the night pacing up and down in the corridor, in a fever to get home; reaching Paris, I was so impatient that I got a taxi to the airport terminal and took the next available plane to London. I phoned Wendy and caught a train that took me as far as Preston. Wendy drove down in the middle of the night, with Conrad asleep in the back of the van, to pick me up.

That return to the Lakes was a return to reality, to the joy of our life together, to a newly found satisfaction in getting down to the book, which at last seemed to flow with some prospect of, one day, being finished – even to a renewed and fresh enjoyment of climbing, unsullied by worries of maintaining a reputation, or building a career round the mountains.

6   Home Ground

A Lakeland autumn: the hill opposite turning a rich golden brown, leaves falling in the little artificial lake at the bottom of the drive, and rock warm to the touch under an autumnal sun. I had three weeks before my lecture season started – three weeks to skirmish with my book, lie in the sun and climb when the will took me, or friends arrived to drag me – all too willing – away from work. Two of our most regular visitors were Mike Thompson and Martin Boysen. Mike was one of my oldest friends. We had first met at Sandhurst, back in 1956, when he joined my company. He was already a climber, having been born and brought up in Cumberland. He went to St Bees, a school more renowned for prowess at rugby than academic learning, and had wandered the hills in his spare time, either with or without permission.

He also had gone into the Royal Armoured Corps – into the cavalry – spending three years in Malaya and then returning to this country to complete a university course at the Royal Military College of Science, Shrivenham. Mike was getting tired of army life at the same period that I was becoming discontented. His problem, however, was that having started the science course, the army insisted on getting their money's worth from him and therefore insisted that he complete at least another five years after finishing at Shrivenham. At this stage, Mike was determined to escape, wanting to get a place at university to study anthropology. He struck on an ingenious solution to his problem by standing for Parliament, since no member of the armed forces can become involved in politics, and yet it is anyone's constitutional right to stand for Parliament if they so desire. In 1962 he stood as Independent candidate for Middlesbrough West. Much to his surprise, he got around fifty votes, but lost his deposit. This freed him from the army.

In the autumn of 1964 he was just starting his final year at University College, London. Besides his interest in anthropology he had a flair for property – many of our Lakeland climbing trips had been spent exploring ruined barns as possible conversions. He had spent a couple of summers converting one such ruin above the Duddon Valley, and, in London, had secured the lease of an unfurnished flat high above Dean Street, living in it for three years nearly rent free, by sub-letting rooms to friends. In Mike's make-up there is a property tycoon and an anthropologist sometimes working hand in hand – at other times in conflict. He is one of those people who never seem in a hurry, never seem to do very much, yet quietly and effectively succeed in carving out a life of their own choosing.

Martin Boysen had slotted into a more conventional mould. He was one of the most brilliant rock-climbers that this country, or to be more accurate, Germany, had produced since the war. Born in 1941, at Aachen, of a German father and an English mother, he spent a terrifying infancy, of which he could have barely been aware, with his mother under constant surveillance by the Gestapo, and constant threat of arrest. After the war they came back to England, and Martin was brought up in Tonbridge, near Harrison's Rocks. He started going to the rocks when he was fourteen and it was here that I first met him, a shy, gangling boy who drifted up the most difficult problems with an easy grace, showing no visible effort. He went to Manchester University in 1961 to study biology, met Maggy in his first term, took her climbing and they have been together ever since. Maggy, slim, vital, dynamic, compensates for Martin's easy indolence. We spent many delightful weekends with him when they visited us at Woodland. They both had a deep abiding love for the hills which went further than just a passion for rock-climbing. Martin had an extensive knowledge and interest in the fauna and flora of the mountains – and this was how one of the best routes I helped to put up in the Lake District came to be called the *Medlar* – named after a rare tree, reputed to be found only in Southern England, but growing at the foot of our climb.

Martin and Mags arrived one weekend shortly after I had got back from the Alps. Mike was over in the Duddon Valley, working on his cottage at Bigert Mire. The weather was perfect and Martin knew of the ideal new route for us to try.

'I had a go at it a couple of weeks ago,' he admitted, 'but I wasn't climbing well, and turned back.'

'Where is it?'

'Wait and see – we'll have to make sure it's fine tomorrow.'

Such is the secrecy that surrounds any possible new line – there are so few left in the Lakes.

The morning was fine and Martin revealed that our planned ascent was on Raven Crag of Thirlmere. From the road it is lost in the conifer woods that cling to the slopes of Thirlmere – the crag is a good 600 feet up the hillside, steep and slender, with jutting, angular overhangs. A light green lichen clings to the rock, making patterns similar to amoeba or bacteria seen through a microscope. The crag was discovered, in 1952, by Harold Drasdo and Pete Greenwood. Its very character, yielding bold lines on very steep rock, attracted some of the outstanding post-war climbers to its flanks. Pete Greenwood was a leading light of the Wall End Barn mob, a group of climbers who temporarily opted out of the rat race, long before beatniks or hippies had been thought of; they raced round the Lakes on high-powered motor-bikes, and went in for prodigious drinking sessions. As with many of the hard climbing groups, their members later settled down to successful careers in a number of widely differing fields. Pete Greenwood, finally deciding that he had had enough of bumming around, worked his guts out as a labourer on the Spade Adam project, saved enough money to buy a plot of land, built a house, borrowed more money, and is now a property tycoon in Cumberland. Jack Bradley, who made the first ascent of *Necropolis*, an attempt to tackle the huge cave that is carved out of the centre of the crag, seemed to be one of the wildest members of the Wall End mob. He became a successful financier in Leeds, floating companies with the same *sang froid* that you or I would display buying a few premium bonds.

Communist Covert, a fine line that works through the big overhangs of the cave, and airily across the upper part of the buttress, fell to Arthur Dolphin, a climber whose brilliant career was cut short in 1954. He was Lakeland's leading rock-climber, making the same impact in the Lakes that Joe Brown and Don Whillans were making in Wales. Even today, some of his routes rank as the finest and most difficult in the area.

The final stamp of recognition for the crag came in 1956, when Don Whillans forced the overhangs of the cave with his route, *Delphinus*. It was a typical Whillans route, a direct onslaught at the most obvious, and certainly the most formidable, challenge of the cliff.

And now, on a fine September's day, Martin Boysen, Mike and I were picking our way through the sweet-smelling woods towards the foot of the crag.

'That's the line,' said Martin. 'Up that undercut ramp to the left of the cave.'

'It looks bloody hard,' I replied. 'Are you sure it's possible?'

'Oh yes, you'll do it all right. I'd only just recovered from glandular fever when I tried it.'

And so I found myself at the sharp end. I was well armed with a wide selection of nuts. We were still in the primitive nut era, when you simply scrounged a collection of nuts from the local garage and threaded them on a few slings. The smallest were Meccano-style nuts on thin bits of line that would barely have held a man's deadweight, and the biggest were over an inch across and weighed a pound a time. The purists drilled out the threads, but I hadn't bothered.

I didn't feel like leaving the ledge – the rock leaned back the wrong way; the holds seemed minute, tiny flakes, cracks that took a finger tip and no more; and after forty feet or so, a nasty little overhang jutted out at least a foot.

'I'm bloody sure I won't get up this. There's nothing for protection.'

'Course there is,' replied Martin. 'I got a good spike runner about six feet up – look, you can see it.'

With a careful look I could – and it was minuscule, but at least it provided some kind of haven to head for. I balanced up gingerly, weight on fingertips slotted into horizontal cracks; a couple of moves and I'm at the spike; it's just big enough to balance a thin line sling round. Another move and I manage to slot a small nut into one of the cracks. I begin to feel better. Even if I fall off, I shouldn't hurt myself.

My arms are beginning to ache, but the long disappointing season in the Alps is beginning to pay off. I am at least fit and mentally attuned to the rock. I am even beginning to enjoy myself; I stop threatening to turn back; edge my way from hold to hold, relaxed, wary, looking for possible runners. Forty feet up, and the base of the overhang, a perfect thread belay, just big enough for a piece of line. I untie the knot of a sling, using one hand and my teeth, push the end of the line into the crack and get out my wire threader to thrust and manipulate the nylon string behind a bulge in the crack – I'm like a safe-breaker, playing the tumblers of the safe in the Bank of England – total concentration – a touch of exhilaration. And the sling is through. More one-handed contortions to tie the knot – my other hand is getting tired. I'm safe again and happy – a master of the steep rock around me, master of my mind and muscles. I jam a hand in the crack beneath the overhang, place a foot in just the right place to give me leverage, and swing up, reach up; fingers play over the ledge above the roof, slot naturally on to a dimple in the rock – it'll suffice – and I step up on to the ledge with ease, muscle and mind tensed, knowing it's hard, yet everything slipping into place. This is the joy of climbing, the absolute freedom of mind and body, a short-bloomed euphoria that flowers in the process of climbing, and can be savoured while resting on the stances before another pitch, lasting through to the top of the climb and down to the pub that evening – the logical end to every Lakeland climbing day. And then next day, with the confrontation of work, of day-to-day problems, the euphoria fast vanishes and the climb is just one more incident docked up in the past. But still it has an importance, as a moment of total relaxation, of unspoilt joy, the repetition of the experience, a goal to seek for other days, till one day, when muscles will no longer respond to the command of mind, this precious euphoria might prove unattainable. I wonder what then?

But I'm at the top of the overhang; a black groove beckons me on, and Martin shouts out from below:

'How about belaying there, Chris?'

He's worried I'll get the whole climb. Fair enough, after all the line was his concept, not mine. And so I hammer in a piton, slot in a couple of nuts and, half hanging off my belay, take the rope in. As Martin climbs up, I gaze down over the dark tops of pine trees, across Thirlmere, a twisted sword stabbing at the vitals of a Lakeland Valley. Not so many years ago there were no sombre pine trees; farmhouses nestled in the bed of the valley and a Lakeland road, narrow, between dry stone walls, wound across the valley bed. This has now been changed by the hands of man – the valley bottom was flooded, forests were planted on the slopes, and a new beauty has emerged, more sombre, brooding, but nevertheless with its own attraction. I can feel the heat of the sun on my face; feel the warm rock against my back; rub a little patch of dried moss into a powder and watch the specks of dust float down towards Martin, as he moves slowly, but oh so easily, up towards me.

And then it's his turn to go out in front. He tries the groove behind me but makes no progress, swings out on to the wall. It's steep and flaky, with tiny spikes for finger- and toe-holds. Another few feet, he pauses, goes back a bit; most unlike Martin, but he's still recovering from glandular fever. I'm bored, the rope begins to cut into my back and I think of pints of cool beer, the reward for victory.

Martin seems to be struggling; a tension is transmitted down the rope. He's standing in a sling balanced over a small flake; the flake breaks off, Martin slips, seizes a hold and somehow manages to remain hanging on to the rock; another struggle and he's up. I quickly bring up Mike Thompson to join me, and then, in turn, we climb to the top of the crag.

Pints of beer, jubilation at snatching a fine new route and talk of other possible lines. Mike is the great strategist. We've been climbing together for nearly twenty years, and on hard ground I have done most of the leading, but almost all the new routes we have done together have been Mike's discoveries. In the same way that he quietly seeks out interesting old houses, he searches for new lines on the crags. That day he had seen another possible route, straight up the centre of the crag. We returned, just the two of us, a couple of days later, to complete a route which was slightly easier than the *Medlar*, but longer and with a more satisfying line, straight up the centre of the crag to the barrier of overhangs that guard the top.

And so September slipped into October, a gently vanishing Indian summer that blended imperceptibly with the chill clouds of late autumn, and the start of a new lecture season – our sole source of income, £20 a time at luncheon clubs, lecture societies or mountaineering clubs. I hated the nomadic existence – the series of one-night stands, the driving, the filling in of time before another lecture, and, above all, the worry that I was getting nowhere. The carefree joy of a summer's climbs vanished in the reality of making a day-to-day living.

7 Hogmanay

It is not always the mammoth successes or the major ascents that are the most memorable. Sometimes an epic failure – a combination of struggle with wind and storm, and the interaction with one's companions – turns what could have been a very minor, low-key incident into one that will never be forgotten. This was the case over New Year, 1965. It started normally enough. We had been invited to see the New Year in with some friends just north of Glasgow, and were then going to meet Tom Patey on New Year's Day, to get in some climbing. But I should have known better – things happened when Tom was around. Mary Stewart, our hostess on New Year's Eve, also has this catalytic quality.

Mary is a vet who lives in the most wonderfully chaotic house I have ever known, with her five children, dogs, other animals, and a succession of friends – often flotsam from the competitive society, who finally end up under the ever-open hospitality of her roof. The house is in the middle of a golf course outside Glasgow, was once a stable but now has a couple of big rooms and a kitchen downstairs and a warren of rooms upstairs.

After graduating, Mary, an American by birth, came over to Scotland to do postgraduate work and had fallen in love with the hills and the country. She had taken up climbing and had married a member of the Glasgow Mountaineering Club. Unfortunately the marriage had not worked. Her husband was a solicitor, and Mary was a warm-hearted Bohemian with little interest in being a suburban housewife.

Strongly built and wiry, with a hand grip as firm as a man's, Mary would have been the perfect frontierswoman on a ranch at the edge of Indian territory in the Far West. Her hair is a rich copper, long and thick, and her face seems perpetually weather-beaten; but there is a rare warmth and kindness in her face that cancels out any danger of over-masculinity. I can always see her in my mind's eye – barefooted, clad in a pair of old Levis and a simple sweater worn outside her trousers, ornamented by a big, broad, patterned belt.

Wendy and I drove up to Scotland on New Year's Eve, with Conrad, now one year old, asleep in the back of the van. The trip was starting badly; I could feel depression creep over me – the result, I suspected, of the proximity of a New Year and its festivities, with my own doubts for the future. The book was barely half-finished. I had just completed a gruelling lecture season, giving the same lecture on the North Wall of the Eiger, which was now two years old, over and over again. It wasn't just the boredom of repeating the same lecture, it was the worry that this was something of the past – that I was leaning backwards, unable to go forwards.

The party was well under way when we arrived. A record player throbbed out its beat. People were dancing, dark gyrating shadows in a candle-lit black-draped room. We were deafened, confused, out of tune with the rhythm of a party that had been under way for some time. Martin and Maggy Boysen, who had been staying with us at Woodland, were already there. So was John Cleare, a climber who was also a professional photographer; he had with him a statuesque, very extrovert, very blonde girlfriend, and seemed the symbol of the success and self-confidence which at that time seemed to be eluding me. He had a real skill – a positive career. This shell of self-confidence probably hid much the same uncertainty that I felt, but that night it seemed real enough to me.

Another friend, who seemed to have found happiness in another way, was Eric Beard. Slightly built and wiry, with an attractive ugliness about him, big ears framing a crew-cut head of hair and a gnomish face that was one big grin, he had devoted his life to becoming a brilliant fell runner. He held the records for running the Welsh three thousanders, and a host of other records. Stripped off, he was all legs – strongly muscled, bonded to a lean, compact body and topped by his big grin.

He had no qualifications, had spent some time as a Leeds chippy, before abandoning steady jobs for a nomadic existence, instructing at climbing centres, or working as an odd-job man. He was the traditional life-and-soul-of-the-party, joking, singing, exuding a simple warm-heartedness, and yet behind this there was an indefinable wistful sadness, as if, in his complete freedom from material pressures and the ties of family or a fixed base, he also was a lost soul, searching for some kind of fulfilment.

I sat on the floor in a dark corner, and tried to drag myself out of my own mood of depression. But it was no good – the New Year was very nearly on us and the spontaneous enjoyment of the others was alien to my own feelings; the New Year was full of foreboding and before it arrived I sneaked up to bed. Wendy, upset, confused, tearful, followed me, trying to understand the depths of my mood, trying to pull me from its dark trap, till at last love and sleep curled round us, and we were lost in oblivion.

We woke to a bright sun, cloudless sky and a hard, keen frost. No depression could survive against such a stimulus – New Year's Day, 1965, didn't seem so bad after all, and anyway, who cared about the distant future when, with a bit of luck, there would be some good snow and ice conditions in Glencoe? I had one plus from my mood of the night before – I had drunk comparatively little and had gained a lot more sleep than the others. We got up, helped clear the debris of the party, and planned the rest of the weekend. Tom Patey was going to meet us that day in Glencoe, and soon we had three car-loads of climbers ready to set out for the hills. Even Wendy was coming, leaving Conrad behind for the first time ever, with Mary's children.

As we drove up to Glencoe, she looked anxious and worried, like any animal taken away from its newborn litter. But I had now recovered completely from the previous evening's low. There was a sprinkling of snow on the foothills as we drove round Bearsden to Balloch, and then, as we came to the foot of Loch Lomond, we could see Ben Lomond near its head, serene, magnificent, plastered in snow.

It was like one's first trip to Scotland, as we careered round the bends on the shores of the loch and then chased over the great sweep of Rannoch Moor. Buachaille Etive Mor, a cathedral of black rock interlaced with snow, beckoned us on our way. We stopped at Altnafeadh, a stalker's house with a couple of barns by the road, and wondered what to do. It was already past midday, and it would be dark by six that night. There were three of us, Mary Stewart, a friend of hers called Jock, and myself. It was obviously too late to tackle any of the harder routes, and anyway we were too polyglot a party. I suggested the Left Fork of Crowberry Gully – the guidebook assured us: 'It is fairly certain that this fork will provide an exciting finish to the gully.' The Right Fork is one of the great classic gully climbs of Glencoe – comparatively straightforward by modern standards, but nevertheless sufficiently long and difficult to trap the unwary into enforced bivouacs.

The Left Fork is slightly shorter than the Right, but makes up by steepness, being a narrow fissure capped by a jutting roof overhang. It was a joy to leave the car and walk through a light covering of powder snow towards the towering mass of the Buachaille. Soon we were at the foot of Crowberry Gully itself. Lined with firm snow, it curled up between the steep, dark rocks of the Crowberry Ridge and the North Buttress – and on this sunny New Year's Day, there seemed little threat or foreboding about the climb. We put on crampons and started soloing up the lower snow-slopes in the gully, boots kicking with an easy assurance into the firm snow. As we gained height, and came to the first little step, we put on the rope – and on we went, till we reached the foot of the Left Fork, a narrow gash in the upper rocks leading on to the crest of Crowberry Ridge. I was itching to tax myself, to get on to some hard climbing.

The Left Fork was little more than a wide chimney, lined with ice, and blocked near its top by a smooth roof. I swarmed into the chimney, wriggled and thrutched up its narrow confines, to a point below the roof. The capstone jutted smoothly over my head – there were no holds, and the chimney widened so that I was nearly doing the splits in my effort to straddle both walls. Providentially, someone had left a piton in place, so that I had some protection in the event of a fall; I was now nearly a hundred feet above the other two. It was the kind of climbing that I have always enjoyed, gymnastic, contortionist, and yet, by using either side of the chimney to the best advantage, I could avoid putting too much weight on my arms – just as well, for there was nothing to pull on anyway. The holds above the roof were all sloping, glazed in ice. The jut of the overhang forced my body backwards; I was dimly aware of the situation as I was forced out of the secure confines of the chimney, but I knew no fear. My concentration on those few feet of rock in front of my nose was too great. Crampons scraped on rock, dug a fraction of an inch into the glaze of verglas. The world contracted into those few feet immediately above me – a pull, a straddle and I was up; a few more feet and I was in the gap just below Crowberry Tower. I knew a delicious sense of achievement – of freedom – of pure, simple joy at my situation; how different from the dark mood of the previous night. Climbing, the great healer, had restored my self-confidence.

It was now the turn of the others. Mary was justifiably apprehensive; although strongly-built and a good climber, her family and work commitments had kept her away from the hills, and this was obviously going to be considerably harder than anything else she had ever tried.

Jock swarmed up the pitch to join me; and then it was Mary's turn. I got into a good position to give her a tight rope. By this time I was getting worried about having brought her on a climb which was obviously too difficult for her. She started up steadily enough – slow, but steady progress – the sound of panting and scraping of crampons on rock drifted up the fissure, getting stronger as she came nearer. The scraping and panting got louder, the rope crept in more slowly as she came up to the roof overhang and came to a dead stop. I was getting cold and gave the rope a reassuring heave.

'For heaven's sake, don't pull, Chris, you're pulling me off,' came a shout from below.

The rope was arched over her head round the roof, so that any pull tended to pull her outwards and off what precarious holds she had managed to find. There was another long pause, a lot more scraping:

'Come on, Mary,' I shouted. 'We're bloody freezing up here. Straddle across the chimney and just bridge up. As soon as you get free of the chimney, we'll be able to pull you out.'

'I can't make my feet stick on the rock,' came the reply.

'Just slap them on,' I shouted. 'They'll stay there. Come on; one big effort.'

'Okay, I'll try now. Hold the rope tight.'

Another long pause and the rope moved a few inches – more scraping from below, and suddenly the rope tugged at my hands and body, pulled me off my stance, and I found myself hanging on the belay with the rope nearly cutting me in two. Mary had lost contact with the rock, had spiralled out into mid-air, and was now hanging in space below the overhang – even with the correct knot, it's no joke hanging on the end of a rope. You can survive about ten minutes before losing consciousness and suffocating.

'For God's sake, let me down,' shouted Mary.

'Hang on, we'll have a go at pulling you up,' I replied. There were two of us, and with a bit of luck we should be able to haul her up to the holds above the roof overhang.

'Be quick, I'm being cut in half,' she shouted.

Jock climbed down to me and we both heaved on the rope, but it was no good. There was too much friction as it went over the overhang, and anyway it is nearly impossible to haul up the deadweight of a person without some kind of pulley system. We heaved and hauled with very little effect, until the pleas from below, to be lowered back down, became irresistible.

Reluctantly, we lowered Mary about thirty feet, till she came in contact with the ice once more. I then gave the rope to Jock and climbed down to a point where I could see her. She was slumped, exhausted, on the ice.

'Come on, Mary,' I shouted. 'I'll talk you up. You'll be all right.'

'Okay. I'm sorry, Chris, for being such a nuisance, but I just couldn't stay on, and I think I'd have been cut in two if you'd kept hauling much longer.'

It was typical of Mary to apologise for a situation that was mainly my fault. Anyway, she soon started to climb again and, exhausted, cajoled and shouted at, she struggled over the overhang.

By this time it was beginning to get dark and in the dusk we scrambled, well content, down the Curved Ridge, back to the cars. We drove down to the Clachaig Hotel, where we had arranged to meet Tom Patey, Martin and the others. So far, the weekend had been enjoyable, but in no way specially memorable from any other winter's weekend. But Tom had a way of turning the ordinary into the extraordinary, and this was to be no exception. Tom was a great traveller; he thought nothing of driving from his home in Ullapool to Speyside, in the Cairngorms, a good hundred and fifty miles on narrow roads, for an evening drink and a sing-song. His standard weekend could include an itinerary that most mortals would spread over a week – a lecture on the Friday night in Cambridge (to pay the expenses), then a quick flip over to Wales to see Joe Brown, and on the way back he would often make a fifty-mile diversion to call in at our cottage in the Lakes. He was a genius at concocting complicated plans for a party's entertainment, which might include a ceilidh a hundred miles away, followed by a day's climbing in the opposite direction. In fact, climbing with Tom Patey was a kind of magical mystery tour, in which no one, except perhaps himself, knew what was coming next.

He was already ensconced in the bar at the Clachaig, his squeezebox out, a dram of whisky at his side and a cigarette in his mouth.

'The snow conditions are no good here,' he greeted us. 'They'll be a lot better on Creag Meaghaidh and I've got a good line you'll be interested in.'

'I don't know,' I replied. 'The Buachaille seemed in great condition to me.'

'Ah, but on Meaghaidh it'll be even better, and we'll be able to drink at the Loch Laggan Hotel.'

And so we drank and argued till closing time at the Clachaig and, well oiled with beer and whisky, were ready for anything. We left Glencoe at eleven o'clock, and raced in convoy round Loch Leven, through the still, silent streets of Kinlochleven and Fort William, past Ben Nevis, massive, squat, gleaming in the moonlight, and up to Glen Spean, over a road white and shiny with hard-packed snow. This was Patey country, and he drove his Skoda like a Timo Makinen, careering round the bends at a steady fifty. I followed, dogged, rather nervous, but determined not to be left behind – apart from anything else, I didn't know where we were bound.

At last we came to a stop outside a hotel. It was dark and silent, but there was a bothy, Tom said, down by the side. The bothy was an old hen house, with holes in the floor and gaps in the door, but it had a roof and walls, and we all got sleeping bags out and snuggled down. Wendy muttered about the cold, and snuggled close to me. She's a comfort-loving girl with an appalling circulation. It was three in the morning when we got off to sleep; even so, we woke quite early. There was little temptation to stay in bed – it was too cold, draughty and uncomfortable.

Breakfast in the hotel with bowls of porridge, Aberdeen kippers and plates full of toast; time slips by and it's midday before we get away.

'It's only a wee walk to the crag,' Tom reassured us. I suspect he enjoyed the perpetual confrontation with time, the game of brinkmanship, of leaving at the last minute, and then snatching the chosen climb from the oncoming night. Tom didn't believe in coolly laid plans – his climbing was one of instant pleasure, based on his own close knowledge of the hills and the most intimate details of almost every crag on the Scottish mainland.

But it was more than a wee walk to the foot of the crag – snow was knee deep, in places thigh deep, and our progress soon slowed to the laborious plod of the man in front who was making the route. There were six of us – Martin Boysen, Tom Patey, Eric Beard, Mary Stewart, John Cleare and myself. Only Tom had ever been to the crag before – but he, of course, knew every foot of the way, every indentation on the crag. We didn't need a map or guidebook, for we were with the local expert. And so, thoughtlessly, chatting, joking, wading, we walked towards Creag Meaghaidh.

This was just another light hearted day in the hills; it was too late to think of trying any of the more difficult climbs, and in any case we were all feeling tired after only a few hours' sleep the night before. The weather was overcast with a ceiling of featureless grey, merging with the grey-white of the upper slopes of the cliff. There was no wind, no sound; everything was muffled by the snow. It took us two hours to reach the foot of the crag – it seemed lost, smothered in the mountainside. At three o'clock in the afternoon there were only two and a half hours to dark.

'Do you think Martin and I have time to do *South Post*?' I asked Tom.

'Och yes, it'll only take an hour if you move fast,' he replied. 'You go straight up that tongue of ice above the big gully in the centre.'

We waded through the snows into the gully. There was no sense of perspective or scale; everything was black or white, black rocks and snow merging into mist, merging into snow. We stumbled through the snow with the exaggerated slow-motion movements of a cinematic dream-world – raise one leg, plunge it into the snow, transfer weight to it and sink, down, down, down into the clinging morass of soft powder snow. It didn't matter how much you cleared with your hands, you still sank into it; we never reached the foot of the climb – it was only fifty feet away, but we just never seemed to get closer to it. Martin lost patience first, suddenly erupting into a frustrated rage at the soft, cloying mass, hammered it with his axe and cursed at the top of his voice, curses that were instantly muffled in the snow around us.

'Come on, let's bugger off from here – we're wasting our bloody time.'

I agreed, and we turned round to flounder back down the gully to the foot of a snowy ramp which the others had followed to complete an easier route. We soon caught them up, near the top of the ramp, at the foot of the head-wall of the cliff. A steep ice pitch spiralled upwards into the mist, and we could hear Tom hacking away somewhere up above. Flakes of ice, loosened by his axe, tinkled down the rock, and we sat huddled at the foot, waiting for him to finish his work.

It was now four-thirty, only an hour to dusk. At last, there was a shout from above and Mary, who was tied on to Tom, followed him up on a tight rope. I went into the lead, trying to keep up with Mary, but the ice was steep and I found that I needed to cut the odd extra hold. As a result, I soon got left behind. By the time I reached the top of a narrow scoop that led out on to the summit plateau, Tom and Mary had already vanished. I could just discern a line of footsteps, fast drifting over in the wind. John Cleare and Beardie had tied on to our rope, which meant that Martin and I had to wait until all four of us were on top. It was very nearly pitch dark before John Cleare reached the top.

I had been getting increasingly worried. Tom was the only person in the team who knew the way down. Neither Martin nor I had map, compass or torch. We didn't know the general configuration of the mountain with any degree of certainty. 'Has anyone got a torch?' I asked.

'Not me,' admitted John.

'I've got one,' said Beardie, and dug it out of his sack.

'We'd better keep on the rope,' I said. 'We could go over a cornice too bloody easily in this light.'

I started to follow Tom and Mary's tracks, but after a few paces they vanished, drifted over by the ever-shifting snows. We stopped in the pitch dark, somewhere on the top of Creag Meaghaidh.

'Has anyone got a map?'

'No.'

'No.'

'No.'

'Compass?'

'I've got one,' said Beardie, and produced it with the aplomb of a conjuror. It turned out that he had some food as well. He, who had least experience as a mountaineer, was the only one who had the bare essentials of equipment.

But a compass without a map is of only limited value. We sat down on the snow and I tried to draw, with the tip of my glove, the configuration of Creag Meaghaidh from what we could remember from a glance at the map on the hotel wall, and from what little we had seen on the way up.

'I think the line of the cliffs should be north and south,' said John.

'I suppose Tom went down one of the gullies,' suggested Martin. 'We could try to find it and go down it ourselves. It would be the quickest way back down.'

'How do we know which is the right gully, though?' I pointed out. 'I think we should try to get to the col on the north of the crag and cut down that to the gully bottom. If we follow the line of the top of the crag on the compass, as soon as it starts curving round to the east we should know we are heading for the col. Then all we've got to do is keep going down till it starts climbing again, and that must be the col – we turn right and we'll get back down into the corrie.'

It sounded simple, but we weren't even sure if the cliffs did lie in a north-south line. Cloud merged with snow at the end of the torch-beam – it was very difficult to tell where snow ended and space began; it was like being in a white box. I started off leading, the others following at intervals of about fifteen feet, all linked by the rope. It was a strange, elating feeling – the situation was undoubtedly serious, for a bitterly cold and gusty wind was playing across the undulating surface of the plateau. We had no bivouac equipment, very little food and only one torch which we couldn't expect to last for more than a couple of hours' continuous use.

In addition, Martin had only recently recovered from a bout of 'flu, and was already feeling tired and weak. Without Beardie's food, the position would have been even more serious.

'You'd better take the torch,' I told Martin, who was just behind me. 'If I go over a cornice, there's less chance of us losing it if you have it.'

We peered into the mist, trying to differentiate between the edge of the cliff and space, kept checking the compass, and advanced slowly and carefully, keeping what I thought was a safe distance from the cornice edge. But it was very difficult to tell just where it was. Martin shone the torch from behind. It cut a bright swathe through the snow-filled clouds, so that the line of light also looked like the line of the slope.

'I think we've come to the place where we can start dropping down,' I shouted. 'Martin, can you come up to me so that we can see just how far this slope goes down?'

Martin came up to my side and altered the angle of the torch so that it was shining straight down. We were standing on the very lip of a huge cornice, looking straight down into a bottomless void. Had the cornice collapsed, the pair behind us would have had very little chance of holding both of us, and almost certainly, all four of us would have fallen to our deaths.

It didn't take a second to sum up the situation. We both scuttled back to safety, and resumed our tortuous progress, trying to follow the top of the line of cornices to where we thought the slope should drop away to the col between the two mountains – and imperceptibly the ground did begin to drop away – we were losing height in our tiny cocoon of dim torchlight. Surely, we must be heading for the col – but were we? Our blade of light was no longer a brilliant white; it had faded to a smoky yellow – a sure sign that the battery was dying. Once dead, we should be unable to read the compass – unable to see the line of a cornice – and should have no choice but to stop where we were and wait for the long night to end. But would we all survive it? The wind was now gusting hard, tearing gaps in the thin layer of cloud above us, to give glimpses of a black, star-studded sky.

With hope buoyant, we plunged down the easy slope, trending eastwards as we had visualised the descent to the col. But there was no sign of any col. We could just discern what seemed a steep drop to the right, and on the left and front, the slope dropped away, undulating gently.

'Are you sure this is the col?' asked John.

'I don't know,' I had to admit. 'It could be a depression on the main ridge-line, or I suppose we could have missed it altogether. Anyway, we'd better keep going while we've got a bit of light left in the torch.'

We kept plodding on, now going gently upwards. Suddenly, glancing at the compass, I realised that the steep drop was now to our west. Had we somehow doubled back on ourselves? Surely not – the steep slope was still on our right. But where the hell were we? Without a map, without any more than a vague impression of the configuration of the land, we were basing all our movement on a series of guesses – an edifice of decisions as fragile as the proverbial card house – but once we stopped reasoning out each move based on these fragile hypotheses, we should be totally lost. I was uncomfortably aware that the mountains to our north and west stretched for miles, without road or human habitation. We might have been in the middle of the Antarctic, our situation seemed so isolated, the immediate surroundings so bleak.

Looking at the compass, it seemed just possible that we had crossed the col we had been seeking, and were now on top of the hill immediately opposite Creag Meaghaidh. But if this were the case, were the slopes immediately below us precipitous, or would we have an easy run off? There seemed only one way of finding out – to start down and hope for the best. The torch battery had, at last, died on us and we could just see the ghostly glimmer of snow against rock. I worked my way to the brink, fearful that I might be trying to step over a cornice, prodding the snow in front of me like a blind man with his stick. It dug into snow – I was on a straight slope. Slowly, we worked our way down – each little drop assumed the scale of a major cliff – even three feet seemed a bottomless pit, and it was only by lowering oneself gingerly down each step that one could find just how extensive it was.

At last the angle of the snow around us began to level out, and we came out of the cloud to see, spread below us, dark and ghostly, the corrie we had left so thoughtlessly the previous afternoon. It was nearly midnight, but we still had an hour of floundering in front of us before we could get to the road. Beardie now came into his own. Throughout our adventure he had kept up a patter of jokes and sensible suggestions. Now he forged into the lead and broke trail almost all the way back, wading thigh deep through the snow. Just short of the road, we saw the glimmer of torches. Patey was there with the beginnings of a rescue party. He, also, had had his share of adventures.

'Why didn't you follow my tracks?' he asked.

'They were covered over by the time we got up.'

'I'm sorry about that. I never thought you'd have any trouble following them, and I wanted to get Mary down the gully before it was pitch dark.'

On the way back down the valley, Mary had fallen through a snow bridge into a stream. She had been soaked to the skin, and her clothes had frozen solid on her. Tom, who had just recovered from a bad attack of 'flu, had been on the verge of collapse.

Altogether, we were all lucky not to have had at least one serious casualty from exposure. We had, undoubtedly, broken just about every rule of mountain safety that had ever been made.

And yet I am unrepentant – it had been an extraordinary, rather wonderful experience. Half the attraction of climbing is playing with danger and the unknown. It would have been lunatic to have consciously sought the particular set of circumstances that faced us, but having landed ourselves in our predicament through lack of forethought, extracting ourselves from what could have been a dangerous situation presented an intriguing challenge.

If we had been taking out school students our conduct would have been unforgivable – but we weren't. All of us were experienced mountaineers who should, perhaps, have known better. Each individual had his own responsibility, to wife and child in my case, to girlfriends or parents in that of the others. If we had died, it would have been our own responsibility. It would have been more difficult to define our responsibility to a search party, if it had been called out. Had we got ourselves well and truly lost, and then collapsed from exhaustion, it could have needed the efforts of several hundred searchers to find us. In this instance, we should have come in for a lot of justified criticism for causing others inconvenience entirely through our own lack of preparation. But we had got away with it, and I suppose, rather like mischievous schoolboys, who have successfully played truant, were filled with the excitement of the experience, feeling closely united through the way we had worked together.

It was two o'clock in the morning before we got back to the hotel. Tom played his squeezebox, and we all dissected the experience with as much satisfaction as we would have done a major first ascent. Wendy and Maggy had spent a chill day in their sleeping bags in the bothy, getting more and more worried by our non-appearance, but neither was prepared to show her fears to the other; neither wanted to increase the worry of the other. In every way, they had had the most trying time, as I am afraid women almost always do in such circumstances. There was none of the excitement of being involved in danger – just the long, cold wait, with nothing to do but worry. They needed much more self-control and courage than we might have shown, and yet it was all too easy for us to take it for granted. Fortunately, they were so glad to have us back, uninjured, that they chose to put aside the agonising hours of waiting.

Are we being selfish or irresponsible if we go on climbing once we are married? I suspect we are, but equally, I know – and Wendy knows – that I would not be the same person if ever I were to give up my climbing. I think this is something that every girl who marries a climber has to come to terms with. At the same time, the married climber should probably take greater precautions to avoid unnecessary risks and danger, though this is difficult to undertake, as was demonstrated by our own near-debacle which occurred because we had taken the hills for granted – something one can never afford to do in Scotland in winter.

But we survived, and we learned a lot and, in a strange kind of way, thoroughly enjoyed our experience.

Thus the New Year of 1965 was launched, in a way symbolically; for out of depression and near-disaster had emerged great experience. And 1965 was to prove a turning-point in my own new-found career as a freelance climber, writer, photographer and lecturer.

8   Tele-Climbing at Cheddar

There was no telephone at Woodland. If anyone wanted to contact me in a hurry they had to send a telegram and I would then go to the nearest phone, which was about half a mile away. One morning, shortly after getting back from our New Year in Scotland, a telegram arrived:

PLEASE PHONE BRISTOL 43112 ABOUT POSSIBLE TELEVISION PROGRAMME – KELLY.

Ned Kelly was a producer working for TWW – Television Wales and West.

'We're thinking of the possibilities of making a film of one of your climbs in the Avon Gorge. Would you be interested?'

'Of course I would. What were you thinking of doing?'

'Well, that would be very much up to you. We want something that will be easy to film, with good camera positions and which, at the same time, looks impressive.'

'Could I think about the best climbs, and then come back to you?'

'Okay. Give me a ring as soon as you've thought of something.'

I have made comparatively few first ascents in Britain – a small fraction of the number made by someone like Joe Brown – but the one place where I did help to make a breakthrough was in the Avon Gorge during the mid-fifties. I was at Sandhurst at the time, and the Avon Gorge gave the best climbing of any area within reasonable range. Set within a couple of miles of the centre of Bristol, immediately above the busy road to Avonmouth and the muddy waters of the River Avon, it had an atmosphere of its own. It can claim none of the magic of a high mountain crag, and yet it has a unique fascination.

The River Avon cuts its way through a line of hills: the Clifton Heights on one side and the Cleveland Hills on the other. It carves out a gorge dominated by quarried cliffs, which is spanned, in one splendid leap, by Brunei's suspension bridge. Today, the river is a trail of muddy effluent, carrying the sewage and polluted waters of the city of Bristol. At high tide, small coasters nose their way up and down the river, drowning the steady roar of traffic with the occasional ear-splitting shriek of their klaxons. In 1956, only one cliff had been fully explored by climbers; this was a buttress of quarried limestone that swept at a comparatively gentle angle down towards the road, its flanks guarded by smooth clean slabs. Hugh Banner, Harry Griffin and Barrie Page, all at Bristol University, had put up most of the early routes on the crag, and these were the ones that we first tackled from Sandhurst. You parked your car at the foot of the cliff and at the top, as you poked your head over the brow of the climb, and scrambled over a barred railing, you found yourself on a footpath, often having disturbed a courting couple. From the top, a brisk five-minute walk took you to the Coronation Tap, where you could down a pint of scrumpy cider and eat homemade pies.

We had exhausted the possibilities of the existing routes after a few weekends. Inevitably, our eyes were drawn to the steep flanks of the Main Wall, a 200-foot bite out of the Clifton Downs, quarried without leaving any of the broad ledges that graced some of the other cliffs in the gorge. It looked blank, loose and frightening. We skirmished around its base for several weekends, making tentative half-hearted attempts to get off the ground before I, at last, committed myself to a frighteningly loose and steep wall in the centre of the cliff, pushing myself beyond the point of no return. We managed to reach the top and named the climb *Macavity*, after T. S. Eliot's cat, who defied the laws of gravity. In some ways, this first route was the least obvious line on the entire wall. A few more routes followed, some put up by myself, and others by friends at Sandhurst, amongst them Mike Thompson, and Jim Ward, a wonderfully eccentric and very untidy officer cadet, destined for the Gurkhas.

At the beginning of 1965 the Main Wall still held its mystique. Mike Thompson and Barry Annette had made an exciting girdle traverse of the cliff, and Barry had put up several more hard routes up the Wall itself. One feature of the Avon Gorge climbs is that, being man-made, without the weathering of centuries, the rock structure has a characterless uniformity, with very few crack-lines. All the climbing is similar: balancing up on sloping holds, using small, incut ledges for hand-holds, and stepping delicately up little roof overhangs. It certainly would not provide drama for filming – it was difficult enough getting interesting still photographs on it.

But Cheddar Gorge – that could be very different. Cheddar Gorge is a true gorge in every sense – certainly the most dramatic in Britain – squeezed between a steep crag-dotted slope on one side, and sheer, vegetated walls on the other, winding from Cheddar Village into the Mendips in a series of sinuous curves. On a summer's weekend the bottom of the gorge is crammed with cars and the Cheddar Village end is packed with crowds of tourists flocking to see the caves. This can present a real problem for the climber, for the cliffs overhang the road and any rock that is dislodged will inevitably hit it. The cliffs, for the most part, are festooned with ivy and every ledge is overgrown with vegetation. As a result, the climber has no choice but to tear down great swathes of ivy and unpeel the heavy moustaches of grass that cling to the smallest ledge; these, in turn, can dislodge rocks and all end up somewhere near the road.

The safest time for climbing in the gorge, therefore, is mid-week in the winter. Then, there is a lurking, exciting mystery about the place. The gorge, empty, has grown somehow in stature, and is as mysterious as any high mountain crag.

Surely there must be a route to be climbed in the Cheddar Gorge, which would have the attraction of being virgin and, at the same time, be very much more dramatic than anything in the Avon Gorge!

I suggested this to Ned Kelly, and we arranged to meet in the Cheddar Gorge the following weekend. My next problem was to decide on a climbing partner for our TV spectacular. I was anxious to keep it to someone who had been involved in the development of climbing in the region, rather than go for one of the great names, like Joe Brown or Don Whillans. Mike Thompson seemed the obvious choice; he was one of my oldest friends, had done as much as anyone to develop climbing in the Avon Gorge, and was a very pleasant companion. We also wanted a support team and someone to take still photographs, so I phoned John Cleare.

One weekend in late January, I drove down to the gorge with Tony Greenbank, having arranged to meet John Cleare there. Unfortunately, Mike was in bed with 'flu, and couldn't make it. We were to find the perfect television route on the Saturday, prior to meeting Ned Kelly on the Sunday morning.

A light sprinkling of snow covered grass and vegetation, turning the gorge into a stark, black, grey and white study, skeletal black arms of the leafless trees reaching into the flat grey sky; grey rock etched with the black of cracks; and the white of snow on every ledge and slope.

The challenge was obvious. Near the lower end of the gorge, just above the commercial caves, is a huge, 400-foot wall, certainly the biggest in Southern England, and one of the largest stretches of continuously vertical rock in the country. It goes to the top of the gorge in a single leap from a newly-completed car park at its foot. Immediately above the car park, the rock is sheer, and seems unpleasantly friable, stretching up to a band of blank overhangs which, in turn, lead to a band of weakness which is guarded by an entanglement of brambles clinging to the near-vertical rock. To the right of the main wall is an ivy-filled groove that seemed to provide the only breach in the wall's defences. This had been climbed some years before, by Hugh Banner, and had been named *Sceptre*, but it avoided the main challenge, making an escape to the right on to steep and heavily vegetated rocks. Graham West, a Derbyshire peg-climber, had made an attempt on the Main Wall, trying to peg his way straight up it but had been defeated after a hundred feet or so by the scarcity of cracks and the friability of the rock. The previous year, Barry Annette had straightened out *Sceptre*, continuing directly up the groove system above the climb's initial corner, but his route still skirted the High Rock.

We looked up at it – in awe – slightly appalled by its challenge.

'There's a line all right,' I said. 'Look, you've got a bit of a groove going out to the left of *Sceptre*. Peg over that overhang, up that overhanging corner, and then you could traverse left along that break into the centre of the face, and the big groove leading to the top.'

'Looks great,' agreed John. 'But what if the rock's bad? It's bloody steep. Do you think you're on good form?'

'Bloody sure I'm not; I haven't done any proper climbing yet this year.'

We delayed the moment of commitment, and went down to the cafe at the caves to have tea and sandwiches.

'It might be an idea if we did something else – just to warm up,' I prevaricated.

'It's a bit late to start on the big wall, anyway,' said Tony. 'How about looking at the top of the gorge? I noticed a good line there on the way down.'

We all walked up to the head of the gorge with a comforting feeling of release from what was obviously going to be a serious and nerve-racking climb. Near the head of the gorge was a fine rib of rock, rising above a small, covered-in reservoir; it was only 150 feet high, and looked ideal as a training climb. It was just the right standard of difficulty – just hard enough to give us confidence for our effort the next day.

We met Ned Kelly on the Sunday morning. He had a perpetual boyish look, is of medium build, with a pleasant smile and a ready enthusiasm in his manner. He came from London originally, and had done a little climbing. Having started in television as a cameraman, he had progressed to directing. The programme had been his idea, and would be squeezed in amongst his run-of-the-mill work organising quiz programmes and beauty contests.

'What I want to do is a form of live broadcast,' he told us. 'We'll record the climb on videotape the day before it actually goes out on the air; to all intents and purposes, though, it'll be a live broadcast, because we'll have the cameras in position, and I'll be mixing the pictures – we'll be sending it out exactly as it happened.'

The difference between a film and this type of broadcast is that with a film probably only one camera is used, with the facility of switching to a dozen different positions. Thousands of feet of film can be shot, in any sequence, taking close-ups of hands on holds, and fingers curling round pitons which, of course, might be conveniently situated at ground level. The whole lot is then edited, and the resulting film is probably more perfect than a genuine, live broadcast. But the public, all too used to seeing stunts in films, view anything they see with a fair level of scepticism. In a live broadcast, on the other hand, there is no room for this type of cheating. The cameras are already set up, and only the action of the climbers at the time can be recorded. To the viewer the thrill, no doubt, is one of – will he fall off? This is the kind of emotion that dominates the watching of motor racing, though in either sport, there is the fascination of watching someone mastering a skill which the viewer knows he could never accomplish.

There had already been a few live climbing broadcasts put out by the BBC, but I had never been involved. The first was a joint Franco-British production in 1963, an ascent of the South Face of the Aiguille du Midi, above Chamonix. The only Briton to take part was Joe Brown. Though very dramatic, it must have been comparatively easy to put on. A téléphérique goes to the top of the Aiguille du Midi, and another goes, in a single giant span, right across the Vallée Blanche, giving superb views of the South-West Face. The South-West Face itself is little more than a small rock buttress, under a thousand feet high, but its position, dominating one of the greatest glacier basins in the Alps, is unique.

The programme was such a success that the BBC decided to do a repeat of their own, this time bringing a single French climber, Robert Paragot, over to England, and using three British climbers. They chose Clogwyn du'r Arddu, the finest crag in Britain south of the Scottish Border; Joe Brown, Don Whillans and Ian McNaught-Davis climbed with Paragot. This was a very logical choice since Joe and Don, in their early partnership, had made the great post-war breakthrough in high-standard climbing on 'Cloggy', and Mac was undoubtedly the best, and funniest, talker on the climbing scene. He had already become a climbing spokesman on radio, and combined a flamboyant personality with a strong sense of humour. He was also a very competent mountaineer having been with Joe Brown and Tom Patey on their four-man expedition to the Mustagh Tower in 1956; he had always succeeded in maintaining a fair climbing level, at the same time as following an exacting and successful career in the computer business. He is an interesting example of the amateur professional, since he has a career outside climbing and is essentially amateur in his attitude to climbing – that it should be great fun and an escape from day-to-day work – but makes a certain amount of money as a climbing commentator on radio and television.

I had happened to be climbing in North Wales that weekend, and must confess I was envious of the climbing actors cavorting across the mist-enshrouded walls of Cloggy. And now I had my chance. Ours was not to be a full-blown live broadcast, but a cut-price substitute. In some ways it was the more satisfying for that, being on a small, informal and friendly scale, and we were just dealing with Ned Kelly who, rather like myself in my role of a professional climber, was getting himself established in the world of television. We were doing something different, for we were looking for a new route to present as an outdoor broadcast – a line which, as we gazed up at it that morning, looked feasible – but only just. The whole concept was immensely exciting, for up to this point, outdoor broadcasts of climbing had been made on established routes. I suppose the truest film of all would have been a live presentation of our efforts to make the first ascent, though the trouble here is that climbing tends to be a very slow process, especially when pioneering new ground. We had to show the public how we climbed, but at the same time we had to make it visually interesting, and to do that, we had to be able to climb quickly, to a set schedule.

Climbing broadcasting has evolved rapidly over the last eight years, and in 1965 we were still in the very early stages of live, or semi-live, presentations of climbs. Our first problem was to make our new route. Once made, we would then be in a position to climb it for television. It was bitterly cold, certainly not the weather for high-standard rock-climbing, but our audience, in the shape of Ned Kelly and his girlfriend, were waiting, and we had to show him that the wall could be climbed. John Cleare was going to act as my second, and we got our gear together for our first winter ascent.

The groove of *Sceptre* which led up to the point where we hoped to break into the steep, unclimbed wall of High Rock, was smothered in snow. I was hoping that this part of the climb would prove quite straightforward, while the upper, unclimbed part was so steep that it held no snow and so, except for the cold, would be no harder than it would have been in summer. P.A.s on, draped with slings, pitons and nuts, I started up the bottom rocks, clearing snow from every hold, and soon my hands had lost all feeling. The smooth soles of my P.A.s skidded on snow-dusted rocks.

'It's too bloody cold,' I shouted down. 'We'll never get up it today.'

'Course you will,' shouted John. 'Just keep going, and it'll work out.'

I kept on going, grumbling and muttering to myself, as I tend to do when I am climbing. Once I'd got used to numb fingers there was even a strange enjoyment in picking my way up the groove. I avoided the snow where I possibly could – a little like those games you played as a child, avoiding every other paving stone on the pavement, the only difference here being that it was a game in the vertical. The route had originally been tunnelled through a barrier of ivy and the strands, now weighed down by a clinging layer of snow, were on either side of the groove, ever pressing in, in a hopeless battle with the invading climbers.

The slow progress I made upwards seemed quick to me, because time races by for the leader on a climb. But the others, down below, were stamping in the snow. I reached a small ledge, about a hundred feet up the groove, just below the point where it bifurcates. The original *Sceptre* route went up to the right, our new line to the left, up an improbable corner to a square-cut, smooth, triangular roof, that looked as impregnable as a ceiling at home. There weren't even any cracks in it.

I brought John up to me, left him belayed to a piton and started gingerly towards the roof. I was weighed down with about twenty pounds of ballast, a wide assortment of pitons and nut runners, for we fully expected our route

Cheddar Gorge: *Coronation Street*

to be high-standard peg-climbing the whole way. I bridged across the groove, prepared to find it near impossible, but somehow, all the holds fitted into place. They weren't obvious – a side hold here, a bridging movement, a pull on an invisible little jug, and I was below the overhang. I leaned out and felt over it – I couldn't find a hold, but there was a crack. Time to put in my first peg: I got out a small one, nudged the tip of it into the crack, gave it a tap and it bounced straight out, tinkling down to the ground, 150 feet below. Have another try; arms now tiring, legs aching and beginning to tremble from my bridged-out position. This time the peg held, another half-dozen whams of the hammer, and it was in to the hilt. I clipped in a karabiner, pulled gently on it, just to get a bit of height, to see what was over the lip of the overhang. I could straddle out still higher; the angle above dropped back just enough to allow me to pull over the overhang without using an étrier. I pulled up, balanced on to the slab, and let out a victory yell. We'd cracked the first problem.

The slab led up to a niche below a ferocious-looking overhanging chimney, comprising a whole mass of blocks that seemed morticed into each other, but there were cracks in between the blocks, and surprisingly, the structure seemed sound. I slotted in a nut, felt more confident, and once again straddle out. This was the kind of climbing that I have always enjoyed – steep and technical, where one could use one's skill to avoid putting too much weight on one's arms. The bridging holds kept arriving; another nut runner – it was going free. I could hardly believe it. I now seemed straddled out over the car park more than 200 feet below, and could see the ground between my legs. A hand over the top, a final heave, and I was standing on top of a flake, only twenty feet below the line of overhangs that led back into the centre of the face. The time seemed to have gone in a matter of minutes, though in fact I had been working for two hours. John followed up slowly, because he was frozen stiff from the long wait below. As he worked his way towards me I kept glancing behind me; a crack jammed with earth led up to the great jutting roof above, but characteristically there was a line of weakness below the roof, a horizontal dyke that would give hand-holds, and what seemed to be another intermittent crack line that relented to give the occasional foot-hold. This led to a great shield of rock that jutted out from under the roof, and barred the way to the start of the groove which we knew led to the top.

John poked his head over the top of the overhang I'd just led. He was as bemused as I by the fantastic nature of the climbing. It had not been desperately hard, just wonderful, sensational climbing, in a magnificent situation.

But it wasn't over. The day was now drawing to a close – only a couple of hours to dark, and we still had a long way to go. I started up the crack behind the pedestal – it was just the right width for hand-jamming, but I had to clear the earth before I could slot in my hands. I was now cold and stiff from the delay while I had brought John up to my position. There is an additional nervous strain while doing a new route which one never experiences in repeating a climb, and on this one in particular, the scale and steepness, combined with the cold, almost gave the climb Alpine proportions.

I was nervous and a little frightened as I struggled up the crack, making heavy weather of something that should have been easy. By the time I reached the overhang I was trembling with exertion and my own nervous tension. I had now reached the traverse into the centre of the Face – at first quite easy, but very steep to tiring arms. Step carefully, swing across, and then the Shield. Close up, it looked even less reassuring than it had from below.

'There's a crack this side of it,' I shouted back.

And I hammered in an angle piton, just under the overhang in the solid part of the rock. Swinging out and across on it, I was just able to reach across the

Shield to feel round the other side.

'There's a bloody crack going right back behind it; it's detached from the rock,' I shouted again.

'Looks pretty solid to me,' said John from below. He's a very reassuring second.

'It's all very well for you, you don't have to try swinging round it. If it came away, I'd have a ton of rock on top of me.'

I tapped it with my peg-hammer. It sounded hollow – but it didn't shift at all. About six feet high and four feet across, it seemed cemented to the sheer wall immediately below the roof in some completely inexplicable way. There was a good line of hand-holds along its top, but I was frightened to trust them; I could imagine, with dazzling clarity, myself clinging to the top of this shield of rock, and feeling it keel outwards and then crashing down with me beneath it.

I hovered and teetered on the edge of the Shield, trying to summon some courage and then John released me.

'You'd better do something soon,' he remarked. 'It'll be dark in half an hour.'

That settled it – we couldn't possibly get to the top before dark. We'd have to try to escape – no question of abseiling back down. However, there was the possibility of traversing right instead of left, into the top of Barry Annette's *Direct Finish* to *Sceptre*. It wasn't easy, but anything that avoided that terrifying Shield seemed welcome, and I thrutched up the final crack that led to a small pinnacle on the edge of the High Rock. I got up as it was growing dark, and John felt his way up behind me to the top.

We hadn't succeeded, but it had been one of the best days' climbing I had ever had. We soon convinced ourselves that there was a way across the Shield, that it was a lot more solid than it looked – and then we began to plan when we could return. There was no question of finishing the climb the following day; John had an assignment as a photographer, and I had a lecture to give in the North – but what if someone else came and snatched our route.

'I know of at least three others who've got their eye on it,' warned John. 'Pete Crew was talking about it only last week, and I believe Chris Jones has been sniffing around the gorge.'

Pete sounded the most formidable competition. In the early sixties he had established himself as one of the best young rock-climbers in the country, and was certainly the most prolific. Perhaps not as brilliant a technician as Martin Boysen, he had a restless dynamism and drive which enabled him to snatch a huge number of good routes, often in direct competition with others. He came from Barnsley and his father had worked on the railway. Pete had got a scholarship to Oxford, had been bored and irritated by the academic strictures of the University, and had abandoned his university career to start a small mail-order climbing business in Manchester, in partnership with another

Oxford man, Pete Hutchinson. After a time, Pete Crew had tired of this and had gone into computers, working in London. Most of his climbing was based in North Wales, but he had made one or two very successful forays into other areas to snatch the odd 'last great problem'. He had done this very successfully, a few years before, in the Lake District, when the local Lake District climbers, led by Lakeland's most formidable modern pioneer, Alan Austin, had been laying siege to the prominent unclimbed pillar on Esk Buttress. This had already defeated several parties, and one of the contestants in the Austin team, Jack Soper, while drinking in a Welsh pub, had been unwise enough to mention the fact that they were going to try the climb on the next fine weekend. Crew overheard this remark, and the very next weekend set out, hotfoot for the Lakes. The Soper/Austin party, blissfully unaware of any competition, had made a leisured start for the crag, only to find Crew and Baz Ingle, his normal climbing partner, embarked on their carefully planned line. The moral of the story is that all's fair in love, war and bagging new routes, and if you want to preserve a new line, the only solution is to guard it with a mantle of security that would shame MI5!

We all swore each other to secrecy, and arranged to meet in three weeks' time, when we hoped the weather might be a little warmer – but only two days had gone by when John phoned me from Guildford, where he lives.

'I think we'd better get moving,' he told me. 'I've heard that Crew has been talking about our line, and is planning to go down next weekend, to climb it.'

'Does he know about our effort?' I asked.

'I don't think so, but he's had the line itself in mind for some time. I think he's planning to do it with Chris Jones.'

'I can't possibly get down till next week; I've got a couple of lectures, one on Thursday, and the other on Saturday.'

'Well, it could be too late by then; they could easily have a go at it this weekend.'

'We'll just have to hope for the best; I can't possibly make it. Could you get away early next week though?'

'Yes, that would be okay.'

'Right. How about trying to find out whether Pete is planning to go down. You know him pretty well, don't you?'

'Don't you think there's a risk of his smelling a rat? He still mightn't know anything of our plans.'

'That's true – we'd better just hope for the best, and hope they don't go for our route. It's still bloody cold.'

And we left it at that. I phoned Mike Thompson and Tony Greenbank, arranging to meet the next Wednesday, and then went through agony, imagining that the rival team might be on our climb.

At last Wednesday came, and Tony and I drove down in my Minivan. It was still very cold and a fall of fresh snow covered the hillside and car park. Our route looked reassuringly virginal, but how could we be sure until we had made a closer investigation?

There was no point in repeating the lower part, and so we abseiled down our escape route, to a small and uncomfortable stance immediately below the overhang. Mike Thompson was looking ill, and complained that he still had not recovered from 'flu, but none of us took much notice; we were too intent on trying to complete the climb, and I was already tensed by the thought of that big, seemingly precarious shield of rock that I would have to swing round.

Reaching it fresh, at the beginning of a day, it didn't seem quite as frightening as on the previous occasion. The peg I had left by the side of it was still there, and somehow, because it was already in place, seemed sounder than when I had first hammered it in. The Shield looked more solid. Even so, I didn't like the idea of swinging round it, hand over hand.

I tapped a piton into a crack in the middle of the Shield – it didn't shift at all – clipped in an étrier and gingerly put my weight on the rung. If it does come down, I reasoned, I should be swung to one side by the rope, out of its path, and with this prayer I trusted my weight to the step of the étrier, reached round the other side of the Shield, and swung across, on to a small ledge the other side. These days, the move is made free by a hand traverse over the top of the Shield. It has stood the test of time, and is probably as solid as the cliff it is cemented to – but on a first ascent, you view the rock in a different perspective, everything being unknown, untried. As a result, you, the climber, are keyed up to a degree unknown if you are following a guidebook ascent. There is always the doubt as to whether the next move is possible, the worry of how to get back down if it isn't. And that is the joy of making first ascents – one way we can taste the thrill of exploration on our cluttered, over-developed planet – a pioneering experience that can be had above the Cheddar car park, on a cliff in Wales, or on a secluded crag in the heart of Scotland.

The groove stretched above me, both threatening and inviting. It looked hard. First, I had to set up a belay and bring Mike across. He had been feeling progressively more ill as I had teetered and struggled on the Shield.

'I don't think I'll be able to make it,' he called. 'I feel bloody weak. It'll be better if one of the others could do it.'

Tony Greenbank had been looking after John Cleare's rope while the latter took photographs, and so, after a lot of manoeuvring, Mike and he changed over and Tony came across to join me. One of Tony's special charms, and a quality that makes him a brilliant second, is his enthusiasm and ability to flatter.

As he swung around the Shield, he kept up a constant barrage of 'Great, man, great. You must feel terrific about leading that.' 'This'll be the greatest route ever.' 'You're climbing fantastically.'

My ego swelled accordingly, and as we changed over the belays I had another look up the groove. It was vertical all the way, with a couple of small overhangs protruding, at about thirty and sixty feet. Surely, it couldn't possibly go free – or could it? There was certainly a good finger-jamming crack to start it; you could bridge out on either wall of the groove, which even on this vertical rock meant you could stay in balance.

I started out, wafted upwards by a barrage of enthusiastic praise by Tony. It was superb climbing – I could look straight down between my straddled legs, to Tony half hanging on his belay on the narrow ledge, and then on down to the car park, now nearly 300 feet below.

A few cars had stopped; Mike, below, tried to persuade their drivers to move out to a safe distance from the base of the cliff. But our figures must have seemed too remote to pose a threat. I reached a small ledge, with a boulder perched precariously on it. I couldn't possibly get over it without dislodging it, and perhaps hitting Tony.

'Look out, I'm going to drop a rock,' I shouted.

The onlookers just gawped.

'Get out of the way, I've got to chuck a rock down.'

They didn't seem to hear me – I had to push it outwards to get it away from my second. I gave it a heave, and it described a graceful arc down to the ground, landing with a resounding thud about twenty feet from the nearest parked car. The onlookers moved back to a respectable distance, and I continued climbing.

I had reached the first overhang – miraculously a hold appeared round the corner – a pull and I was up round it; more bridging, another nut runner in, the next overhang – concentration, yet a sensation of acute enjoyment, of being in control over mind and muscle. Another few movements, a ledge in sight, and it's finished. And then, a feeling of pure ecstasy, at the end of a superb piece of climbing. One more pitch that was interesting, but not as hard as the previous pitches, and we were on top of the gorge. We had completed our climb. What had started as a route for a television broadcast had turned out to be the most satisfying I have completed in this country. It had all the makings of a classic route. It was a magnificent line up a stretch of unclimbed rock; there was only the one escape on it, and somehow, that didn't detract from the feeling of commitment while climbing. Most satisfying of all, it had yielded almost entirely free climbing, with only the odd piton for direct aid or protection. In subsequent ascents by others, even this comparatively small level of aid has been eliminated.

The idea of the climb had been evolved from commercial motives, but did this destroy any of the pure enjoyment that one should experience from climbing? I don't think so. I have often been asked whether I can continue to enjoy climbing when I know I am dependent upon it for a large part of my income. I think this shows a confused interpretation of motives and values. I certainly couldn't tolerate teaching other people how to climb, or even taking less competent people climbing, as a guide. But it is not the payment which would spoil it for me, it is merely that I like stretching myself to my own limits in climbing, and one can only do that when climbing with someone of similar calibre.

To do the things I love doing and get paid for them at the same time seems the perfect answer and, I imagine, is the motive for professionalism in the majority of sportsmen. However, I was worried about one facet of this type of career: I disliked the idea of total dependence upon being a performer, or gladiator, in high-standard climbing. For a start, one's career would be limited to the period whilst at the top of the sport; and there was another objection – that of being pressurised into climbs which were outside the boundaries of risk that one was prepared to accept. I wanted to develop my own powers as a writer and photographer so that I should become more broadly based in my career.

But finding our way up the High Rock on Cheddar gave us everything that climbing can offer – even down to a bit of healthy competition, in the shape of the threat (which, in the event proved baseless), of someone else snatching our route from us.

Having got the route in the bag, we now had to wait until May, when we were due to climb it in front of the cameras. In the meantime, back at home in the Lakes, I was storming through the final stages of my book, and we were looking for somewhere else to live. We were tired of the inevitable restrictions imposed on anyone living in furnished accommodation and, not having enough money to buy a house, decided to try to rent an unfurnished cottage. But hunting for unfurnished cottages in the Lake District is like searching for the lost Grail. Having given in our notice for Easter, we were beginning to contemplate erecting our tent in a field somewhere, when at last our search bore fruit. I was tired of the South-West corner of the Lake District. It is very beautiful, but is outside the main climbing area. I fancied getting closer to Keswick, which is the closest the Lake District has to a climbing centre.

One morning, at the end of a wild goose chase to the north of Keswick, we saw an advertisement in the paper for a cottage at Kirkland, near Ennerdale. It was farther into West Cumberland than I had originally intended, and would obviously present problems in getting out of the Lake District to give lectures. Even so, we were desperate, and therefore went over to see it.

West Cumberland is a small world of its own, isolated to the west by the Irish Sea and to the east by Lakeland fells. As a result, it has developed its own special character, charm and problems. In the space of a few square miles are concentrated some of the most beautiful and remote valleys in the Lake District, rolling fell country where, even on a bank holiday, you won't meet anyone all day. As you approach the coastline, dead slag heaps rise from little mining villages of terraced houses, brave in the face of dying pits, with bright-painted door lintels and woodwork. On the coast itself, a trinity of industrial seaports combine some of the worst relics of industrialisation with a peculiar fascination of their own.

The route from Keswick to Kirkland goes through no-man's-land, between the fells and the industrial belt, through sleepy, unspoilt Cockermouth and then over a winding hedged road, to Cleator Moor and Egremont. Kirkland itself is like most of the little mining villages whose original purpose for being there has long vanished with the closing of the mines. It is a terrace of houses, perched on the crest of a hill, as if dropped there by a careless god. Somehow, they do not belong to the patchwork of pastures around them; are not sculptured into the land, as are Lakeland's farms and cottages. The road, fast narrowing, winds down a hill towards Ennerdale village. To the east is the great sweep of Ennerdale, with its lake and pine-clad slopes, which culminates in the rounded mass of Pillar Mountain.

Bank End Cottage was on a lane through two gates, tacked on to the end of a farm. This was part of the land, cradled in the arms of two grassy spurs that framed an ever-magnificent view of the hills around Ennerdale. The lake and valley bottom were hidden by dimpled hillocks to our immediate front, but above them rose the fells, a view more limited than the one from the road down from Kirkland, but in its way more attractive, with a tantalising quality of hidden secrets that I came to appreciate; and at Bank End Cottage we were to know a stronger feeling of homemaking than we had before experienced. But first, we had to rent the house. The owner lived at the farm at the end of the track – a quiet man, whose life, and probably those of his children, would be devoted to farming the land immediately around him. He had advertised the cottage at thirty bob a week. It had two bedrooms, a bathroom, kitchen, a big living room downstairs, and a small dining-room to the side of it, which was tailor-made for my study. The staircase was a half spiral of stone; the floor was stone flagged; the walls three feet thick; there were small, deep-set windows and a low-beamed ceiling. Even the garden was perfect – a little patch of deep, sweet-smelling grass, bounded by a high hedge with an old wooden seat, softened with age and wood-rot, in the corner. The fact that there was only an Elsan for a toilet seemed unimportant when balanced with the beauty of the cottage.

'I've had twenty applications already,' he warned us.

'But we're desperate,' I replied. 'We've got to move out next week, and have nowhere to go.'

Fortunately, Conrad, now eighteen months old, was on his best behaviour and looked cherubic.

'I'll have to think about it. Could you give me a ring at the end of the week?'

We were on tenterhooks. We phoned him that afternoon and offered £2 a week for the cottage. Whether this clinched the deal, or whether we had managed to capture his sympathy, I don't know, but at the end of the week he told us we could move into Bank End Cottage. We were to live there for two years, the first year of which was to be idyllically happy. Conrad was growing into a rare, self-contained, adventurous yet gentle child. We went exploring together in the fields around the cottage and I shall never forget one wild, windy day, when I took him in the papoose, and we walked over the fields to the open fell and climbed Murton Fell, a 1,400-foot hummock. The wind hammered at our faces, and great grey clouds scudded across the rolling fields from the sea to break on the high fells of the Lake District. To the north we could see Ennerdale's slate-grey waters, torn with flecks of white by the fierce wind, and back below us, a mile away, our own haven, almost lost in undulations of the land. Then, back home to a coal fire and mugs of tea, to a cottage in which, slowly, we were implanting some of our own individuality. We had started with a single desk – the only piece of furniture we had owned at Woodland – slept on the floor, used a camping stove for cooking; then, slowly over the months, we picked up some furniture at sales and were given even more by relatives and friends.

Our proudest acquisition was our cat. He came with the cottage, but in fact, acquisition is the wrong description, for Tom Cat was more a distinguished guest than a pet. He was a magnificent tabby with a white blaze on his chest, who could boast that no one would ever own him. One morning, shortly after we had moved in, he walked through the door and gave a firm but courteous mew to indicate that he expected to be fed. Most of the time when we were at home he stayed with us, though on occasion would vanish for a few days at a time, always returning sleek and immaculately clean. When we left the cottage – even for quite long periods – a day or so after our homecoming, Tom would slide in through the door, plump, self-possessed and friendly in a remote kind of way.

It was shortly after we moved into Bank End Cottage that I went down to Cheddar Gorge to perform in the television broadcast. Wendy and Conrad came too, and we set up camp in a field in Cheddar Village. The broadcast was exciting in the sense that this was my debut as a climbing television performer, that I had to become accustomed to climbing with a pair of headphones crackling in my ears and that I had to talk while I climbed. We practised the climbs many times over, however, so that I knew every move backwards and, in the process, of course, lost a great deal of the spontaneity and adventure which, ideally, one should pass on to the viewer. But that first time, it was sufficient challenge in itself.

Our week at Cheddar was hectic and exciting. I was meeting and working with experts in the communications field; was constantly learning from them. The climax – the actual broadcast of the climb – becomes in a way, an anticlimax compared with those nerve-stretching moments in January, when we had made the first ascent. That, whatever the motivation initiating the attempt to climb the High Rock, had had all the ingredients of climbing adventure. The television performance was a job of work – but was an enjoyable, exacting and very interesting job. To me, the climbing took second place – there was no mystery, because I had done it before. The challenge was to try to put across to the lay viewer what climbing entails – not just the obvious sensationalism, but how I, the climber, feel, as I work my way up a stretch of rock which is commonplace to me, but unbelievably difficult and dangerous to the beholder.

Finally, to tidy up the whole affair, we had to think of a name for the climb. We decided to call it *Coronation Street* – because it was next to *Sceptre*, and we were doing the broadcast for ITV.

9 *Rassemblement* International

Things were looking up. At long last, a mere two years behind deadline, I had finished my book. My fee from the Cheddar broadcast provided a little money in the bank and I was full of ambitious plans for an Alpine summer, with some good partners to share them. In addition, Wendy was going out with me, and we had bought a large, Agincourt-style frame tent, especially for our family holiday.

And then, a few weeks before we were due to leave, I had a call from Tom Patey.

'I've just been nominated by the Alpine Club as the British representative for this year's International *Rassemblement*. They've left me to choose my companion. Joe can't make it this year, so I wondered if you'd like to come.'

I accepted immediately, arranging for Wendy to join me later, as planned. A holiday with Tom was guaranteed to be unusual, varied and exciting. The previous year, when Tom had been climbing with Joe, the arrangement had not been satisfactory since, as a team, they were so much faster than Robin Ford and myself. But this time Tom and I would be climbing as a team. In addition, we should be living it up, for the International *Rassemblement*, or meet, was based on the Ecole Nationale de Ski et Alpinisme in Chamonix. The function was held every two years, and national clubs from all over the world were invited to send their representatives. I had already heard tales of superb food, free lifts on all the télépheriques, and free stays at the huts.

The international meet was due to start early in July, and I drove out with Tom. We had with us Tom's bible of potential new routes; in it were a few additions to the previous year's collection, the products of his ingenious research. The cuisine at the Ecole Nationale lived up to its reputation, with succulent steaks for lunch, unlimited red wine and masses of vegetables. The actual meet was a cross between Noah's Ark, with pairs of different nationalities, and the Tower of Babel. Already a healthy element of competition was springing up between the big league climbers of the Alpine countries, fostered by the custom of listing everyone's ascents as they were made. This was a little like a league table, which we all examined with care as we decided what to do next. An ascent of the Bonatti route on the Grand Pilier d'Angle would have rated ten points, probably by virtue of the fact that it was by Bonatti and had not yet had a second ascent, while that of the South-west Pillar of the Dru, once the most prestigious of all Chamonix rock-climbs, was little more than a trade route, and therefore would only rate two points in the prestige stakes.

Climbing with Tom, I was on safe ground – he was interested in nothing but new routes, which really defied any imaginary point count system.

The range of ability assembled at the *Rassemblement* was impressive. From Italy came Roberto Sorgato, one of its finest climbers – among many other routes, he had made the first winter ascent of the North Face on the Civetta, and had also made a couple of attempts on the Eiger Direct – at that time the most outstanding unclimbed problem in the Alps. Never bothering to indulge in competitive stakes, he was happy to eat, drink and flirt with the girls down in Chamonix. Equally uncompetitive were a pair of Mexicans, with neat little black moustaches. They wore beautiful blazers bearing their mountaineering club badge, but had no climbing equipment at all. To every invitation by their French hosts to actually go out climbing, they replied that the hospitality of Chamonix was so delightful and they were gaining so much from meeting their fellow mountaineers that they were happy to stay within the confines of the École Nationale. We shared a room with two inscrutable, but immensely courteous Japanese.

The International side of things started well, with two Americans, Steve Millar and Lito Tejada Flores, going up with us to do a new route on the West Face of the Cardinal, an elegant little rock spire above the Charpoua Glacier. Having cut our teeth on a comparatively small peak, I was keen to get on to bigger things. Ever competitive, I had my eye on the international point count. Tom, ever easy-going, agreed, and we worked through the Patey bible.

'How about the Right-hand Pillar of Brouillard?' I suggested. 'Crew and Ingle failed on that last year. They couldn't even get to the foot of the Pillar.'

'Aye, that could be pleasant enough.'

The Right-hand Pillar of Brouillard, one of a trinity of three, is a rock buttress at the head of the Brouillard Glacier, the widest and most difficult glacier in the Mont Blanc region. Walter Bonatti had climbed the Red Pillar of Brouillard in 1958, and the chapter in his book devoted to this ascent comprises a hair-raising description of his crossing of the glacier and then dismisses the actual ascent in a couple of paragraphs – a tribute to the horrendous difficulty of the glacier. Crew and Ingle had fared no better, getting lost in a maze of giant crevasses, and finally, after falling into one, they retreated before even reaching the foot of the Pillar.

That afternoon, we happened to call in at the Bar Nationale, at that time the meeting point of all British climbers in Chamonix. Crew and Ingle were sitting at one of the tables.

'Just arrived?' I asked.

'Yes. Conditions aren't much good, are they?' Pete replied.

'Hopeless,' I agreed. 'What are you thinking of doing?'

'Probably push off to the Dolomites,' Pete replied.

'You might just as well; nothing's in condition.'

And then we had some beers and started talking about the south side of Mont Blanc. Tom, less competitive than I, even mentioned our interest in the South-west Pillar and then went on to suggest we joined forces. I kicked him under the table, and Crew looked nonplussed, muttering something about preferring the idea of climbing in the Dolomites, and shortly afterwards made his excuses and left.

'I'll bet you anything they're going for the Pillar,' I told Tom.

We crossed over to the south side of Mont Blanc the next morning, availing ourselves of the free télépherique tickets given to us at the *Rassemblement*. At this stage, judging Crew by my own competitive values, I was convinced he was probably on his way to the foot of the climb. I was all in favour of going straight up to the hut and, if possible, stealing a march on them – unless, of course, they were already ahead of us. Tom, the traditionalist, was convinced that no one could be guilty of such overt competitiveness, and insisted that we seek out their campsite in the woods of the Val Veni, and proffer our invitation once again.

We found them in a woodland glade, just out of bed and, over a cup of coffee, we quickly agreed to join forces. It was midday when we got away, plodding through the richly perfumed pine woods of the Val Veni and then up the winding path to the Gamba Hut. It stood on a grassy spur running down from the Innominata Ridge of Mont Blanc, flanked by the frozen cataracts of the Frêney and Brouillard Glaciers. On the other side of the Frêney Glacier soared the West Face of the Aiguille Noire de Peuterey – a petrified brown-yellow flame.

On we tramped, past the new Monzino Hut, solid and lavish, with granite walls and plate-glass windows, to the shell of the old Gamba refuge, a little wooden and stone hut which seemed part of the fell-side. It had seen a thousand exploits – some victorious, some tragic. Bonatti, with his client Gallieni, had staggered here that June day in 1961, through a blizzard, after four companions had died in their retreat from attempting the first ascent of the Central Pillar of Frêney. This disaster had highlighted just how remote are all the climbs on the south side of Mont Blanc. Now the hut had been superseded, and was already partly demolished. I was sad to see it go, for it seemed in keeping with the wild beauty of that outlying spur of Mont Blanc. The new hut represented civilisation's cloying encroachment on the fast-shrinking mountain wilderness, when even the climbing huts begin to resemble hotels. Gone was the crusty old pensioned-off guide, who lived in a little cubby-hole at the end of the single, dark bunk and living room.

But the ruins of the old hut still stood and, to save money, we stayed there. Next morning we watched clouds scudding over the summit of Mont Blanc;

the weather was obviously unsettled and somehow our little team had not coalesced into a determined group. Perhaps it was too early in the season, and we were insufficiently fit, and so we turned tail, went back to the valley and then returned to the flesh pots of the International *Rassemblement*.

The next fortnight passed pleasantly enough, with another new route on the West Face of the Aiguille du Midi, a sortie into the Vercors with the great French climber, Lionel Terray (tragically, to be killed in the same area only a few weeks later), then the final party to close the *Rassemblement*. All the climbing dignitaries of Chamonix attended, and a list of everyone's climbs during the fortnight was displayed, giving full vent and satisfaction to our competitive instincts. There was plenty of champagne, superb food, and Wendy, with a grubby and bewildered Conrad in tow, arrived halfway through the reception. She had driven out from England in our Minivan, with the girl-friend of a friend of ours.

They had had their share of adventures; a broken fan belt, just short of Dover, caused the car to boil dry before they noticed anything was wrong. Then, reaching the ferry only just in time, they were turned back because we had forgotten to have Conrad put on Wendy's passport. They ended up sleeping in the van while waiting for the Passport Office to open, and then, next morning –

'Have you the husband's consent to take this child out of the country?'

'But I'm going out to meet him. He's already in France.'

'But how do we know? I must have a letter of consent.'

Wendy, near to tears with fatigue and exasperation, then remembered that she had my most recent letter in her handbag. I had written that I was longing to see her. She showed this to the Passport Control man, and Conrad was duly entered on to her passport.

Across the Channel, halfway through France, it was getting dark when the dynamo failed. With lights getting dimmer, dazzled by oncoming traffic, they arrived at a garage whose owner allowed them to sleep on the garage floor while waiting for the mechanic to arrive next morning. At long last they drove into Chamonix. In spite of everything, although sweaty and a bit bedraggled, Wendy, in a mixture of tears of relief at finishing the journey and smiles at being with me again, looked fabulous. We all got happily drunk and then I smuggled Wendy and Conrad up to our room in the *Rassemblement*, to have one last night under a roof, before spending the rest of the summer under canvas.

Next morning we drove over to Leysin, in Switzerland, where we had arranged to meet Rusty Baillie. Rusty was a Rhodesian climber who had come over to Europe in 1963, immediately making his mark with the second British ascent of the North Wall of the Eiger, with Dougal Haston. I had met him in Zermatt immediately after he had made this ascent, at the time when

RASSEMBLEMENT INTERNATIONAL

Hamish MacInnes and I were trying to make our Matterhorn film. Having spent the previous year in Kenya, Rusty had been doing various odd-jobs, acting as a life-guard at a beach club, working as a game warden, and enjoying the hot sun.

High on the list of our possible objectives was the North Wall Direct of the Eiger. This had undoubtedly become the current Last Great Problem of the Alps – one of the most over-used cliches in mountaineering literature and talk. In recent times, a new last great problem has been found, attempted and solved, almost every year. European Alpinists were beginning to run out of unclimbed ground – every face and ridge in the Alps had been climbed and had at least one route up it. Wherever there was room for one, a direttissima, or direct route, had been made, straightening out the original route to follow as closely as possible the imaginary line a drop of water would describe in falling from the summit. In many instances, in the Dolomites, these routes had been engineered by drilling a continuous line of bolts, making a mockery of the natural configuration of the rock, and the entire concept of the direttissima.

The possibility of putting a direct route up the North Face of the Eiger, however, did indeed have the ingredients for being the true Last Great Problem in the Alps. No other wall in the Alps combines length, intricacy of route-finding and objective danger to such a degree – a fact grimly proved by the ever-lengthening roll of accidents on the face. True, the original route put up by Heckmair, Vörg, Harrer and Kasparek was not technically extreme by modern standards – there was no pitch on the climb harder than Grade V, one grade below the top grade – but this fact ceased to have much significance to a climber caught in a blizzard, or confronted by rock covered by a thin and treacherous covering of ice; and all too often the North Face of the Eiger was either caught by bad weather, or was in a dangerously iced condition.

Strangely enough, it was Sedlmayer and Mehringer, the first serious party to climb on the face who, in effect, made the first attempt on a Direct Route up the Eiger. In the summer of 1935 they embarked on the bottom rocks of the face and took a fairly direct line up to the First Ice-field, climbing the first rock barrier near its centre. (On all subsequent ascents this line was turned, by the *Difficult Crack* and *Hinterstoisser Traverse*, well to the right.) They reached the Flat Iron, a prominent prow of rock in the middle of the face, and there their luck ran out. Hit by a savage storm, probably knowing they could never have got down, they tried to sit it out, and were frozen to death – the first victims of the Eiger.

Their deaths at least taught those who followed that the Eiger does not lend itself to direct ascents, for the strata stretch across the face in a series of smooth rock bands and ice-fields in the lower part of the wall, and in the upper part the lines are all diagonal, seeking to lead the climber to the edge of the wall.

The route finally completed in 1938 was, therefore, essentially a wandering line, searching out the lines of weakness through this huge maze of ice-filled chimneys and galleries.

Climbers did not start thinking of a direct ascent until early 1963, though on my own ascent of the North Wall in 1962, Ian Clough and I caused a great deal of excitement amongst the ubiquitous watchers at Kleine Scheidegg, by losing the route in the upper reaches, and making one desperately difficult pitch, straight up towards the summit from just above the White Spider, before realising our mistake and coming back down.

In the winter of the following year, two Polish climbers, Czeslaw Momatiuk and Jan Mostowski, made the first recorded attempt to climb the Eiger Direct. They chose winter, hoping to reduce the objective dangers, since the Direct line also goes straight up the main line of stone-fall on the face. In winter the stones would be frozen into still silence. Following the Sedlmayer-Mehringer line, they were forced to turn back by bad weather at the start of the First Ice-field. Between 1963 and 1965 several more attempts were made by various leading European climbers, with little progress; no one did better than Sedlmayer and Mehringer, thirty years before.

From the start, the name Harlin had been closely linked with these attempts. He climbed the original route on the Eiger in 1962, a short time before Ian Clough and I made our ascent. His thoughts had immediately turned to the possibility of making a Direct Route, and he had camped below the face in the summer of 1963, but the weather had been too bad to make an attempt. He did, however, meet the Italians, Ignazio Piussi and Roberto Sorgato, who were also interested in the Eiger Direct. In the winter of 1964 he joined them, and two other Italians, in an abortive attempt, returning in the following June with the famous French climbers, Rene Desmaison and Andre Bertrand. They reached the top of the Second Ice-field before being forced back by bad weather.

Harlin had already made for himself a considerable reputation with a series of revolutionary new routes, using the newly developed technical climbing techniques which had been evolved in Yosemite. Tom Patey drove over to Leysin with us, and sociable as ever, suggested we should call and see John Harlin.

At this stage I regarded Harlin as a potential competitor for the Direct route, and was a little defensive, perhaps, since he had already made several attempts, and presumably knew more of the problems than I. I had already heard a great deal about him – he was known in some quarters as the Blond God – a nickname not entirely affectionate, for his flamboyance and drive had made enemies as well as friends.

His house in Leysin was perched on the hillside overlooking the broad sweep of the Rhône Valley, with the Dent du Midi, standing like a Gothic cathedral on the other side of an empty void, hiding Mont Blanc: the Verte,

Droites and Courts, whose snow-clad North Faces, white-etched with the black of distant granite, peered from behind the Dent du Midi, like three sirens tempting the climber to their cold touch.

We knocked and John opened the door. His title was well earned – he had a Tarzan-style physique and looks, from his blond hair to his thigh-sized biceps. He greeted us warmly, and ushered us into his big downstairs living room. It was sparsely furnished with a few brightly coloured rugs and cushions scattered over the floor, a low settee and some big, bold, rather brooding abstract paintings on the walls. I learned later that these had been painted by John.

In the course of our conversation, my own suspicions quickly subsided – he appeared outgoing, frank, and immensely enthusiastic. I suspect that he had also viewed me with suspicion, as a potential competitor, but as so often happens, now that we met, antagonism vanished in a decision to join forces in our attempt on the Eiger Direct. We decided to make the attempt as a threesome, since I had already involved Rusty Baillie; we resigned ourselves to waiting until the end of the season, when the weather is often more settled, and the long cold nights reduce the stone-fall down the face.

John suggested that we should camp in the quarry immediately behind his house. We could get water from his outside tap, and even have the occasional bath. And so it was all settled, and things at last seemed to be slotting into place. We had a pleasant base for the summer, our team had been strengthened with John's inclusion, and now all we had to do was wait, and climb, until the weather was sufficiently settled for the big North Wall. Our routine in Leysin became a leisured round of sunbathing in the quarry, playing on the abundance of boulder problems the crag offered and, in the evenings, wandering up to the Club Vagabond, the social centre for most of the English-speaking people there. It had been opened some years before by Alan Rankin, a Canadian who had tired of travelling in Europe and wanted to settle down. He had seen the need for a non-institutionalised, free and easy hostel, to provide cheap accommodation for travellers, without any of the puritanical overtones which tend to dominate youth hostels. The result was the Vagabond Club. It had a bar, discotheque and comfortable bunk accommodation. Regular habitués, many of whom eked out a living by working in the Club, were mainly Americans, Canadians or Australians who had, at least temporarily, opted out of the rat-race. Its shifting population encompassed thousands of young people wandering round Europe. Some stayed a few nights, others longer. It was a good place to drink at night – if you were alone, there was an ever-changing supply of attractive girls and a timeless atmosphere of slightly aimless pleasure-seeking, one which could be satisfying for a short period, but which could, perhaps, cloy over a longer one.

In the following week I saw a lot of John Harlin, and came to know him well.

He had an extraordinary mixture of qualities, mirrored, perhaps, in the contrasts of his life and career. He had always been a brilliant natural athlete, excelling at almost every game and track event in which he took part. Since his father was a pilot with TWA, he had had a nomadic childhood, constantly on the move from one city to another in Europe and the United States. At Stanford University, where he first started serious climbing, he flirted with the idea of becoming a dress designer, even knocking on the doors of Balmain and Dior, to no avail, finally ending up at the other extreme as a fighter pilot in the United States Air Force. At university he had met and married Marilyn, an attractive blonde girl studying marine biology, and by his early twenties had two children, a boy and a girl.

He had made little impact on the American climbing scene, mainly because in the early fifties, when he was at Stanford University, climbing in Yosemite (which was later to become the cockpit of world rock-climbing) was still in its infancy. It was not until the late fifties and early sixties that a small group of American climbers were to develop fully the new equipment and techniques, which were to enable them to tackle the sheer granite walls of Yosemite, and then to revolutionise rock-climbing throughout the world.

John was posted to Germany in 1960, and it was in Europe that he established himself as a mountaineer. Strangely, he was not a brilliant natural climber. On a trip he made to Britain in late 1960, he climbed with Ron James, who, at that time, ran an outdoor activities centre in North Wales. John was at a loss on British rock, and did very little leading. In the Alps, however, his ambition was boundless. He walked to the foot of the Central Pillar of Frêney in 1961, at the same time that Don Whillans and I, with Ian Clough and the Pole, Jan Djuglosz, made our first ascent, and turned back only because there was already too big a crowd there, in the shape of a rival French party In 1963, he established his reputation with his first ascents of the South Face of the Fou (in the Chamonix Aiguilles), and the Hidden Pillar of Frêney. John had been the architect, the driving force behind the venture, though Tom Frost, a brilliant Yosemite climber, had led the most difficult pitches of the climb. This was to be the pattern of many of John's ventures – he provided the inspiration and drive, often using climbers who were technically more skilled than he, to lead the key section.

Taking the step I had taken two years before, he left the United States Air Force in 1963 to become Sports Director of an American private school in Leysin. Even with Marilyn teaching biology at the school and, in fact, earning a higher salary than he, their incomes suffered a considerable drop from his Air Force salary. That summer of 1965, when I came over to see him, he had taken a further step in commitment, leaving the American school to start his own International School of Modern Mountaineering. With an impressive brochure and a few students, recruited entirely from the United States, the new school was launched.

He had invited Royal Robbins, one of the leading exponents of Yosemite climbing, to be chief instructor, and the two men, both prima donnas in their own right, could not have offered a greater contrast. John, flamboyant, assertive and impulsive – Robbins, very cool, analytical, carefully avoiding any ostentatious show, yet every bit as aware as John of his own position in the climbing firmament. The pair planned an attempt to make a super-direct route up the West Face of the Dru, a line which John had attempted on several occasions with a variety of weaker partners, with consequently little success. With Robbins he was to succeed, and in doing so, to complete a route which to this day ranks as one of the most difficult and serious rock routes in the Mont Blanc Massif.

After the climb, Robbins had devoted himself to running John's climbing school, whilst John himself put in spasmodic appearances, dreamed up new plans and snatched training climbs for our planned ascent of the Eiger Direct.

One such was on the Dent du Midi – a direct start to one of its ridges. The climb itself was undistinguished, but our way of climbing it was indicative of the nature of the team. We set out spontaneously after a fondue party in our tent in the quarry, which was followed by a long night's drinking. In the early hours of the morning, staggering back from the Vagabond Club, we noticed that it was a superb, clear night – the first for some time.

'We could do a route tomorrow,' I suggested.

'I know a new line on the Dent du Midi – how about trying that?' suggested John.

'How long would it take?'

'We could be up and back in the day, if we started early enough.'

'That'll have to be now. It's two o'clock already. We'll have to pack some gear, and we've got to get there.'

'What are we waiting for? Let's go.'

And go we did; having packed the sacks, we piled into John's Volkswagen bus, driving through the dark, down into the Rhône Valley and up the other side to the foot of the Dent du Midi. We reached the top of the road and walked through the woods to the sound of the dawn chorus, then up above the tree-line, and by seven in the morning we were at the foot of the vertical step in the North Ridge of the Dent du Midi, which had never been climbed direct. It was our intention to try out the American Big Wall climbing technique. In this technique the lead climber attaches the rope to a piton and then the second man climbs the rope, using jumar clamps. While he climbs, the leader can either rest or haul up the rucksack carrying all the gear for the climb. This was the technique we proposed to use on the Eiger, even though I had never used jumars before. We tossed up for who should have the first pitch, and I won. It gave pleasant straightforward climbing, leading up to a huge roof overhang. Rusty led the next pitch, disappearing round the corner of the roof and climbing a long groove. He reached the top. John was to follow him, being taken up on the rope, while I was to have my first try at jumaring.

'Nothing to it,' said John, as he climbed off the ledge, and disappeared round the corner. 'Just clip on, and swing out on the rope.'

The trouble was, the rope was going straight over the lip of the overhang which jutted a good fifteen feet outwards above me. We had scrambled several hundred feet up steep broken rocks before starting to climb and, as a result, there was a giddy sense of exposure. I clipped on to the rope and stood poised like a trapeze artist under the big top. Had Rusty secured the rope correctly? I had to trust him. Did it pass over any sharp flakes of rock? God knows. I hated the thought of committing myself to that slender strand of rope – was even more determined not to show I was frightened, especially to the Blond God – and so, with a shudder, I stepped off the ledge, and went spiralling into space. The rope dropped with a sickening jerk – it had been caught round a flake. My own heart, already pounding, seemed to plummet down into my stomach. And then my swings decreased – the rope was intact, and all I had to do was climb it.

I now discovered that the length of the slings, which connect the jumars to one's waist-loop and foot, is of vital importance. Mine were all wrong. They were too long, and incorrectly proportioned to each other. As a result, climbing the rope, especially with a rucksack suspended from my waist harness, was a murderous struggle. Later, I learned that an essential precaution for any jumaring is to tie a knot in the rope, so that if the jumars do slip on the rope, you don't slide straight off the end. This was a precaution of which I had been blissfully unaware. Climbing with Harlin was a hard school – a constant game of Chicken, with no one prepared to call off first.

The rest of the climb was a romp, and we were back late that night, tired and happy, having completed a 2,000-foot climb and having walked round the entire Dent du Midi – about fifteen miles in all.

And so the summer wore on – the Eiger Direct always in our thoughts, but the weather never settled enough for us even to think of going over to Grindelwald. Rusty and I did, however, attempt a climb which was to give one of the most tense and memorable experiences of my climbing career. There was a fine weather spell in mid-summer and John used this for his ascent, with Royal Robbins, of the Direct on the West Face of the Dru. Rusty and I decided to have another try at the Right-hand Pillar of Brouillard.

We sorted out our gear one morning, assembling our meagre supply of American pitons. I wanted to travel light anyway, hoping to get away with a fast ascent. So much of the pleasure of climbing can be destroyed if you are weighed down by too much equipment.

When John saw our equipment layout, he raised an eyebrow and commented: 'You guys sure do believe in travelling light.'

He was destined to be proved unpleasantly right.

10   The Right-Hand Pillar of Brouillard

And so through the Chamonix tunnel once again – car lights, psychedelic, wink in front, automatic speed controls flash their warnings, and we're excited, like small boys escaping from parental control. At the end of the tunnel, a distant blink of white suddenly rushes up on us, and we've passed under Mont Blanc – under a thousand million tons of rock, ice and snow, and back into the dazzling sunshine and a cloudless sky. This was the perfect weather we had been awaiting all summer. It was difficult to believe that it had ever been bad – could ever be bad again.

Before racing up to the old Gamba Hut we go to the little cable station which carries food and supplies, and send up our packs. Both Rusty and I are intensely competitive; there's already a tension in our relationship – I am the established climber, with sufficiently obvious weaknesses to make stardom questionable, while Rusty, the young climber still to establish himself, has enough good climbs behind him, together with the self-confidence gained from knocking around the world from an early age, to feel himself every bit as good as I.

I lengthen my pace, sweating hard, enjoying the undeclared competition. I have been out in the Alps a few weeks longer than Rusty and am therefore slightly fitter. Reaching the garish new Monzino Hut first, I am pleased at my hollow little victory. It is three o'clock in the afternoon, and I want to get high on the Innominata Ridge tonight, ideally to the little bivouac hut which is opposite the foot of our objective. Rusty, swept along by my enthusiasm, agrees, and we collect our sacks, leave the soft comfort of the new hut, pass the site of the old one, now sadly cleared down to its last timber, and start plodding up the long scree slopes leading to the crest of the ridge which bars the view of our objective.

A fine weather forecast aided my decision to press on as far as possible that afternoon, though this was hardly borne out by existing signs. An even ceiling of dark grey cloud clung to the top of the Pic Innominata and completely hid the main mass of Mont Blanc. From the crest of the ridge we could look down on the chaotic jumble of ice towers forming the Brouillard Glacier – obviously a place to avoid if we possibly could. The route up to the Eccles Bivouac Hut lay over comparatively easy-angled snow-slopes, below the crest of the ridge, up towards the Col de Frêney, and then up a slightly steeper slope. We could just discern the hut – a tiny box, clinging to the slope of the Innominata Ridge, just below the cloud ceiling. From there, we could see that a straightforward traverse led into the upper Brouillard Basin, from which we should be able to reach the foot of our Pillar.

We started wading through wet, sugary snow towards the Col de Frêney. This was obviously the wrong time of day to be crossing these slopes, but unless we wanted an unnecessary bivouac, we should have to keep going to reach the hut before dark. Reaching the Col de Frêney an hour before dark we were, finally, defeated. The steeper snow leading up to the hut was a bottomless morass of soft sugar, but having retreated to the Col we found a small island jutting out of the inhospitable snows, and settled down there for the night. At least the forecast had proved correct. As night fell the cloud ceiling disintegrated, and a myriad stars stabbed through it. It was reassuringly cold, always a sign of settled weather, and as dawn broke we began to cook our breakfast. Then began a chapter of accidents which were to dog our entire attempt. With frozen fingers I dropped the burner of our stove as I struggled to light it. I heard it trickle down into the dark void below. No longer did we have the means to melt snow for drinks – something that was even more serious than losing all our food. But it was a fine morning, and we couldn't possibly turn tail and return, so packing our sacks we started up towards the hut we had struggled so hard to reach the previous night. In the hard frost of the dawn, the snow was crisp and firm, crampons bit into it with a satisfying snick; no longer wallowing, we were able to move steadily, easily upwards, passing the hut, empty and silent, traversing across steep frozen slopes into the upper basin below the Pillar. We could now gaze across at our objective. The face of the Pillar was sheer, clean and dry, but the slabby flanks were dotted with snow patches and running with melt water. Cutting into the left-hand side of the face was a great clean dièdre, which ended in a number of huge roof overhangs, but to its left was a series of cracks that seemed to offer the easiest line. We resolved to try this.

Quickly, we crossed the firm snows that led to the base of the Pillar, and started up the broken rocks at its foot. These led to a steep rock buttress and two good pitches up a series of steep cracks which, in turn, led to a ledge that stretched across the Pillar. Above it, the rock stretched steep, smooth, seemingly impregnable. We traversed the ledge, trying to outflank this obstacle. Time slipped by. We were on the side of the Pillar; the rock, no longer redbrown and firm, was that dusty shade of grey that almost always means bad rock with a lack of crack lines. Suddenly, the climbing had lost its attraction, and we started fumbling around, wasting time in changing belays. We were hesitant, indecisive. It was now early afternoon, and we had still gained no height above our traverse line.

'This is no bloody good,' I said; 'we'll have to get back into the centre of the

Pillar. At least there are some decent cracks there.'

As we travelled back into the centre of the Pillar, we felt hot, tired and thirsty. Looking up at the rock above, the line seemed obvious enough – up that big clean dièdre – but what about the overhangs above? We had lost too much time, and felt very small, weak and helpless as we sat on the ledge, still near the foot of the Pillar, in this remote spot.

'Let's bivouac here. We'll have a go at the groove tomorrow,' I suggested. Rusty didn't take much persuading, and we settled down for the night. A trickle of melt water gave us a little to drink, though barely enough to slake our thirst. Packets of soup and tea bags were a hollow mockery without the burner on the stove – but still, we had a good large ledge on which to sleep, and the weather seemed settled.

Next morning, we started up the gangway that led to the groove. Rusty led the first pitch up steep but perfect rock – the red granite of the south side of Mont Blanc is superb climbing rock. I followed up to the foot of the big groove. It curved up in a single sweep, just off vertical and without a ledge and hardly a single hold – only the crack in its back provided a mixture of hand-jamming and lay-back holds.

I sorted out some gear and realised just how optimistically light we had travelled. I had only four pitons large enough to use in the crack – over 200 feet of climbing; and what about those serried roofs above?

I set out, half-hearted, already beaten. I worked my way a few feet above Rusty, hammered in a peg, hung on to it, and stared upwards. The crack seemed endless, full of unknown threats.

'We just haven't got enough gear,' I shouted down.

'What are you going to do about it?' asked Rusty.

'There's only one thing – we'll have to go and get some more.'

Go and get some more! Go down 7,000 feet of snow, scree and grass, all the way back to the valley and Courmayeur, just to get a few pieces of hardened steel – and then all the way back! That is what we did. We abseiled right down to the lowest rocks of the Pillar, for the way we had followed the previous morning was now being swept by a continuous hail of stones, dislodged by the afternoon sun. Abseil after abseil, until we were nearly down; nearly, but not quite, for between the foot of the Pillar and us was a monstrous bergschrund, a huge, mind-boggling chasm about fifteen feet across, with its lower lip about twenty feet below. The schrund itself vanished, seemingly bottomless, in dark shadows. Always frightened of jumping from heights, I hate leaping over crevasses. In theory, it is easy enough; you leap out on the rope, let it slide through your fingers and land on the other side. But what if it snags – if you miss the other side and go swinging back against the sheer ice wall, to be left hanging in the void? I stood there, determined not to show Rusty how frightened of the jump I was. Pride giving me the necessary impetus, I leapt, reached the other side, let the rope go and rolled down the slope. Rusty followed, and we plodded back to the Eccles Bivouac Hut, to reach it just before dusk.

After sleeping in the comfort of a bunk, the next morning, in the dawn, we raced back down towards the valley. An afternoon was spent shopping for pitons, more food, and a burner for the gas stove. We were ready for another onslaught. We walked back up to the Monzino Hut that very same afternoon and spent the night in its lush comfort. No more wallowing in wet snow for us.

This was to be a serious, systematically organised attempt; we had a mass of high protein food; nuts, cheese, salami, chocolate, tea bags and tubes of condensed milk. The warden of the hut called us at three in the morning, with boiling water for our tea. Piling our gear at the side of the table, the food neatly packed in a single nylon stuff bag, we packed our rucksacks. We were being so methodical – so uncharacteristically efficient. I knew that Rusty had packed the food – he thought I had packed it – and we both left it, in its stuff bag, sitting on the table.

We set off through the night, head torches throwing small islands of light in a glittering black world as we progressed up the long scree slopes, cramponned across the snow slopes, and reached the Col de Frêney just as dawn broke – time for a first breakfast.

'Might as well have a quick brew,' I suggested. 'We've got enough food with us for a five-day siege.' We sat down and looked at each other expectantly.

'How about some cheese?' I asked.

'Good idea.'

'You'd better get it out.'

'But you've got the food.'

'Have I, buggery. You took it.'

'No, it was up to you to take it. I've got all the pegs.'

Recriminations followed quickly, each determined that it was the fault of the other. Having searched our rucksacks, we discovered we had six tea bags, a bag of sugar and a handful of almonds – we were back to normal – disorganised. But at least we had some means of melting snow for drinks, and enough pitons to climb the big groove.

Swift easy movement over the hard, frozen snow was balm to our anger and worry about the loss of the food. We soon reached the bottom rocks of the Pillar and climbed to our highest point.

I set out, once again, up the groove. With sufficient pitons to hammer one in every twenty feet or so, it no longer felt either so long or so committing as before. It was certainly magnificent climbing. I ran out 130 feet of rope, hung on a piton to bring Rusty up, and then led another pitch, up towards the big roofs. The angle had steepened and the cracks had thinned down, but the peg-climbing was straightforward, and I was happily lost in the concentration that good, hard climbing always offers.

The Right-hand Pillar of Brouillard

It was now Rusty's turn to lead. The way above was barred by the roofs, and the only possibility seemed the crest of the buttress to our right. The wall between was steep and blank and Rusty fussed around it. Holding the rope I began to notice the passing of time and the big clouds that were growing out of nothing in the blue air around us. Just afternoon cloud – or something more ominous? The cloud line to the south, like the front face of a giant tidal bore, seemed to carry a more serious threat, but with its own wild beauty, enhanced by the very vulnerability and isolation of our position. The maze of crevasses and chaos of ice towers in the Brouillard Glacier were etched as black shadows drawn by the afternoon sun. Then, as the sun became diffused, blanked out by the fast-piling cloud, shadows also vanished, the snow and rocks around being flattened into menacing greys and whites by the even lighting.

The rope in my hand had gone still. Rusty had vanished round the corner. I cursed him, to myself, for his slowness and shouted:

'What are you doing? Have you reached a belay?'

But there was no reply.

At last – 'Come on, I'm belayed.'

The rope pulled in tight. I followed it, uncomfortably aware that if I did fall off, I should go spinning round the corner, as the rope was going away from me horizontally, offering scant support. Rusty was on a ledge round the corner;

a crack line vanished upwards into the mist that now enveloped us. It was impossible to see if it led anywhere.

'I think this pitch is mine,' said Rusty very firmly. 'You had the two in the groove.'

'All right, but you'd better be quick, I think the weather's breaking.' Rusty set out, hammering his way up the crack, at times nearly invisible as the mist swirled around us. I had sweated up the groove and now my clothes were cold and clammy. I shivered, cursed Rusty, and shouted up:

'If you can't get up any faster, you'd better come back down. We've not got long before dark.'

No reply, just the ping of the hammer. He was now sixty feet up. He paused, obviously enjoying himself, let out some rope and swung back and forth across the face, trying to work out the best line. 'Bloody idiot,' I thought, 'what the hell does he think he's doing!' There was a roll of thunder in the distance to emphasise the danger of our position.

'It's great up here,' came wafting down. 'I think we can get across to the right. You'd better come up.' And so I followed.

It's strange: once you're out in front again, all fears vanish. We had nearly reached the top of the Pillar; a blank slab barred our way. I climbed a few feet, managed to place a peg and then tensioned out from it, working my way, though constantly pulled back by gravity, till I was able to reach a series of ripples in the smooth granite. I let go the rope and balanced up; six feet, and I was on a sloping ledge. Rusty followed up, and I began hunting for a way up those last feet. But our luck ran out. The mists suddenly turned to flurries of snow; snow ran down the rock, covering every hold and, in a matter of seconds, what should have been quite easy climbing was rendered impossible. The change had all the dramatic suddenness that makes mountaineering the exciting and exacting sport it is. At midday, we had stripped down to our shirtsleeves under a blazing sky. The transition from sun to blizzard had taken about three hours, but the final transition from cloud to scudding snow-flakes had been instantaneous, turning a straightforward climb into a struggle for life.

I slithered down to the little sloping ledge, which was already banked up with snow, and we started preparing our bivouac, hammering in pegs, spread-ing the rope on the floor of the ledge to act as a rough cushion and insulation. It was now snowing too hard to think of dressing for the night, unless sheltered by the bivvy tent; so we got out our red nylon bag and Rusty got under it to get ready for the night. This meant slipping off his breeches to put on his long wool underpants, then removing his anorak to put on extra sweaters and a down jacket – the whole time being careful not to drop anything. The perpetual nightmare on any bivouac is of dropping your boots. I stood and stamped and shivered outside, as the storm which had hit us so quickly rose to a crescendo.

At last it was my turn to crawl into the bivvy sack. It was almost impossible to brush all the snow from my clothing – as fast as I brushed it off, more cascaded down from the rock above. Finally, I gave up and crawled into the tent-like sack – it was just a big bag of lightweight, proofed nylon, which we could pull over our heads. With me inside it as well as Rusty, there was hardly any room to move, let alone change my clothes. I managed to pull my boots off, slipped them in my rucksack and then pulled the pied d'éléphant over my legs, ending up with my feet in my rucksack.

By this time the storm had reached a new fury; it was nearly dark, and flashes of lightning lit the outside of the tent. Thunder crashed with ever-increasing reverberations. Our position was undoubtedly dangerous, but we felt a strange sense of security, almost contentment, while squeezed on that little ledge. The wafer-thin walls of the sack guarded us from the cruel talons of the wind and inside, uncomfortable though we were, there was an element of relative luxury, compared with what it could be outside.

We got out the gas stove and started melting snow which we collected from just outside the tent. We were already nearly buried in it on our ledge. After a few minutes, the flame went a dark colour, and then went out altogether. We had sealed ourselves in the sack too efficiently, and were fast running out of oxygen. The cold and snow gusted in, as we pulled up one side of the tent to admit some air. The flame of the stove flickered into life, and after half an hour or so we had a panful of lukewarm water in which to drop our precious teabags. The night passed slowly. We dozed, talked spasmodically, and tried to climb back up our sloping ledge, down which we were perpetually sliding. I thought (as no doubt Rusty also thought) about just how desperate our position was. There was the memory of the 1961 disaster, during the first attempt to climb the Central Pillar of Frêney, when four had died in a retreat after a storm very similar to the one which was striking us. There was, however, one big difference – we had the Eccles Bivouac Hut as a retreat – though even reaching that in a severe storm could prove a cruel test.

When morning came, the wind was as fierce as ever, and, to delay the moment when we should have to abandon the partial shelter of our bivouac tent to fight with tangled ropes and snow-buried gear, we had another brew and a handful of almonds. With no other excuse for delay, we struggled with frozen boots, and at last emerged from the sack into the full force of the wind. In an emergency like this, one must be very, very slow and systematic, checking everything twice, and three times, to ensure that knots are tied correctly, karabiners are clipped in, pitons secure. At last, with ropes untangled, a piton in place, we hurled the rope so that it disappeared down into the void. Rusty went first. There was a long delay – I couldn't hear anything – just stood shivering until the rope went slack. It must be my turn. I clipped in and started abseiling. We had never heard of the karabiner brake abseil, and were using the old-fashioned method, where you thread the rope through a karabiner clipped into a thigh loop, and then pay the rope over your shoulder. It offers the minimum of friction, and as soon as I launched myself out on it I realised there wasn't enough. The face of the rock was encased in wind-blown snow, the rope itself had an icy sheath, and I just went plummeting down, barely in control. It was just as well that Rusty had secured both bottom ends to a piton he had hammered in, otherwise I doubt whether I could possibly have stopped myself. How Rusty managed to stop himself, I just don't know.

'Nearly went off the end,' he stated tersely. There was no ledge, just a horizontal crack into which he had hammered a couple of pitons. We now suffered the nightmare: were we going to be able to pull down the doubled rope? We pulled one end; it jammed solid, and was so badly iced that even with jumars we could never have climbed back up to free it. We heaved again, and it gave a little, another pull and it started running through our hands. I threaded it through the piton for our next abseil as Rusty heaved. It was my turn to go down first, into the unknown.

Down and down we went in a succession of abseils, through the wind and snow and storm, building up a rhythm with a weird enjoyment at our sense of control in the face of the fury of the elements. I regarded Rusty in a new light. At ground level, even on the climb when things had been going well, many of the quirks of his personality had irritated me, in exactly the same way as I am sure I had irritated him. Now, confronted by the sheer scale of our struggle, we were closely united, and I was able to respect his calm, methodical approach to our problem.

We reached the great bergschrund at the bottom, hardly noticing its size as we leapt across and then groped through the white-out, towards the crest of the Innominata Ridge, where we knew the hut should be. But what if we couldn't find it? If we went too high or got on to steep ground? But then, in a break in the cloud, we saw the gleam of the tin roof below us.

We were tired and hungry, but with a few more hours to dusk, we kept on going down, hoping that the great piles of fresh powder snow would not avalanche under us. At the Monzino Hut, the guardian gave us a bowl of soup, but the goal of wives and food and sleep kept us going down, automaton-like, till we reached the valley and great mounds of antipasti, litres of red wine, and long, deep sleep. We had reached a point fifty feet below the summit of the Pillar, had come tantalisingly close to success, but somehow it didn't seem to matter. The experience had been exacting and rewarding, and at no time had either Rusty or I felt out of control of our own destiny, even though the margin for error was nil. This, perhaps, is what climbing is truly all about. You would never seek out the situation, but once in it, fighting your way out stretches nerves and mind and body to the limit, and in so doing brings new levels of awareness of yourself, and your companions.

We slept in the van and next day drove back to Leysin to two very worried girls. There, we had an interlude; the weather continued unsettled, and Rusty was getting married. He had met Pat, a practical, down-to-earth girl, while in Kenya – she had followed him to Europe. The ceremony took place in the Mayor's office and then in the church in Leysin; I was best man. Returning to John's house, we had a magnificent buffet lunch, prepared by Marilyn and Wendy.

Rusty did not have much time for a honeymoon. The weather improved after a few days, and we resolved to make another attempt at the Right-hand Pillar of Brouillard, this time increasing our team to four by including John and Brian Robertson, who had just arrived in Leysin.

Once again, the walk through the Alpine meadows, and up the steep path to the Monzino Hut; a night at the hut, and another dawn start – this one threatened from the beginning with auguries of bad weather. Wispy clouds of grey were playing round the dark sabre tooth of the Aiguille Noire, and an ominous mackerel-shaped cloud perched over Mont Blanc. It was too warm, and we wondered whether to set out at all, but the forecast was good and John, perhaps as a result of his Air Force background, had a fanatical confidence in the powers of weather forecasters. The ascent was untoward. This was the first big climb I had been on with John, and I liked the steady rhythm of his movement, the confidence of his decisions and his speed of climbing. We were on the same wavelength, climbing with the minimum of verbal communication.

We had reached the top of the Pillar by four in the afternoon; clouds, once again, were boiling up around us. Another storm was on its way. We left a rope in position for the other pair to follow up the last pitch of the Pillar, and began to climb together, up the broken snow-plastered rocks that led towards the crest of the Brouillard Ridge. Even when we reached that, we should still have over a thousand feet of climbing before we reached the summit of Mont Blanc. And as we climbed, the snow came gusting in, blanking out the peaks around us and enclosing us in our own little world. If we had just been a pair, I have a feeling we should have risked all and made a bid for the summit – we were climbing well and strongly enough. But there was no sign of the others – they were not as swift. So, with hardly a word exchanged, we turned tail and retraced our steps to rejoin them near the top of the Pillar.

Another storm-racked night in a small bivvy tent; a straight repetition of the previous experience, but now we were four and not two. We knew the way down, and our descent next day was merely an exercise in patience.

We had climbed the Right-hand Pillar, though total success still eluded us; we had not tasted that delicious moment when, on reaching the top of a mountain, the ground suddenly falls away on every side, and new vistas are opened before your eyes. We had been pinned within the close confines of the Brouillard Cirque, with its now familiar, magnificent views of chaotic icefall, the jumbled mass of the Pic Innominata, the split tooth of the Aiguille Noire and, to the south, the haze of the Italian foothills and the gentler peaks of the Gran Paradiso.

But we had gained all there was from the Right-hand Pillar, and we should not go back. Although we were supremely fit, ready for the Eiger Direct, and all it had to offer, the weather was not. August crept into September; October was approaching with commitments back in England.

There was no choice, we would have to delay our attempt on the Eiger Direct until the winter, and so, towards the end of September, Wendy and I took the tent down, packed the Minivan and set out for home. In some ways we were relieved to escape from the close confines of Leysin and from the demanding, all-embracing presence of John Harlin. For eight weeks I had been caught up in his dreams and plans, like so many others before me, having arranged to climb the Eiger Direct, help with the International School of Modern Mountaineering and with plans for a mammoth flight down through the Americas.

As we drove from Leysin, the spell lifted and the ideas seemed distant, far-fetched and improbable. Reality was the touch of Wendy, Conrad, and our cottage at the foot of Ennerdale, with Tom Cat waiting for our return. We drove hard on the way back, overjoyed to be in England once again. We couldn't wait to see our Lakeland hills.

11   Eiger Direct: Preparations

Our return to the Lake District was like an escape from enchantment. Becoming too involved in John's fantastic schemes, I had felt my own individuality and freedom of action curtailed. From the sane quiet of Ennerdale, even John's winter plans for the Eiger seemed filled with question marks. For one thing, I had never climbed in the Alps in winter, and knew too little of the problems involved. John reckoned that the climb could take up to ten days in winter, and that there was usually a period, some time every winter, when the weather remained settled for ten or more consecutive days. My worry was the thought that you could not possibly tell, at the start of any one good weather spell, just how long it was going to last. What would happen if you got three-quarters of the way up the face after seven or eight days, and then the weather broke? Would you have the strength left to fight your way out or retreat – especially in a winter blizzard? I doubted it.

Nursing my doubts, I became involved in another expedition for the summer – to climb Alpamayo, a spectacularly beautiful peak in the Peruvian Andes. Conveniently, I put all thoughts of the Eiger Direct to the back of my mind, until one day in November the telephone rang:

'Is that Chris Bonington?'

'Yes.'

'My name is Peter Gillman. I work on the *Daily Telegraph* magazine and they want me to do a story about your planned route on the Eiger Direct this winter. Could I come up and talk to you? I'll bring John Cleare along as well, if I may, to take some pictures.'

'I suppose so. When do you want to come?'

'Day after tomorrow, there isn't much time.'

As I put the phone down, all my doubts welled up. This would commit me to the climb and, in facing this commitment, I realised just how worried I was about the entire concept. I could not bottle it up any longer and expressed my doubts to Wendy; doing so rendered it impossible for me to go on.

Wendy has always been prepared to accept any climbing project, providing she can sense that I am confident about it, but it would have been too much to have expected her to be stoical about something with which I was so obviously very unhappy. Quite apart from this, my own uncertainty rendered unwise any attempt to carry through such a scheme. This one seemed all wrong, somehow. Although I had complete confidence in John Harlin as a mountaineer, and had struck a rare accord with him on the Right-hand Pillar of Brouillard, I was less certain about his practical planning ability. With these doubts already in my mind, talking to a journalist about the planned climb would be impossible – I couldn't possibly let him see them. On top of this was the worry of becoming a gladiator, at the mercy of the watching public. It is one thing to exploit the interest of the media, and through them, the public, to carry out something you truly want to do, but quite another to feel forced to go on a climb about which you are not happy, because you have publicly committed yourself to do so. I was, perhaps, trapped in the cleft stick of the professional mountaineer, faced with the pressure to climb for the sake of a position in the climbing firmament, and it was a position which I abhorred. After an agonising day of indecision I rang up Peter Gillman to tell him that I had decided to withdraw from the climb. At the same time, I wrote to John telling him how I had let him down. It was now early November and he was not going to have long to find a replacement.

There followed a very flat few weeks. I had the nagging feeling that in standing down I had dropped out of top-class climbing – that, for the first time, I had rejected a climbing challenge at a time when my ability as a climber was my only tangible asset. As a writer and photographer I had had published only one short article in the *Daily Telegraph* magazine, together with a couple of pictures.

Just as my morale reached its lowest ebb, I had a letter from John Anstey, editor of the *Daily Telegraph* magazine, asking if I would be prepared to act as the magazine's photographer covering the climb. Having bought the exclusive rights to the story, they planned to send Peter Gillman out as their reporter, but wanted to get pictures from the side of the face and to have someone to meet the team on the summit, should they prove to be successful.

Suddenly, everything had changed. This was the very chance that I had been waiting for. I should be able to use my ability as a climber to exploit a creative skill which could put my entire career and life on to a sounder, and what seemed to me a more worthwhile course. I accepted immediately, and it was arranged that I should fly out to Switzerland as soon as John was ready to start climbing – probably sometime early in February.

Other opportunities then presented themselves. The BBC wanted to put on another live climbing broadcast, this time on the steep cliffs of Anglesey. Presumably as a result of my performance on *Coronation Street*, Chris Brasher, who had masterminded the BBC's outside broadcasts from the very start, approached me asking me not only to perform in it, but to help find a suitable site for the broadcast as well.

I was to meet him on the weekend of the 7/8 February 1966, on Anglesey, above the South Stack Lighthouse. The trip was ill-fated from the start.

Wendy and Conrad came with me and we drove down early on the Saturday morning. Our little Minivan was now four years old and had done just under 100,000 miles. It was fast falling to bits, and on the way it developed some kind of distributor trouble. In spite of three years in the Royal Tank Regiment, and a driving and maintenance course, my mechanical ability has never gone further than opening the bonnet, pulling at wires and, finally, kicking the vehicle in exasperation, hoping that this would make it go.

We reached Holyhead that evening only to find that the BBC team had long departed. Tired and bedraggled, with Conrad bored and whining in the back, we drove to the Pen Y Gwryd Hotel, where the recce team were staying. We hardly had time for introductions when I was called to the phone. It was the *Daily Telegraph* magazine – John Harlin had just informed them he was about to set off for the face; could I fly out first thing the next day? John Cleare, a member of the recce party, drove me to Holyhead that night to catch the midnight boat-train to London. Leaving Wendy in the Pen Y Gwryd Hotel with a lonely bed, I was in the air by ten o'clock the next morning on my way to Zurich. I couldn't help being wildly excited at the prospect of covering the climb, and had no regrets about not being a member of the climbing team.

I reached Kleine Scheidegg that evening; there seemed little risk of the team having set off, for the sky was covered by a scum of high grey cloud, and the forecast was bad. The team, which numbered three, were comfortably installed. Dougal Haston and Layton Kor had joined Harlin and I found them all in the room which had been allotted to them, at cut rates, by Fritz von Allmen, the hotel proprietor. It was an attic in one of the outbuildings and presumably was used for putting up his staff.

I only knew Dougal in passing, and had never climbed with him. On early acquaintance he seems silent and withdrawn – even contemptuous of others. He dresses with an almost foppish elegance, in a very mod style, but any risk of effeminacy is avoided in the cast of his features. His eyes are hooded, his face long and somehow primitive – a strange mixture of the sensual and the ascetic. Relaxed to the point of laziness, he has a single-mindedness which, when the need arises, enables him to direct his entire powers in the desired direction.

Layton provided a complete contrast. Over six feet in height, he reminded me of a big, awkward cowboy in some kind of Western comedy. He had the biggest hands I had ever seen, and they were constantly in motion, drumming on the table, clasping and unclasping – not so much from nervousness, more as a culmination of restless energy which could not be contained. In background, Layton and Dougal were very different. Dougal, the son of a master baker, had studied philosophy at Edinburgh University, had been bitten by the climbing bug and as a result had never completed the course. Even so, he was basically an intellectual, widely read, introspective and essentially philosophic in his interpretation of life. Layton, on the other hand, was a bricklayer, never aspiring to much else other than his own climbing. Whereas Dougal gave the impression of being completely self-contained, Layton was like a big, slightly mixed-up puppy, in need of love and care. He was a brilliant rock-climber and was one of the few American climbers, outside the small Yosemite bred and trained group of climbers, who had actually tackled routes in the Yosemite Valley. As a potential member of the Eiger Direct team, I found him intriguing, for this was to be his first taste of winter mountaineering and he knew even less about it than I.

They made me welcome and told me that the face had been in perfect condition a few days before, but that the weather pattern had now changed, leaving them to wait until it was more settled before making their push. This suited me; I was in the pay of the *Daily Telegraph*, staying at a comfortable hotel, with some of the best skiing in Europe on the doorstep – and I was very happy to spend a week or so skiing. There were problems, however. My relationship with John was no longer as easy as it had been, now that I had split loyalties between my paymasters and the team. I was the middleman. John wanted me on their side, getting as much support from the *Telegraph* as I could for the team. On the other hand, as representative of the *Telegraph*, I was hopeful that this would be the first of many assignments and I also wanted to ensure that my masters had a fair deal. This strain grew as the days slipped by without any sign of the promised spell of fine weather. I was becoming increasingly worried about the chances of the team. They had collected an impressive array of food, gear and clothing, but it seemed an awful lot for three men to shift up the face. John, recognising this fact, bent his own climbing ethics. The weight of the gear would have been particularly awkward on the lower part of the face, which was comparatively straightforward with long stretches of snow slopes broken by ice walls. At the top of this section, at the base of the First Rock Band, was the window of the Eiger Station. This was an eternal contradiction on the biggest, most unattainable wall in the Alps – that a man-made tunnel should spiral its way up inside the mountain, with a peephole from which the curious could gaze out on to the face.

John saw a way of utilising this. If we took all the gear up on the train, we could lower it out of the window and leave it there, thus saving two to three days' hard work, ferrying it up the lower part of the face. These two or three days could, at the end of the climb, prove crucial. This was the argument: they were trying to climb the face in the most aesthetically pleasing manner, not by laying siege to it with thousands of feet of fixed rope, and therefore, surely, they should be allowed to make their own rules. I wondered. If you want to lower gear out of a window, why not use the train yourselves and start the climb at the window? But it was their climb – not mine; it was they who were going to take the big risks once they set forth up the Rock Band. So I suppressed my own doubts and, one afternoon, with Dougal, caught the train up to the Eiger Station and lowered three rucksacks, full of gear and food, out of the window. And there it stayed – for the weather still showed no sign of improving.

We skied, did a few practice climbs on the little pinnacles above Eiger Gletscher, drank in the Gastubel in the hotel and, on occasion, danced to the stolid, slightly Teutonic music pumped out by the three-man band resident there for the winter. February was drawing to a close – and I began to wonder whether the team would ever get off the ground – when the weather showed signs of improvement. Then John had an accident. He loved being the centre of attraction, dropped easily into Tarzanesque poses, and enjoyed showing off the odd feat of strength. Skiing down the Lauberhorn, he tried balancing on only one ski, tripped and dislocated his shoulder – the Blond God immobilised! The team decided to retire to Leysin to lick their wounds, leaving me to hold the fort in Kleine Scheidegg.

A couple of mornings later, one of the waiters called me and told me that someone was starting up the face. Looking through the powerful binoculars kept by the hotel proprietor outside his private sitting-room, I saw a number of tiny figures at the foot of the wall. One was undoubtedly starting up the first pitch. John had warned us that a German group was also preparing for the climb but we had never taken the threat seriously, having also heard that the team numbered eight. This was a ridiculously large number for an Alpine route – where on earth would they find sufficient bivouac spots for a team of that size? And so we had tended to discount them. But there they were – actually starting on our climb whilst our men were in Leysin with John out of action for some days to come. I telephoned him immediately. Though non-committal, he said they would return to Scheidegg immediately.

'You might as well get over there and have a look at what they're doing,' he suggested. Next morning I skied over – rather diffidently, since I am a very poor and timid skier – not at all sure of the kind of reception I could expect from the rival team. My fears were justified, for when I tried to get close enough to photograph them, one of their members started throwing snowballs. Retiring to a respectable distance, I carried on taking my pictures with a long-focus lens.

It didn't take long to work out why they had a team of eight. Their entire concept of the climb was different from ours. It was obviously their intention to lay siege to the face, fixing ropes as they went, hauling up a mass of gear. Superficially this seemed a logical approach, for they were able to start out up the face even though the weather forecast was poor and snow was falling, while we had been sitting impotent at the foot of the wall for three weeks, and might well have remained there for another three, before starting it up. I was impressed by the systematic approach used by the Germans – it was obviously slow, but nevertheless very effective.

That night I told John what I had seen, and we determined to start climbing the next day. John was still out of action, and so Dougal and Layton were to climb up to the base of the First Band in order to start finding a route through it. I led them across to the foot of the face the next morning, and waved good-bye as they started up the fixed ropes left by the Germans the day before. Following these for about 1,500 feet, and using them part of the way, they made their own route in places. They reached the foot of the Rock Band in early afternoon and Layton started up. It presented very difficult piton-climbing and from a distance it looked completely blank – but this was the kind of climbing at which Layton excelled. At ground level he seemed gangling and awkward, barely able to control his great limbs whereas on rock he came into his own. He had an extraordinarily good power:weight ratio for a man of his size, with a delicacy and precision of movement that was a joy to behold. On the Rock Band he discovered tiny pockets in the rock, filled them with little wedges of wood and then tapped in a peg. He spent all afternoon making about thirty feet of progress and then retired to the small ledge that Dougal had cut out of the snow immediately below the Eiger Window.

That night the weather broke and they found themselves in the direct path of a constant torrent of spindrift which came pouring down from the upper reaches of the face. It penetrated behind their tent, and pushed them inexorably off their ledge, till they were hanging from their ropes. Inside a bivvy tent in bad weather it is almost impossible to remain dry – breath and steam from cooking condenses on the walls and inevitably runs into clothes and sleeping-bags. By morning their gear was soaked through, and they were beaten. They baled out at dawn and fled back to the valley. The Eiger – and the Germans – were winning.

The following day the weather improved and the Germans were back on the face, where they continued to work their way slowly up to the foot of the First Band. They dug out a snow cave immediately beneath it and this was to prove to be the secret of survival on the face. A tent bivouac sack is of limited use, since once the weather breaks, it is almost impossible to remain dry inside one – as Dougal and Layton had just discovered to their cost. In a snow hole, however, it doesn't matter what the weather does – once the cave is dug you can remain inside it for as long as your food lasts. There are no condensation problems and there is an inexhaustible supply of water from the snow that comprises the walls. Even if there is a hundred-mile-an-hour gale outside, the air is quiet inside the cave and the temperature remains the same – just below freezing mark.

But we still had to learn the snow-hole game. It was becoming increasingly obvious to me that our little team of three was inadequate for the style of siege operation which was seemingly essential if we were to have any chance of success. At the very least we needed four – two men to go out in front to make the route, and place a continuous line of fixed ropes, and two men to ferry loads behind. The entire concept of the climb had changed and with it my role. Before, there was no question of my venturing beyond the bottom of the face, since the team planned to cut adrift from the bottom and make a single push for the top. Now, with a continuous line of fixed ropes it was possible for me to go very much higher up the face, getting better photographic coverage of the climb and, at the same time, helping the team by being a fourth man. When they got high enough to make their bid for the summit, I could then either come back down again or accompany them all the way to the top. At an early stage of the climb, John had invited me to join them fully, but though I toyed with the idea, I never felt totally committed to the climbing; whether because of the strength of my own interest in the photographic coverage of the climb, or an awareness of the risk-level still involved in that final push, I am not at all sure. Having got out of the project once, I never really felt like committing myself totally to it again. Nevertheless, there was a part-commitment. We now had to adapt to the Germans' siege tactics, digging a snow cave at the foot of the Rock Band and laying siege to the Band. They had already started at a point about 200 feet to the right of the Eiger Station window, up an obvious fault. The line Layton had chosen was very much more direct, and also looked considerably harder. Layton, Dougal and I set out in the early hours of the 28th February, for the foot of the face. The Germans were already ensconced below the Rock Band. We climbed the fixed ropes of the bottom third of the face in the dark, reaching the foot of the rock-wall in the dawn. Whilst Layton climbed, and Dougal held his rope, I was to dig a snow hole. The first problem was to find the right kind of snow. I needed compacted old snow of sufficient depth to tunnel into till I reached the rock, and then to be able to make a room large enough for four to sleep in. It had to be in a place where the hard under-lay of ice was well covered, for it is near-impossible to cut away large quantities of ice – in winter it is much too hard and it would take all day to dig away a small ledge, let alone a room.

I was learning the hard way. We hadn't thought of taking a shovel and I quickly discovered how inadequate an ice axe is as a tool for digging. But how about the Germans, next door? They had dug a vast cave which they called the Ice Palace. They had everything, and were sure to have a shovel. Could I ask them? If so, would I make our team beholden to them? What would John think of that? We were still deeply suspicious of each other and had had only the briefest of conversations to determine some kind of *modus vivendi* on the face.

We had agreed that both parties should use the line of fixed ropes from the bottom up to the foot of the Rock Band. Thus far, honours had been fairly even, for although the Germans had made the bulk of the route in the first 1,500 feet, Dougal and Layton had climbed the last 500, which gave, technically, the most difficult climbing. Now we had chosen separate lines, ourselves going for a series of ice gullies once we had reached the top of the First Band, and the Germans heading up the line of a rock buttress to its right. The big problem would come above the Flat Iron bivouac, in the upper part of the face, for there seemed only one feasible line up this, and whoever got there first would be able to stay in the lead. It was like Patagonia all over again, with our team once again outnumbered. This was not mountaineering in the pure, uncompetitive sense, but there was no doubt that the competitiveness added a touch of spice.

But now, on a more practical level, I wanted to borrow a shovel from our competitors – but should I? No, it could possibly put us in their debt; and so I chipped away with my miserable little axe for another half-hour. Or could I? What harm was there in it, anyway? They could only say No. Finally, I made up my mind, swallowed pride and crawled out of the short burrow I had dug, to borrow from the hated next-door neighbours.

There was a purr of a petrol stove from their burrow; a delicious aroma of fresh coffee wafted from its entrance. I poked my head through. 'Guten tag.'

A grunt.

There was only one of them in the cave, looking very comfortable wrapped in a sleeping bag on a foam mat. I tried some English. 'Do you think we could borrow your shovel?'

'I don't know at all. Why didn't you bring one up yourselves?'

'We never thought of it.'

'Perhaps this will make you think a little better before you set off,' he said, sounding very self-satisfied – the cat teasing the mouse. It was time to start a different tack – if he was going to be pompous, then two could play at that game!

'Don't you believe in some fellowship amongst mountaineers? I know you're not particularly glad that we're here, trying to do the same route as you, but what possible difference to the eventual outcome can it make if you lend me your shovel? It'll just make it either easier or a hell of a lot slower for us to dig out a bloody snow hole.'

'I cannot possibly let you have the shovel before consulting my colleagues,' he replied. 'I shall be talking to them on the walky-talky in an hour or so, and shall let you know then.'

I returned, mortified and very angry, to our miserable little burrow and vented my feelings on the snow – every blow of my axe plunging deep into a Teutonic head. The trouble was, you needed an awful lot of axe blows to clear very little snow. About ten minutes later, there was a little cough from behind me. I turned, and there, wearing a wicked little grin, was the German. I was to learn later that it was Peter Haag, co-leader of their team: 'I have been think- ing; it is petty not to let you have the shovel. I haven't waited to ask the others.

You can use it if you want – come and have some coffee cognac when you've finished.'

We had begun to establish a sensible relationship on the face, and as time went by, and we got to know each other as individuals, our lurking sense of competition was accompanied by a growth of real friendship. Peter was one of the few members of his team to speak good English. He had recently finished a degree course in engineering, and was a cheerful happy-go-lucky individual who could never have maintained a savagely competitive stance for long. Jorg Lehne, his co-leader, on the other hand seemed the typical Teuton – harsh in manner with a limited, beer-cellar style of humour, competitive to the end.

Peter and I talked for a bit until, with renewed vigour, I set to work on the snow hole with my borrowed shovel. It made all the difference. You could use the blade of the spade to shape out big blocks, and then could shovel them out from behind quickly and easily By the end of the day I had a room big enough for two. From time to time I climbed out of the hole to photograph Dougal and Layton. Dougal was belayed about halfway up, hanging from a piton and, above him, Layton was slowly and methodically pegging his way up the wall.

Climbers are never easily impressed by the progress of others, but Layton's ascent was truly amazing, for the rock appeared to be completely blank, with no cracks for his pitons. Most climbers would have drilled holes for expansion bolts and, in fact, the Germans used several on what seemed an easier line round the corner. This big, gangling man, however, who seemed so ill at ease and awkward on the ground, was in his element, using every little weathering he could find on the surface of the rock. After taking a few pictures, I returned to the hole to dig out some more snow.

The weather seemed to be getting a little worse. It had started with a perfect dawn: a carpet of cloud at our feet shut out the intrusion of Kleine Scheidegg, its railways and ant-like skiers; overhead the sky was a clear pale blue. But the weather can change fast on the Eiger, and is always unpredictable. A line of high grey cloud had raced in from the west, settled on the summit rocks, and imperceptibly had slid down the wall. A few snowflakes drifted lightly round the grey air – first a flurry and then a steady fall. In a matter of minutes, the spindrift avalanches began to career down the face, their augur a dark shadow, a sibilant whisper, and then an all-penetrating, suffocating downpour of snow crystals infiltrated every chink of clothing and froze any exposed skin. It piled on top of the climber, trying to take him down, down, down into the snows at the foot of the wall.

Climbing was impossible in these conditions. Dougal and Layton started to bale out. Worried about them, I looked out of the hole. I could hear shouting, didn't want to leave the shelter of the hole, but the calls became insistent, with a raucous quality of emergency. I swung out on to the fixed rope and worked my way across in a lull between avalanches. Dougal was about a hundred feet above me, hanging upside down!

'I'm stuck,' he announced, very matter-of-fact. 'The bloody rope's jammed. I think I'll have to cut myself free. Can you get a knife?' At this point he disappeared in another spindrift avalanche. I hunched into the snow, waiting for the worst of the torrent to rush past and then swung across to the Germans' snow hole to borrow a knife. Dougal must have been hanging for about half an hour before I managed to tie the knife on to the end of the rope for him to pull up. His position was still risky. Had he made a single mistake, cutting the wrong rope, or unclipping himself incorrectly, he would have fallen, with little chance of survival. He succeeded in cutting away the jammed rope, and got back to firm ground. A few minutes later, Layton, frozen solid and tired from his nerve-racking climb, joined us.

'I've had enough, man,' he told us. 'I'm going back down till this stuff clears up.' At this, he plunged down the fixed ropes and soon vanished in the swirling snows. Dougal and I decided to stay up there, spending the rest of the afternoon digging out the snow hole. Outside, the snow was gusting in a high, blowing wind, but inside we were happily unaware of it. Snow holes were, undoubtedly, the secret for tackling big walls in winter.

Next morning, on finding the snow scudding down the face, we did some more digging, to make the cave big enough for four, afterwards retreating to the bright lights of Kleine Scheidegg. The contrast was, at one and the same time, confusing and yet attractive. On the face life was simple – merely a question of survival. From there, the tiny black dots of the skiers skimming down the Lauberhorn and round the Eiger Gletscher Punch Bowl, were as remote from us as if we had been on another planet. Nearer at hand, the tourists who gazed down at us from the Eiger Window, like so many people goggling into an aquarium, were completely removed from our own private world of wind, snow and rock. What was real – their world or ours? I suspect it was theirs. Back at Scheidegg, we were still in a make-believe atmosphere – this time with a touch of MGM or Paramount included – a world of glamour-story fantasy, of Chateaubriand for two, eaten by one hungry climber, of bucketfuls of champagne, all paid for by the *Daily Telegraph* magazine, and the endless interest of the press and tourists.

This kind of atmosphere is meant to be totally abhorrent to climbers and climbing – men of the mountains should be seeking the quiet of the hills, escaping from the vainglory of press coverage – yet I wonder. My position was different from that of the other three. I was part of the media; was the exploiter rather than the exploited and, I must confess, I thoroughly enjoyed it, with the excitement of calls to London and the challenge of getting film, taken on the face, back as quickly as possible. Pete Gillman shared in his side of the story. His own report was factual and accurate. Certainly in no way did he sensationalise the story as so many reporters working for the popular press are tempted to do. Was what we were doing against the interests of mountaineering? I don't think so. It certainly made a lot of people aware of what climbing can be like. Some elements of the press played on the level of competition which undoubtedly existed between our team and the Germans, but this, in fact, was a competition that was slowly being reduced through our growing knowledge and interdependence upon each other during the climb itself. This also came through slowly in the press reports.

I sometimes wonder how John, Dougal and Layton felt about it all. John, undoubtedly, revelled in it. This did not mean that he was doing the climb solely for honour and glory – his love of the mountains, his need to extend himself to the limit, to find new horizons, went much further than that – but the glory was part of the attraction, as it is with most men.

Dougal on the other hand – silent, introspective – went through it all as though hardly aware of it. I think he accepted the circus at the bottom of the mountain for what it offered him – a comfortable bed, limitless food and booze – the means to carry out his ambition, to stretch himself to his own limits on the face. And Layton, very much the same, had the least ego-drive of the three. He just liked climbing, finding a fulfilment of his abilities and confidence in himself on a vertical rock face which he did not find in everyday life. At Kleine Scheidegg he ate huge meals, paid long and earnest court to the attractive, but perhaps a little straight-laced postmistress at the station and, after a few days, became impatient to do something – go up on the face – go skiing – go to Leysin – it didn't matter, but Layton was always searching, a little lost, with a touch of indefinable pathos in his make-up.

In those early stages of the climb we yo-yoed back and forth between Kleine Scheidegg and the Rock Band, forcing a few more feet, and then retreating through the bad weather. There was always the temptation of the comfort of the hotel. The only man of either team who firmly rejected this indulgence was Peter Haag, who steadfastly stayed on the face, living in the Ice Palace.

Back at Kleine Scheidegg, our own party was now increasing. Peter Gillman was permanently installed. I had asked for an assistant, and the picture editor of the *Telegraph* magazine had signed up Don Whillans, who was staying in Leysin at the time. He was working at the American School, as the sports master and proctor, the latter being the equivalent of housemaster, or custodian of the pupils' morals. I felt a little apprehensive about the choice, since I knew that John Harlin and Don Whillans had little in common. Don had previously turned down John's invitation to join him on the face, distrusting his logistic planning and, I suspect, resenting his flamboyance. In Don's down-to-earth description – 'A load of bull-shit!' In the event, he was able to give only limited physical help, either to me or to the team. On the one occasion he ventured on to the face with me, he was troubled by an acute attack of vertigo, an illness which has troubled him from time to time over a long period, and he was consequently forced back down. He did help, however, in getting together much of the extra equipment which we now found we needed and, at the same time, providing a practical and at times drily humorous element of common sense to our councils.

We had a courier, in the shape of Dougal's current girlfriend, an attractive Canadian girl called Joan. Her job was to carry my exposed film in a hired car from Grindelwald to Zurich Airport. Unfortunately, she was not the most brilliant of drivers, and after she had crashed the car twice, writing it off completely on the second occasion, we felt it was time to look elsewhere. This seemed a heaven-sent opportunity to get Wendy into the act, and I phoned her one night, to suggest that she fly out to Zurich to become the team's courier.

'But what about Conrad?' she asked.

'Can't you find anyone to look after him for a couple of weeks?'

'I don't know.'

'Please, love, it'd make all the difference in the world if you could get out here. I'm missing you like hell, and it's such a heaven-sent opportunity. The *Telegraph* will fly you out, and pay you whilst you're here.'

'I just don't know. I don't like leaving him.'

'Think about it. I'll phone you back this evening.'

Wendy thought about it and, finding she was able to leave Conrad with some friends in Moor Row, a nearby village, finally decided to come. However, when she arrived at Kleine Scheidegg three days later, thoughts of Conrad and how he was, constantly nagged at her.

I had desperately wanted her with me, but in fact we saw all too little of each other. When she was at Kleine Scheidegg, I was on the face helping the climb and taking pictures – and as soon as I got back down, she had to collect the film from me and dash off to Zurich, an exhausting three-hour drive on icy roads.

It was now early March – getting near the end of winter. The First Band had, at last, fallen to the onslaught of Layton, Dougal and John, now recovered from his dislocated shoulder. We were ready for the final push up the face. I was going with them, up to whatever should prove the high point of the fixed ropes; I would then leave them for their climb to the summit, race back up by the West Ridge, and meet them at the top.

12   Eiger Direct: the Climb

It was the 7 March and we were at last committed to the face; with a bit of luck the constant yo-yo between Scheidegg and the snow cave would be over. John and Dougal, out in front, had forced the Rock Band the previous day, spent the night in a small snow hole they had hollowed out under a rock overhang on the ice-field between the two bands, and were now climbing up towards the Second Band. Layton and I were hauling gear up the First Band. Ours was the support role. Layton had jumared up first, and most of the day went slowly as he hauled sack after sack up the face. I alternated between the snow hole and the foot of the slope. As in war, siege tactics on a mountain entail constant long periods of inaction, broken by spasmodic moments of frenetic activity. There is one big difference though: the moments of inaction are precious in their own way – you can gaze over the hills, feel the peace and silence of the mountains – peace that is the more real for the very presence of a lurking threat of change in the weather, or a mistake on a fixed rope.

Then it was my turn to follow Layton up the fixed rope – the second time I had ever been on jumars. The rock was sheer and the rope dropped down in a single span of 300 feet. Economising on weight, we had used 7 mm perlon, being the thickness of an ordinary clothesline and, in theory, strong enough, with a breaking strain of 2,000 lb. – in practice it inspired little confidence. Wherever the rope went over a sharp edge of rock, it flattened out under tension till it was not much thicker than a piece of tape; how much wear before it was cut through? Only time and experience could tell.

You clip the jumars on, one for your thigh harness, one for your foot. I got the lengths of the slings wrong again, and as a result turned that first ascent into a terrifying struggle. You have to first pull in all the spring in a 300 foot length of rope by putting your weight on it, then shooting down the ice slope about thirty feet, bouncing like a red ball at the end of a string, all the time imagining what is happening to the rope, high above your head, as it saws over sharp edges. But you can't afford to think of that. Blot it out of your mind and start jumaring, pushing up the clamps alternately, your life depending on that thin thread that stretches forever in front of you. Glance over to the left; you're level with the Eiger Window. A train has just pulled in and the tourists are gawping through the window, just a few feet away – a few feet which might as well be a thousand miles, for your life and your whole world revolve round that thread of rope. You've moved above the window – no longer in sight – no longer exists – nothing does, except the need to push the jumars up, alternately, with your rucksack, attached by a sling to your waist harness, dangling spinning below your feet.

A jerk – you drop three inches. It's the rope – it's gone – broken; death, tumbling horror, fear, and a heart that pumps at twice its normal rate. But you're alive! The knot in the sling attached to the karabiner in your waist harness has jammed on the gate of the karabiner, and had then freed itself, letting you drop those few inches. Although this happened quite frequently, the jab of horror was always there – frightening in a way that climbing emergencies rarely are. You are so helpless, the pawn of a rope fixed in position by another man, the potential victim of a piece of rock that might be slowly sawing through your life-line as you, your own executioner, bounce and struggle your way up.

The angle began to ease. Nearly up, I reminded myself to adjust the length of the slings to my jumars for the next rope length, and then took stock. Layton was already near the top of the next rope-length, up a steep ice runnel. A cluster of rucksacks, all of them our responsibility, hung from a peg, and the evening sun was just touching a rocky spur over to the right. Clouds had come rolling in that afternoon, blotting out Kleine Scheidegg, and we were now alone in the world. John and Dougal were somewhere above – I could hear John's yodel. No sign of the Germans, they were somewhere to the right, but exactly where, I did not know. They had favoured the rock spur, but with a bit of luck they would now be in difficulties. We had chosen the short hard road, had conquered it, and now had an easy run out to the foot of the next major barrier, the Second Band.

No time to dream. Layton had reached the top of the next rope-length and I started after him. Swing across to the right, up over a short steep wall, and the angle eases. No need for two jumars here. One's enough – just kick into the snow and push the jumar up. Suddenly it is steeper, the rope's at an angle and the jumar jumps off; I begin to topple over backwards, but grab the rope with one hand – a moment's struggle, and the jumar is clipped back on again. A narrow escape, but I just keep going. A little hole in the snow – the cave where John and Dougal had spent the previous night and, presumably, where Layton and I would spend tonight. But there's more work to do in the evening sun, more loads to ferry up to the foot of the next barrier.

Now I can see John and Dougal, small insect-like figures against the white of a snow ramp cutting across a great rocky depression in the Second Band. The Germans are to their right, hammering away up an impossible-looking rock-wall, sheer, featureless and seemingly very high. There's a shout. One of the Germans has fallen – it happens too quickly for my straying eye to catch – one moment he is spread-eagled on the rock, and the next, he is dangling about twenty feet below. More shouting – he's talking and sounds cheerful, so he can't have hurt himself.

The sun fades fast, washing the rock and snow in a soft yellow glow which gives an illusion of warmth. John and Dougal, 300 feet above, are climbing into the dusk; they reach a ledge in the dark and have an uncomfortable, cramped bivouac. I return to our own little hole between the two Rock Bands, to find Layton already folded into it. It is very small, womb-like, reassuring. The petrol stove roars in the night, and we brew ourselves rose-hip tea to wash down our ration of *viandes sèchées* (a wafer-thin dried meat) and assorted nuts.

The raucous excitement and melodrama of Kleine Scheidegg has vanished. We are back on the big mountain wall, confronting our own special over-simplified reality. I love the rock and the snows, and these few moments of peace give me supreme comfort in my sleeping bag. I lie curled in the tight confines of the snow hole, tired but able to rest, hungry and able to eat – sheer contentment for a few moments of time.

Next morning the weather was still fine, and we jumared up to the camp site prepared by the others. We were now to experience the fable of the tortoise and the hare. Undoubtedly, we seemed able to climb more quickly than the Germans, and tended to pick the better routes. This enabled us frequently to get out in front, but because of our fewer numbers, we were never able to sustain our advance and, on several occasions, the Germans were to move through us, taking advantage of their reserves in numbers and their greater carrying power.

This is what happened that morning. John and Dougal had had an exhausting day and little sleep that night, their bivouac having been so poor. As a result, we were forced to spend the day after their successful ascent of the Second Band consolidating our position, ferrying up loads and digging out a good bivouac site.

The Germans were better rested and, having failed on their line up the rock buttress, climbed our fixed ropes in the early morning. They pushed on through, up the easier ground that lay above the Second Band leading up the side of the Second Ice-field. That night their front pair bivouacked about 500 feet above us, to the side of the Flat Iron, having pushed on without leaving any fixed ropes behind them. This meant we had no choice but to reclimb the route they had followed, leaving the fixed ropes in position. In the meantime, Layton, ever energetic, had raced back down to Kleine Scheidegg the previous night to pick up some more supplies, returning in the dawn to join us for our push towards the crest of the Flat Iron.

Once again, John and Dougal took the lead, while Layton and I followed, humping loads. Jorg Lehne and some of the Germans were immediately behind us, using the same fixed ropes. It was strange: even though we were still undoubtedly in competition, with each party prepared to steal a march on the other, there was also a growing friendship as we came to know, and at times to help, each other. Peter Haag and Karl Golikow, a delightful, friendly character, who always wore a broad grin and had a few cheerful words for us, or for anyone, were out in front, tackling the rocks leading up the side of the Flat Iron. Dougal and John, alternating the lead, slowly worked their way up the side of the Ice-field, and I humped my big rucksack, taking the occasional photograph and chatting to Jorg Lehne or Layton.

At last, we seemed to be nearing a summit push, though I was not at all sure, at this stage, what part I was to take in it – whether I should continue with the team once they abandoned their fixed rope, or go back down. I had surprisingly little ambition to be out in front, with my mind attuned to the challenge of getting a photographic record and not to the climbing itself. As a result, I became more aware of the risks than if I had been more deeply involved in the climb.

The day slipped by and as morning merged into afternoon a few herring-bones of cloud acted as forerunners to the smooth grey ceiling that was always a sure herald of snow. We had more loads than we could take in a single carry, and it meant that I had to go back down to haul the last rucksack up to the top of the Flat Iron. It was a heavy, awkward load and I was beginning to tire. By the time I reached the top of our line of fixed ropes, it had started to snow. There was less than an hour left to dusk, and we still hadn't found a deep enough bank of old snow in which to dig a snow hole. The Germans, who had got there before us, were already ensconced, their hole dug, petrol stove roaring, and the bleakness of our own position became more evident. We had felt carefree and confident that morning, but all this had vanished in the cold grey of twilight.

'There should be something on the top of the Flat Iron,' John suggested.

'I'll have a look,' said Dougal, always ready to tackle the hardest, most unpleasant job, especially if it meant leading out in front. He worked his way across the steep snow slope, immediately below the rocks of the upper part of the face. There was a thin layer of powder snow on top of hard ice.

His progress was painfully slow, his protection apart from the occasional ice piton, non-existent. It was nearly dark before he reached the crest of the Flat Iron, site of the infamous Death Bivouac, where Sedlmayer and Mehringer had frozen to death in 1935. He still had to find enough built-up snow to dig a snow hole and seemed to spend an eternity prodding about on the crest of the arête before finding the right kind of snow and, equally important, a place to anchor the rope.

'Okay, you can come across,' he shouted. 'Be careful on the rope, the peg over here isn't too good.'

It was impossible to pull the rope in tight, and it described a sagging arc across the rock-studded ice that lay between us and the crest of the Flat Iron. By this time, chilled to the bone, tired and apprehensive, I had lost much of my enthusiasm for the North Wall of the Eiger.

I was the last to traverse across. By this time it was pitch dark and I couldn't see where to kick in with my crampons. I slipped and hung sagging on the rope and, in my fear, cursed and swore into the blind night. Being a traverse, it was particularly awkward, with the constant risk of a jumar jumping off the rope. By the time I reached the others, Dougal had disappeared headfirst into the snow, burrowing away like some new species of mole. There was no shortage of volunteers to do a spell of work in the snow hole; there was warmth in digging, shelter from the wind, and a comforting sense of enclosure in the bowels of the snow. Another hour slipped by, feet frozen, hunger gnawing, we dug away or awaited our turn to dig, crouching in the snow on the threshold of the hole. It was past midnight before there was room for all four of us. We piled in, crammed together between the rock-wall of the Death Bivouac and the outside snow wall, which seemed precariously thin. But there were still two sacks on the other side of the fixed rope – one of them Dougal's, for he had led over the crest of the Flat Iron without a rucksack. The other one contained our precious brew kit and stove.

'I guess someone'll have to get them,' said John.

There was a silence, each person dreading the prospect of another traverse on that sagging rope in the dark of the storm. We could hear the powder snow avalanches, soft yet menacing, swoosh down the face.

I was cold, frightened, and knew that under no circumstances did I want to leave the security and relative luxury of the snow hole.

'I've only come this far as photographer, and I've done a hell of a lot more than that. I'm sorry, but I'm not going back over that traverse!'

Layton muttered something about his feet being bloody cold; then Dougal, without saying a word, swung himself out of the hole to make the dreaded traverse. We sat there, in the cave, silent – each held by his own special thoughts. Mine were of shame at my cowardice – guilt that I hadn't volunteered – mingled with the relief of being still huddled in the snow, sheltered from wind and danger. As the time dragged by, John kept looking out of the entrance, shouting into the wind, but getting no reply. Then, at last, Dougal came back, fulfilled in the challenge he had accepted, in a state of peace that at that moment and for some time to come, Layton and I could not know.

John volunteered to get the other sack, and was back sooner, since Dougal had succeeded in tightening up the rope, thereby rendering the traverse much easier. At last we could have a brew, and we fumbled in snow-filled rucksacks for candle, matches and gas stove. Dougal lit the candle, tried to light the stove, but the cartridge appeared to be empty. He started unscrewing it; with a sudden whoosh, the gas, perhaps blocked in the jet, escaped. It ignited with a flash, and the whole cave seemed filled with fire. I was nearest the door, and the instincts of survival took over. Diving for the entrance, I only just stopped in time as I remembered there was a 3,000-foot drop on the other side. At the same time, John, with a great presence of mind, grabbed the blazing canister and hurled it through the entrance.

I received a dark look. At that moment my stock was very low. I have often thought back on this incident. No one enjoys memories of a situation which became too much for him, of panic in the face of an emergency when he reached that fragile borderline of giving up. Compare this with my reaction to the storm on the Brouillard – a situation which, in actual fact, was potentially more dangerous than this one on the Eiger. Then, I had been in control; on the Flat Iron I was not. It all comes back, I suspect, to one's level of involvement and responsibility. In an emergency, I realised and felt I was just the camera-man – I did not intend to go to the top, having already opted out on grounds of risk, and therefore was all the more risk-conscious. John, on the other hand, behaved magnificently, reaching his own heroic stature to the full, and more, the depth of his involvement in the venture, his responsibility as leader. And so did Dougal, his involvement provided with a cutting edge of desire to explore the very extremities of his own potential.

Fortunately, the damage had been slight and the fireworks more spectacular than dangerous. We found a fresh cartridge, loaded it into the stove and in the early hours of the morning drank our first brew for nearly twenty hours. Then we all slumped into sleep, piled one on top of the other, like young wolves in a crowded lair. In the dawn, we could see the light glimmering through the walls of the snow cave. John poked an axe into the outer floor, and looked down through the hole it left. You could see Grindelwald – a good 8,000 feet below. We had burrowed our cave into the curling lip of a cornice, and the outer wall actually overhung the slope of the Third Ice-field!

It had dawned fine, once again. The Germans were already at work on a line of grooves that led up to a gully in the centre of the face. Because of their greater logistic back-up, they had managed to get away early and stay out in front. We were going to have to find an alternative route if we were to avoid following them for the rest of the climb. The team now seemed poised for their summit bid. There was barely room for four in the snow hole, and I wanted to get my film back to Scheidegg, to send it to the *Telegraph*. There was little enough temptation to stay with the team and complete the climb with them. I don't think it was the risk involved that really deterred me, though awareness of it was ever present – perhaps more so than I have experienced on another route, before or since. It was primarily my lack of personal involvement, combined with concentration upon the photographic coverage of the climb.

I left that morning for the valley, after taking a couple of final photographs of Layton and Dougal setting out across the Third Ice-field to climb a groove leading to a ledge system at the foot of the prominent pillar in the centre of the face. The most obvious way up was by a gully on its right-hand side, but the

Germans were already installed in this. Dougal, however, was doubtful about its feasibility, for it was barred near its top by a huge bulge of unstable-looking snow. They resolved to return the next day, and attempt a traverse of the base of the pillar, across steep blank-looking rock, where they hoped to find an easier gully on its other side. But their hopes were to be dashed.

That evening the clouds rolled back over the face and by morning a full-blown storm was raging. We talked over the problem, on the walky-talky, with me sitting in comfort in Peter Gillman's room at the Scheidegg hotel. The little radio crackled with static, and the voice of John Harlin was frequently smothered, as if it had been engulfed in spindrift.

'Layton's coming down this morning,' he told us. 'There's no point in three of us staying up here. Dougal and I'll sit it out. We can't afford to let the Germans reach the top of the Pillar in front of us; we'll never get in front if they do. Two of them seem to be staying up.'

'What's the hole like?'

'Not too bad. Quite a bit of spindrift gets in through the opening, but we're beginning to get it sealed off properly.'

'How much food do you have?'

'Should be enough for four or five days, if we're careful.'

'Well, good luck, I'm just off to a chateaubriand for two, all to myself, over and out.'

John and Dougal settled down to their meal of dried meat and nuts, followed by rose-hip tea. They had no books with them, but in the ensuing days found little time for boredom. Just fighting the insidious spindrift that crept through every chink in their defences, cooking and keeping their sleeping bags dry, filled the day. Both John and Dougal had a wide-ranging philosophical bent. Perched in a tiny world of their own they had complete freedom to explore their own dreams, aspirations and interpretations of what they were trying to achieve in their lives.

Back at Kleine Scheidegg, the excitement steadily built up as more and more correspondents arrived – all avid for good sensational stories. John and Dougal, in their tiny eyrie, were secure, and deeply content – but to the lay beholder down below, they were trapped in the jaws of the Eiger. The journalists allowed their imaginations free rein, producing a series of sensational stories with headlines that read … 'It started a race … now it's a rescue.'

Each day at Scheidegg, we phoned Geneva Airport for a weather forecast. There was a high-pressure system in the Atlantic, which seemed to be drifting slowly towards Europe, bringing with it omens of good weather. However, t remained sitting off the coast of Ireland, and the winds continued to batter the Eiger. After four days, when John and Dougal had nearly run out of food, John contracted a chest infection. At one point we had no less than six doctors, all on skiing holidays, in consultation at the end of the walky-talky.

We discussed co-operation with the Germans, joint relief operations in order to carry food to the beleaguered climbers – even skied to the foot of the face, in appalling circumstances, but all to no avail. No one fancied the thought of trying to fight their way up those fixed ropes, in the face of continuous spindrift avalanches.

At last the weather improved, but our decision had been made for us. John and Dougal had no food left, and John was too ill to think of anything other than retreat. On the 16th March they came back down. The Germans, having managed to stick it out, were already sending up a relief force, and this meant that in a matter of days they would be able to force their way to the top of the Pillar, then up what seemed the only feasible route into the famous White Spider.

I had no ambition to go back on to the face – even less to do any lead climbing – but now there seemed no choice. John and Dougal obviously needed a rest. I agreed, therefore, to go back with Layton.

We set out on the 16th, myself apprehensive, frightened of those all-too-thin fixed ropes that had by now been in position for over a month, had had dozens of ascents and been battered by several storms. Yet, as so often happens, once committed, I lost much of my fear, began to enjoy the feeling of my own fitness and the rhythmic, steady movement as I climbed the ropes, finally taking them for granted. After all, they'd been here for some time and I'd climbed them all before.

The height that had taken four weeks to gain, now, with fixed ropes in position, took a mere eight hours. The snow hole had a well-lived in look, with a rim of frozen excreta round the door, and holes drilled in the sides by urine. In a blizzard you don't open up the entrance to relieve yourself – especially as, living in a deep-freeze, there is no smell or risk of infection.

It was a good feeling to be back on the face in the quiet peace of the little ice cave – very different from the frenetic hurly-burly of the hotel below. The following day, the weather had brewed in once again, with more spindrift avalanches spewing down the face. No question of going out. I curled up in my sleeping bag, reading a book. Layton lying beside me, tucked in nose to tail, was clenching and unclenching his great hands. He hated inactivity, was like a steam boiler, steadily building up pressure with no outlet to allow escape.

It was just as well that the next morning dawned fine. We set out early; but not early enough to beat the Germans, who were already at work high in the groove above.

'If you can't get across the Pillar, we've had it,' I commented to Layton. 'You'll have a dobbing match to get past those buggers.'

'Don't worry, it'll go all right,' he replied, quietly confident.

I climbed up the fixed rope Layton and Dougal had left in place before the storm. Jorg Lehne, looking rather like a wartime stormtrooper, was paying out the rope to Karl Golikow, who was out in front on their line.

'Morning, Jorg. Do you think Karl will get up?' I asked.

'Maybe. We do not like that snow bulge. It could be dangerous. What will you do?'

'We're going round the side. There's a better groove on the other side of the Pillar.'

'Ah, but the bottom of the Pillar looks very difficult. I don't think it is possible.'

'To Layton, anything is possible,' I replied with less confidence than I tried to put into my voice.

Layton came up and joined me at this point – gone was the cumbersome, rather diffident backwoodsman from the States, gone the nervously tensed companion of the previous day. He was now sure-moving and confident. He went straight into the lead, kicked up a few feet of snow to the foot of the rocks, hammered in a peg, clipped in a karabiner and étrier and stepped up. A short pause; gloved hands, searching, had found another placement for a peg, nudged one into the crack, tapped it with half a dozen sure blows and repeated the previous process. He knew exactly what he was doing and where to find the right placement for his pitons by glancing at the rock rather than by trying a dozen different places. He then knew how hard to hammer the piton into the crack – not too hard, yet sufficiently to hold his weight. He was a craftsman, superbly adapted to this highly specialised form of climbing.

He reached the line of weakness that stretched round the base of the Pillar. From below, it had looked easy-angled, but now I could see that this was a relative term. It was still desperately steep, and loose into the bargain. Clusters of icicles clung to every crevice in the rock, and Layton had to clear each one away before finding placement for his pegs. I don't think any of our own team, or that of the Germans, could have completed that traverse without drilling a succession of holes for bolts, but Layton, making maximum use of his long reach, and uncanny ability to place pitons, got across it, using the cracks and crannies which nature had provided in the rock.

This type of climbing is a slow process, and the morning slipped by as he moved and swung deliberately from étrier to étrier. I talked in a desultory fashion to Jorg Lehne, gazing down at Scheidegg, now 6,000 feet below us, and watching the cavorting black specks of the skiers as they gambolled in their world of bright sunshine.

A cry came down from above. Layton had managed to get round the side of the Pillar, had pulled the rope in, and now it was my turn to follow up his pitch using jumars, and removing the pitons. Following Layton, this could be desperately difficult, because they were placed so very far apart. I found him perched on a narrow ledge which he had cut out of the ice. Above, an ice runnel ran between steep rock-walls to an even steeper ice-field. It looked hard.

I belayed myself and Layton set out once again. At this stage, I had no intention of doing any leading – I had come along in an emergency, was getting some extra pictures, and was happy to hold Layton's rope.

But Layton was no longer moving with confidence. He, a master on rock, had little experience of snow and ice. He messed around, trying to put in an ice screw – you treat it like a corkscrew, and screw it in to its head in the ice, turning it by hand, or using the pick of your hammer for leverage. Sometimes they don't bite easily – there's a knack to it – one that Layton hadn't yet learned. But at last he got it in, climbed another few feet, cutting steps in the wrong places and getting tangled with his crampons.

'Can't get a bloody peg in,' he muttered.

I was getting worried. You can't afford to fall off on ice; the ice screw runners are of very doubtful value, and would almost certainly pull out. If he had a long fall, I might also be pulled from my stance, since his belay pegs seemed none to sound.

'Do you want me to have a go?' I offered. 'At your present rate, I don't think you'll get up before dark.'

'Okay, this just isn't my scene.'

And so I found myself out in front, for the first time on the climb – something that I had never intended to do. I couldn't help but get a thrill of excitement, mingled with apprehension. It looked a long, hard ice pitch, harder than anything I had ever attempted before.

Layton slid back down on the rope, and I set off, kicking carefully up to his top peg, and then pausing to take stock. He had reached the top of the little ice runnel and the ice now flared out, and up towards a band of rock about seventy feet above. It was around 70 degrees in angle, which was sufficiently steep to make it essential to cut hand-holds as well as foot-holds. The occasional island of rock stuck out of the ice, a sure sign that this was only a thin skin over the rock underneath.

You've got to be methodical on ice, working out the sequence of holds that you plan to create, cutting them with the minimum of effort, no bigger than absolutely necessary, all the time remaining relaxed, or aching calves and hand cramps will soon make steady movement impossible.

I cut my first steps; the apprehension slipped away. For the first time on the climb I was totally involved. Swing gently, not too hard or you'll shatter the ice and it won't form a perfect step; make three or four steps – all in the right places; make hand-holds to go for, and then step up, gently, delicately, with precision.

I'm thirty feet above my last runner, time for another, but the skin of ice is too thin to take ice screws. I clear away some ice. The rock underneath is as smooth and polished as a boiler plate – no cracks there. Just keep climbing, you can't afford to fall off. And the ice gets thinner, not more than an inch thick, with a gap between ice and rock, which is nice for fingers which curl reassuringly round the ice rim in the little holes I have cut. But it's frightening in another way. What if the ice around me breaks away? I'll be clinging to an icy toboggan – all the way to Grindelwald. The thought is only fleeting – there's no time any longer for fears, no room for the play of an over-vivid imagination. Just ice in front and the need to fashion a stairway. And a snow gangway, where the angle seems to ease twenty feet away, becomes the focal point of my very existence.

Now I'm a hundred feet above Layton, and the rope drops gracefully down to that one pathetic little piton that he managed to hammer in, some twenty feet above him. That would mean a fall of 160 feet. But I've reached the snow, good hard snow – you could go straight up it on the points of your crampons. I don't feel brave any longer, and cut little steps with my axe, kick my boots in hard, and move up the ramp, slowly, steadily, to the foot of a groove that runs up the left-hand edge of the Pillar.

Cut out a stance, find the rock belay, and I'm safe. We've solved the problem of the Pillar and a great bubbling wave of joy rolls over me. I look up the groove. It'll go all right – no problems there. I can see its top. That must be the crest of the Pillar and there's no sound up there – that means the Germans have failed to get up the groove on the other side. We might have beaten them. I yell down to Layton and bring up the rope. I daren't let him jumar up to me, since I can't trust my belays and am afraid that his deadweight on the rope could pull them away.

As he climbs, I gaze down, across the face, with a rich feeling of content-ment. It had been the hardest, and certainly the most spectacular ice pitch I had ever climbed. The complete lack of protection made it, in effect, a solo ascent, for had I fallen, I don't think Layton could have held me.

It was nearly dark before he reached me. We hammered in some extra pitons and very gingerly abseiled back down the ice-field to the end of the traverse. The day's excitement was not yet over, however. Layton was the first to swing back across the horizontal rope of the traverse, and I followed. Halfway across, my jumar jammed, and I found myself in an inextricable knot. Whatever I did seemed to tie me more securely in position, so that I could move neither back-wards nor forwards.

Layton was waiting on the other end of the traverse.

'Guess it's going to be pretty cold if you have to stay there all night,' he commented.

I continued my struggles on the rope, hanging free from the rock at the lowest point of a V formed by the horizontal rope under tension. The only way out seemed to be to untie completely, maintain my hold on the rope, and then reorganise my jumars and karabiners.

By this time, Layton had vanished back down to the fixed rope, towards the snow hole, muttering about his feet being cold. I felt very much on my own in the gathering dusk. Make a mistake now, and you're dead, Bonington. The thought of the fall was worse, more immediate, than death. At last I succeeded in getting the gear sorted out, and was able to pull myself across the end of the traverse. Tired and hungry, I abseiled back down towards the Flat Iron. On the way across to our snow hole, I passed the entrance to that of the Germans. Jorg Lehne was sitting in the entrance.

'How did it go?' I asked. He looked thoroughly discouraged.

'It is too dangerous,' he said. 'We had to turn back. We could get round by the side, but it would take a very long time. I wonder though, could we use your fixed rope to get to the top of the Pillar?'

'Seems fair enough, provided you wait for us, and follow us up,' I replied.

We had used each other's fixed ropes in the past, but now we had an advantage over the Germans, for we had been the first to reach the one vital bottleneck which offered the only feasible route into the upper part of the face. We had to make sure that we stayed out in front.

That night, I told John the good news. 'Sounds good – you guys have done a fine job. Dougal and I'll come up the day after tomorrow.'

'How do you feel now?'

'I've been checked over by the hospital in Interlaken, and they say the infection has cleared up. I feel fine.'

'Roger, good to hear. Layton and I'll go up again tomorrow, and have a go at reaching the Spider.'

'Sounds good.'

'The brew's ready now. See you day after tomorrow. Over and out.'

Our link with Scheidegg and civilisation cut off with the flick of a switch, we settled down to a victory feast of nuts, cheese and dried meat, with Calcatonic, an effervescent vitamin drink.

Next morning we were just getting ready to go out, when Jorg Lehne appeared. 'Chris, I would like to talk to you. We have an idea.'

'Go ahead.'

'We should like to see this competition end. Would it not be a good idea if today Karl climbed with Layton. Then you would have a truly shared rope, and we could go on like this with our teams climbing together. Then it could not be said that one or other team had been taken to the top by the other. Do you think it is a good idea?'

I was immediately attracted to the suggestion. True, we had everything in our favour, which of course was why Jorg Lehne was appealing to us now. He was making his suggestion from a position of weakness. I responded immediately.

'Sounds like a good idea to me, but I'll have to talk it over with John.'

'Why not let Karl climb with Layton today?' asked Jorg. 'It would give you a good chance to get pictures.'

'That's a good idea. Okay. Layton climbs with Karl today, but as for joining up on the route, John'll have to ratify that.'

Had I been weak in agreeing so easily? I've often wondered. The previous day I had enjoyed some of the most intensely stimulating climbing I had ever known, and had certainly had my best day, so far, on the Eigerwand. The day before us held the same promise, of good climbing which would almost certainly be safer and better protected than the lead I had already made. And yet, photography was still my main priority. I wanted to get the best photographic record that I possibly could of this climb, and when you're actually climbing, or even belaying someone and holding the rope, photography is very difficult. Perhaps this, more than anything, influenced my decision.

Another factor was that co-operation seemed to be the perfect way of ending the competition on the face. I had come to like and respect the Germans, as I know John, Dougal and Layton had, also. If we could all end up climbing together, it would be the perfect climax to the successful conclusion of the route.

There was still the dilemma, whether or not I should stay with the climbing team and go all the way to the top with them. At this stage, it looked as if the final push for the summit would be quite straightforward. I had no pictures in from the side, from the easy West Ridge of the Eiger. More, I had a dream of going to the summit of the mountain by the West Ridge, and then abseiling down the top ice-field on a long rope, to meet the successful team. Thus, I hoped to get the most spectacular pictures of all. I decided to go down, having photographed Layton from the top of the Pillar.

Layton and Karl set off together for our previous night's high point, and I sat and talked with Jorg Lehne. At eight, I opened up the wireless to talk to John.

'We've made a rather radical decision,' I told him with some diffidence, for I wasn't at all sure what his reaction would be.

'It's only a temporary one, until you actually ratify it. Layton and Karl Golikow are climbing together, up the Pillar, today, and I suggest that we let them do this until you get up here. We should then climb in conjunction with the Germans. This seems a good compromise to me, as it is inevitable that we are going to be following the same route to the top. What do you think?'

'Well, it's a lot to swallow at the moment, Chris,' said John. 'I'll have to think about it. Offhand it sounds good – except I think it should have happened later, after we had actually reached the top of the Pillar. How did this decision come about?'

I told him what had taken place and we left it at that. In a way, I had forced the decision on John and his fears were well grounded. There was always the risk that in the final analysis it might have seemed that we had got help from the Germans when, in fact, the very reverse had occurred. Had I climbed with

Layton that day, and had we then actually dropped a rope to the Germans, it would have been obvious that it was they who had needed the help. But I was tired of all this manoeuvring – wanted to get my pictures – so had made the decision.

Layton and Karl reached the top of the Pillar just after midday and dropped a 300-foot rope straight down the groove which had defeated the Germans. I jumared up it, while Layton started up the next pitch, a great rock corner that led to a huge roof overhang.

He moved up quickly and easily. It was very steep, but the cracks were deep and sound – it was just a question of hammering away. I hung on the rope just below Karl as he belayed Layton, taking my final pictures from the face itself. Layton, a hundred feet above, was spread-eagled below the overhang, the do-ing, do-ing, do-ing of his hammer had a joyful ring to it, and I think we all felt that the climb was very nearly in the bag.

It was time for me to start my long descent and I went down without regret. My ambitions were concentrated on the photographs I was taking, not on reaching the top of the Eiger Direct. And I spun down, down, down, precise, careful, for if you aren't, you're dead. Clip on the karabiner, brake on to the rope, check the gates are facing the right way and are closed, lean back, slide and zoom down the rope, in a single effortless leap to the next anchor piton – clip into that with a spare karabiner, remove the brake from the rope, replace it, check it, check it again, and down again.

It took only one and a half hours to get from 300 feet below the White Spider to the bottom of the face. Picking up my skis, I pointed them downhill, and with less grace than on the ropes, plunged through the deep powder snow of the famous White Hair Run below the Eiger, down to the rack-railway track that led up to Kleine Scheidegg. I had finished with the Eiger's face. In four days' time the whole climb should be finished. Next morning I would realise my ambition of climbing the West Ridge to photograph Layton and the Germans as they reached the White Spider. John and Dougal would be climbing the fixed ropes to reach the Death Bivouac that night.

March 20th. The weather still perfect. Mick Burke has now replaced Don Whillans as my assistant and we are scrambling up the broken rocks and snow slopes of the West Ridge. Dougal and John are on their way to the Death Bivouac and Layton is out in front, cutting the final steps up into the White Spider. We reached the crest of the ridge in the late afternoon, hot, tired and sweating. Winter had crept away during our long siege of the face, and spring had now pounced upon us. The afternoon sun had crept round the face, and was now bathing the summit rocks of the Eiger in its soft rays. I could see climbers in the White Spider, tiny little red flies, sitting – too complacently, perhaps – in the middle of the Spider's Web. Two of the Germans were spending the night there. John, Layton and Dougal were at the Death Bivouac, all set for the summit push.

As Mick and I scrambled back down the West Ridge, in the gloaming, it seemed as if everything was, at last, fitting into place. Another couple of days and I should be taking those summit shots as John, Dougal and Layton cut up those last hundred feet or so of ice-field, to reach the top of the Eiger.

13   Eiger Direct: the Summit

When we reached the Kleine Scheidegg hotel, late that night, Peter Gillman had some disturbing news for us.

'There's a bad weather forecast, with a front coming in from the Atlantic,' he told me.

'Does John know?'

'Yes, I told him on the evening call.'

'What's he planning to do?'

'He wanted to make a push for the summit tomorrow, but he's worried now, and says he'll wait to see what the forecast is.'

Next morning we were ready for the radio call at 7 a.m.

'How're things?' John asked.

'Not good, I'm afraid. The front seems to be moving in to the west coast of Europe. Could be here tomorrow.'

'I don't want to be caught out on those summit rocks. We'll stay where we are and see what it's like at midday. Could you give me another call then?'

'Okay. Let's hope it's better.'

Up on the face, a restless Layton decided to come back down to Kleine Scheidegg for more supplies, to have a beer and see his girlfriend. He set off at about 9 a.m. Now, so close to success, all they had to do was to wait for two fine days, and then they could tackle those last 1,500 feet to the summit. Back at Scheidegg I spent the morning preparing gear for my own coverage of the arrival at the summit, and then went through the daily ritual of getting the weather forecast. This entailed phoning not only the airport at Geneva but also the weather centre in London, in order to get a rounded pattern of the progress that frontal systems were making across the Atlantic. There was a touch of superstitious confidence in all this, as if we believed that the favourable interpretation of one forecaster might actually change the inexorable march of a storm – we were the modern-day suppliants to the gods.

The London forecaster was more encouraging than the man in Geneva, saying that the frontal system seemed to have slowed down, and might take another twenty-four hours to reach the Alps. I was just leaving the phone kiosk when Mick Burke came into the hall.

'Have you had a look through the telescope recently?' he asked.

'No.'

'You should. The Germans don't seem to believe in weather forecasts. I've just seen one in the Fly.'

'Christ. That means they could reach the top by tomorrow. I wonder what John will do?'

In the call at midday, we told John both about the improved forecast and the progress of the Germans. This altered the situation completely, for it meant that the going between the Spider and the Fly (the name we had given to the small snow field above, and slightly to the right of the Spider) must be quite easy.

John now had no choice. The Germans were obviously going for the summit, and if he chose to sit it out, waiting for the storm to pass, his own opportunity might well be missed. I urged him to move up the fixed rope to the Fly that afternoon, so that they could make their bid for the summit the next day. It was the obvious course, and one that he had arrived at on his own. He made his decision.

'I guess we'll go for the summit tomorrow. Tell Layton we're sorry we can't wait for him. He can always join the Germans; they look as if they're planning to put a second team up there, once the fixed ropes have been placed.'

John and Dougal sorted out their gear in the Death Bivouac and set out an hour later – Dougal first, followed by John.

Back at Scheidegg, Pete Gillman, who had just happened to come out to the big binoculars to see what progress they were making, swivelled the glasses towards the face, and began following the line of the fixed ropes from Death Bivouac, up towards the Spider. At full magnification the figure of a man could be discerned quite clearly – not just as a black dot, but as a real person, with arms and legs. You could even pick out the thread of the fixed rope through the eyes of these binoculars. The magnification was so great that it was very easy to get lost, having swung the lenses across the bewildering maze of rock and ice.

Suddenly, as Peter followed the line of rope towards the top of the Pillar, something flashed down across the lens. A dark shape; flailing arms – but were they? Could it have been imagination? Perhaps a rucksack had been dropped. A stone? Pete cried out, and soon a small group gathered around the telescope.

'I think someone on the face could have fallen,' he told us.

'Could it have been a rucksack?' I asked.

'I don't think so; I'm sure it had arms and legs.'

I gazed through the binoculars, first searching the face. There were two little figures on the Spider, one of which must be Dougal. Then, by searching the rocks below the Spider, I hoped to find John, slowly climbing the fixed rope, but could find no one. Perhaps he was hidden behind a buttress of rock, or in one of the gullies that led to the Spider. I dropped down the wall, through the eye of the telescope, to where someone was stirring outside the German snow hole on the Flat Iron, then on down to the foot of the face. Scanning the snows at the base of the Eiger, all the time trying to convince myself that it could only have been a rucksack that had fallen, I found something – a dark smudge in the snow. It could have been a rock, or a sack – but I knew, we all knew, that it was John Harlin.

The only way to find out for certain was to ski over, and I set out with Layton, taking with us one of the walky-talky radios. I still tried to convince myself that it was a rucksack that had fallen, but that even if it were John, there could be a chance of his having survived the fall by going into deep powder snow. We skied in silence, each dreading what we might find. We came to some gear scattered in the snow – the contents of a rucksack.

'It was only a sack,' I shouted, in a wave of relief that, somehow, I knew was not justified.

And then I saw something above us. We plodded up through the snow to where John Harlin's body lay, grotesque, distorted by the appalling impact of his 5,000-foot fall, but still horribly recognisable. There was a strange, terrible beauty in the juxtaposition of the bent limbs of this man, who had devoted everything to climbing, and finally to this project and to the face towering above. It made a perfect photograph – a picture that said everything that could possibly be said about the North Wall of the Eiger. I was horrified with myself that I could even think in this way; I knew that I could never take such a picture.

We could not bear to look at him for more than a few seconds. I forced myself to feel his heart, though the fact that he was dead was painfully, totally obvious. Having turned our backs on him, I opened up the wireless, and in a voice that I found impossible to control, told Peter that it was John who had fallen. I asked him to arrange for a party of guides to come for the body, and then Layton and I returned to Scheidegg. I could not have borne carrying him down myself, I was much too upset.

Back at Scheidegg, I became involved once more with the climb as a whole. What had caused the accident? Was it a broken rope, or had he failed to clip in with his jumars correctly? The latter seemed unlikely. John, for all his ambitious schemes, was a supremely cautious and very competent mountaineer. We could only surmise. Now, what would the others do – Dougal and the Germans, poised so close to success but threatened by the change in the weather which was already showing itself with an advance guard of high cirrus marching over the western horizon? Late that evening, we made contact with Dougal on the Germans' walky-talky set. Karl Golikow had come down the fixed rope from the Fly to bring the radio to him.

'The rope parted,' Dougal told us, 'just above the Pillar. It went over a particularly bad spot just there.'

'What do you plan to do yourselves?' I asked.

'We've talked about this,' he said. 'Our first reaction was to come back down, but then we realised that if we did this, John would have thrown away his life for nothing. We want to finish the route. It's what John wanted to do more than anything, and we reckon that this is what he would have wanted us to do.'

'I think you're absolutely right,' I said; 'but what about gear; did much go down with John?'

'All the food and our bivvy tent, but there's just enough up here.'

The next day was spent in getting reorganised for their summit push, and in getting their gear up into the Spider. There were four Germans, Jorg Lehne, Gunther Strobel, Siegi Hupfauer and Roland Votteler, with Dougal. As they worked, the clouds crept over the sky and built up for the storm. The safest course would have been to pull back to the Flat Iron bivouac to sit out the storm, for there was insufficient snow in the Spider or the Fly to dig a proper snow hole. But this was impossible on psychological grounds. After the tragedy they could never have continued the siege in cold blood – it was a matter of making one last desperate attempt, and in doing so they intended to preclude any possibility of retreat, for they had to lift the fixed ropes behind them, in order to give themselves enough for their summit push.

Action absorbed some of our grief. If they were going to make their bid for the summit, I had to be there, not only to record their arrival, but to act as the nucleus of a rescue party, in case they needed help. There was now barely time to climb all the way to the top of the Eiger, and anyway I needed more gear than Mick Burke and I could carry. I decided to use a helicopter, which would cost the *Telegraph* well over £200, but it seemed worth it.

Mick and I spent the rest of the day in preparation, and took off late that afternoon. The helicopter was flown by a squat, tough-looking little Frenchman, who couldn't speak a word of English. The machine itself looked ridiculously fragile, as we piled ourselves and our gear into it.

Clouds were now scudding over the Jungfrau, and the bowl, formed by the two edges containing the North Wall of the Eiger, was filled with cloud. Somewhere in there were Dougal and the four Germans. The helicopter buzzed crazily up the side of the Eiger.

'Est que possible au sommet?' I shouted.

He shrugged. 'Pas possible.'

We were now above the Eiger Glacier, a large cwm between the Monch and the West Ridge of the Eiger. The higher we went, the less possible were the landing spots we saw; crevasses gaped, the slopes stretched up into the clouds.

The pilot muttered 'pas possible' once again, and pointed down towards Scheidegg. There seemed no choice but to go back.

As the helicopter darted downwards I had a sense of failure. We could not, must not go back down – but what else could we do? Obviously he could drop us, far below the summit, on a part of the mountain where I had never been before, but we could never have carried the mound of gear all the way to the summit. Nearly back at Scheidegg, I realised suddenly what we had to do. We could leave most of the gear in the helicopter and get him to drop us on the glacier. We would still be a lot nearer to the summit than if we had to walk all the way from Kleine Scheidegg. I tapped him on the shoulder, gesticulated upwards and he, with a resigned shrug, that said 'these mad English don't know what the hell they're doing', turned the helicopter back up the mountain. Mick and I quickly readjusted the loads, dumping most of the food, all the cine gear, and some of the climbing equipment.

It was a crazy, exciting feeling as we skimmed back up, close to the snows. When high enough, we hovered at about six feet – it was too steep to land – and he gestured for us to jump out, a frighteningly final gesture. So what if there was a hidden crevasse at the point of landing – only one way to find out – jump! And I did. The snow leapt up at me, and I was there, in one piece, with the slipstream of the helicopter hammering at me.

Mick chucked down the gear and came after me. The pilot gave us a wave and the helicopter suddenly careered up into the sky, leaving us lonely and vulnerable, as it quickly shrank into a small speck. There we were, on the flanks of the Eiger, crevasses around us, the North Face of the Monch, dark, dominating to one side, and a great snow slope in front, leading up towards the top of the Eiger. We shouldered our rucksacks and started up the slope; it wasn't particularly steep, but the snow conditions were most frightening. The crust of snow was firm and hard, beaten into position by the winds; but beneath, it was soft and powdery. As we made our way up it, the top surface on either side of us cracked, sending lines racing across the smooth surface of the snow, a sure sign that we were on windslab, the most dangerous of all avalanche snows. The crust was not anchored to the snow beneath, but was merely resting on steep powder and could break away in a single catastrophic slab, as much as a hundred yards across, with us on it. In a place like this, there could be little chance of survival, and none at all of a rescue party coming to dig us out.

We tiptoed up the snow, hardly daring to talk, as if the resonance of our voices might trigger off an avalanche. When, at last, we reached the top of the slope and the ridge connecting the Monch with the Eiger, we were exposed to the full blast of the gale, and it was very nearly dark. Having scrambled up the ridge, finding no suitable spot for a snow cave, we knew we would have to look for a snow bank on the flanks. I stumbled forward in the dark, working my way across a steep snow slope. It was impossible to tell whether there was a drop below of five, fifty or 500 feet. Without somewhere to dig, we would have scant chance of survival.

Eventually I found a snow bank, brought Mick across to me, grabbed the shovel and started digging. At least I was able to keep warm as I worked away in the shelter of the snow, while all Mick could do was to sit, huddled outside, waiting for me to dig out enough snow for him to creep in behind me. There was an odd sort of enjoyment about the entire venture. Perhaps it was because we were on our own, with a simple, independent aim. And although now in the midst of a most savage storm, we still felt in complete control of our destinies. Our position was certainly more dangerous than it had been that night on the Eiger Direct when we had been trying to establish our snow hole on the Flat Iron. Then, I had been nervous, almost cowardly, partly I suspect because I was not in command of the situation, having type-set myself as the photographer. Now, I was in command. Mick depended on me, in much the same way as I had depended on Dougal and John. The very level of this responsibility made me forget any fear that I might have experienced.

It was nearly midnight before we finished. There was no sound of the wind in the hollow we had dug out of the snow, and we were able to relax and sleep. We woke in the morning to cool, filtered light. It was impossible to tell whether the storm was still raging, or whether it had cleared up into the perfect day. I discovered soon enough, by sliding down the short curved tunnel. Fresh blown snow, banked high in the entrance, had to be cleared by digging away with my hands before I could tell what the weather was like in the outside world.

If anything, it was worse than the previous night. Dense cloud surrounded us, and the wind, tearing blindly through it, made it impossible to tell the difference between wind-blown snow and cloud. Back in the hole I found Mick asleep, and gave him a prod to tell him that the storm was still raging outside. He just grunted, happy to be snug and warm inside his sleeping bag. It was nearly eight o'clock, and we had agreed to give Kleine Scheidegg a call on the hour, every hour, if possible. I switched on the set and listened to the crackle of static; then Pete came up, very weak and distorted, as if talking from another planet – which, in our present position, he might well have been doing, he in his centrally-heated bedroom, and we in our snow cave a thousand feet below the summit.

'The Germans on the face got through last night,' he told us. 'They bivouacked in the Fly, but Lehne and Strobel fixed a lot of rope yesterday, and reckon they got somewhere just below the summit ice-field. They think they'll get out today.'

'Sounds great. We'll try to get up there ourselves. It's bloody desperate up here.'

'Have you got enough food?' asked Peter. 'We were worried when we found all that gear you left behind in the helicopter.'

'We're fine, thanks, specially if they get out today. Open up every hour, so that we can get you back if we want you.'

'Okay. Have a good trip. Over and out.'

We were on our own again. I couldn't help worrying that the Germans and Dougal might have got up early and, at that moment, could even be at the summit. This being the case, I would have missed my great opportunity of getting summit photographs. Quickly, I prodded Mick into wakefulness, got the stove going, and an hour later we were packed, ready to go. At this stage I thought we were only a few hundred feet below the summit, but once we started climbing, it became increasingly evident that we were very much lower. It was a savage day, much worse than the previous one, for the wind seemed even stronger and almost impossible to face into, because of the way ice particles were driven into our faces. It was also an almost total whiteout, impossible to tell where the driving snow ended and the mountain began. We just picked our way through it, groping blindly upwards in an enclosed world of our own. It was exciting, stimulating work. A steep snow slope led up to broken rocks covered in snow, then to a wall of hard, green ice, up which I had to cut my way, all the time battered by the wind. Mick was a good companion, always ready with a touch of dry Lancastrian humour, whenever he caught up with me in this world of snow and cloud and wind.

We reached the summit. Had the others been and gone? There were no signs, but there probably wouldn't be anyway. We found a piece of hard, frozen orange peel, jammed between two rocks. Gazing down the steep ice-field of the North Face, we shouted, but the words, torn from our mouths by the rushing wind, were dissipated in the air-blown snow. It was difficult to believe that anyone could survive there, let alone complete a high-standard climb.

We ourselves were beginning to freeze, exposed as we were to the full blast of the wind.

'We'll have to find somewhere to snow-hole,' I told Mick. 'Come on, we'll drop down till we can find enough snow to dig in.'

We tried to keep as close as possible to the crest of the ridge, so that we could look over and peer into the mist and snow, in a vain hope of seeing the others. About 500 feet below, we found a bank of snow sufficiently deep to dig a cave. It was high time, for by now we were frozen to the bone, and I had lost all sensation in my feet. Once in the hole, we got out the wireless and called Gillman.

'We can't see anything down here,' he told me. 'I haven't managed to get any information from the Germans, either. I'll go over now – what's it like up there?'

'Bloody desperate. Let us know as soon as possible what progress the others have made.'

Mick and I got our boots off, massaged our feet, and then climbed into sleeping bags. Fully expecting the Germans to arrive at the summit at the same time as ourselves, we had left all the food at the other snow hole. We now realised that we had only two teabags, no sugar, and a bar of chocolate – pitifully little to keep us going in these conditions.

An hour went by, and I switched on the walky-talky. Pete came up after a few minutes, sounding even more distant and distorted than on the previous call. We had to ask him to repeat what he was saying, over and over again, to get any sense out of the confused jumble of words. Eventually we gathered that, a couple of hours earlier, Jorg Lehne and Dougal had reached a point just below the summit ice-field. This meant they could be at the top in the next hour or so. Immediately closing down the set, Mick and I struggled to get back into our frozen outer garments. It was like trying to put on suits of armour. Out we went, up towards the summit. Each time I went out, I had felt that the weather couldn't possibly get worse, and each time it had. Hardly able to stand against the force of the wind, we certainly could not face into it. Slowly, we crawled up to the top, where we looked over the edge and into the face, where we could see nothing except whirling snow and ice dropping away into the abyss. Having stayed there for half an hour, at the end of which time we were scarcely able to move, it was time to return to the comfort of the snow hole. At least we had a retreat, but what of the climbers on the face? What had they? While we snuggled in our sleeping bags, Dougal was abseiling down frozen ropes to the place where two of the Germans had prepared a bivouac site. Gunther Strobel had come up to the high point, carrying Jorg Lehne's and his own bivouac gear, so that they could bivouac where they were, leaving Dougal to return to the bottom, where his gear had been left with the other pair. He spent the night wrapped up in a bivouac sack, his sleeping bag already frozen solid from the previous night. His stance was too small for him to even contemplate taking off his boots, though he did succeed in removing his crampons and, in doing so, perhaps saved his feet from frostbite.

It must have been a long, cruel night, though talking to Dougal afterwards, one could see that he had derived the same strange enjoyment from an extreme situation as I had experienced that day in wandering around the top of the Eiger in the tempest.

We woke at dawn and lay in our sleeping bags, with nothing to do but wonder about the fate of our friends on the face. It seemed they could have little chance of survival in a storm as savage as this. Outside, the wind was as fierce as ever, with visibility as low. I switched on the wireless at 6 a.m. and Peter told me that three of the Germans, together with Toni Hiebeler (a member of the team which made the first winter ascent of the North Wall of the Eiger by its original route), were going to try to reach us, to bring us more food, and enough rope to lower someone down the face to try to help the climbers trapped on it. It was obvious that Pete couldn't hear my reply, and he ended up by telling me to press the send switch of the radio three times as affirmative and twice for negative, in reply to his questions. We, of course, unable to ask him anything, did gather that the Germans' radio had also failed, leaving Peter with no idea of their progress.

Having had practically nothing to eat on the previous day, we now ate two cubes of the chocolate left from the bar we had brought with us from the lower snow hole. We discussed the possibility of searching for our previous home, but quickly abandoned the idea. We could never have found it in the near whiteout conditions we were experiencing. Although I dreaded the thought of another struggle to the summit, our consciences finally drove us out. We fought our way through the driving snows to a point where we could overlook the summit ice-field. No sign of anyone. We could try, however, to get a higher snow hole, and to this end we started poking about. It was late afternoon when there came a shout from below. I looked down, and saw Karl Golikow, grinning as always, in spite of the blizzard and the seven-hour struggle which they had experienced in fighting their way up to our assistance. He got out his walky-talky and spoke to the base camp man, talking fast and excitedly; then he hammered me on the back.

'They are nearly up,' he shouted against the wind. We abandoned the snow hole and crawled up to the top as fast as we could. Jorg Lehne and Gunther Strobel had just arrived, their faces masked in icicles. Jorg looked surprisingly fit, but Gunther, moving like a sleep-walker, was obviously badly frost-bitten. Grabbing hold of them we shook hands, and thumped them on their backs in our pleasure at seeing them alive. They had fought their way out of the grasp of the face and the weather, entirely unaided. They had, they told us, left fixed ropes behind them for the others to follow, and we helped and guided them back down, towards the other Germans who were now coming up towards us.

We didn't know then, that Dougal was struggling for his very life. There was one section where Jorg had run out of rope, and had left a gap of about a hundred feet. Dougal and the two Germans had no ice axes – not even an ice-hammer. This was all right as long as they were following up the fixed ropes left by the lead pair. But now there was a gap, without even a trace of the steps they must have cut in the ice, for these had all been filled in by the driving snow. His crampons had become loose, and he was unable to tighten the straps because they had frozen into bands like strips of steel. The lead pair had disappeared and he could not even see the top of the ice-field though, in actual fact, he was only about 300 feet below it.

There was no point in staying where he was – all three of them would have died, and so he started out, on what must have been the most difficult lead of the entire climb. He moved, clearing the snow with his gloved hands until he found traces of the steps cut by the others; stepped up into them cumbrously, yet so carefully, always uncomfortably aware that if he did slip he would almost certainly pull the pair below off their stances and that they would all fall to their deaths.

He came to the top of the line of steps. The end of the rope had been blown about twenty feet to one side, and between him and the rope was a smooth ice slope, canted at about 50 degrees. In trying to balance across on the front points of his crampons, he found they were so loose on his boots, so blunt after weeks of climbing, that he obviously had no hope of getting across.

Most climbers would have given up, or made a mistake, faced with such an appalling situation. Dougal did not, and in solving the problem survived and, at the same time, displayed his own genius as a mountaineer. The only hope seemed to be a tension traverse. To complete this manoeuvre you hammer in a piton, clip in a karabiner, and then swing across, almost horizontally, relying on the side tension of the rope to hold you in. Dougal had a piton – the ice-dagger which was his only aid; he had no hammer, but did have a Hiebeler clamp, a little lever of light alloy. He tried to hammer in the piton with this, but it only went in about an inch, then moved from side to side in its hole with frightening ease. It certainly would not have held a fall, and it was highly doubtful whether it could even have taken the strain of a tension traverse.

As Dougal worked his way across, leaning against the rope, placing his feet very, very carefully, he was well aware that a slip meant a plummeting fall of 6,000 feet for both himself and the two others. But having managed to get across, he seized the rope, fastened his own climbing rope to it, and then climbed up towards the summit.

I got back to the top just in time to see him moving up those last few feet. I don't think I have ever been so glad to see anyone in the mountains, as I was to see him. My pleasure and emotion did not stop me taking photographs, although the cold very nearly did. My first camera froze solid and I had another half-frame camera round my neck but that was frozen as well. My last resort was yet another camera, which I had wrapped in a down jacket in my sleeping bag. It worked, and pointing it in the general direction of Dougal, I got half a dozen pictures of him as I manipulated the rewind and trigger with frozen fingers. When my fingers began to go white, I stopped, sucked my hands in my mouth until I got a bit of life back into them, and then shot a few more.

And then back down to the snow hole, moving slowly and cautiously, fearful that after so much had happened, now, in sight of safety, we should have another accident. There were shouts of pleasure as we thrust ourselves into the cosy confines of the hole. That morning it had barely been large enough for Mick and me, but the Germans had enlarged it slightly, until it was just big enough for four. Eleven of us were now crammed into it – there was no room to move, certainly insufficient to get into sleeping bags. A gas stove was purring in the back, someone had a flask of schnapps, and we laughed and joked in our relief at the face team's success and, more to the point, at just being alive. Toni Hiebeler, jammed in the back of the cave, complained of suffocation as the air became thick with smoke and lack of oxygen; I took off Dougal's boots to massage his feet, which seemed cold, but were not frost-bitten. His hands, however, were in a bad way, being covered in great black blisters.

The dawn crept in, and we packed rucksacks. One by one, we squeezed out of the snow cave for the last leg down to Scheidegg – back down to newspaper men, flash bulbs, TV lights, but more important than any of this, as far as I was concerned, to Wendy. Once in the hotel, Mick Burke and I peeled off our boots, Mick grumbling that his were soaked. Rather self-satisfied about my own, which were a different make, I remarked:

'Mine are bone dry. My feet haven't been really cold once, during the whole business. You should throw those away and get a pair of these.'

By this time I was down to my socks, pulled these off to gaze at five blackened toes. I had been frost-bitten without even realising it. Mick and I collapsed into near-hysterical laughter at the come-down from my own pomposity – laughter that was short-lived. A brain surgeon, having a holiday in Scheidegg, volunteered his services and prescribed an injection in the artery in the fleshy part of my thigh. He spent over an hour trying to locate it, digging away with his needle until, eventually, Wendy who was holding my hand began to feel sick and faint, and even my own very limited level of stoicism ran out. We fled from the hotel that night to Interlaken, where there was a hospital. Wendy tearfully left me there to get back to Conrad in England. She had by now been separated from him for three weeks.

I managed to escape from the hospital after three days of boredom. The climb was over – eight weeks of intense excitement, tragedy, superb climbing, farce and the inevitable circus atmosphere that the Eiger always seems to encourage. The climb, undoubtedly controversial, excited criticism in both the popular press and in mountaineering circles. It was said that unfair means had been used to conquer an Alpine face. An extract from a British newspaper article sums up a surprisingly widely held opinion. 'In early March the circus came to Scheidegg again and we were subject to the ballyhoo that now accompanies each North Wall climb … Certainly the courageous contestants were supreme technicians but some of them came down to Scheidegg to sleep at nights and this bears no more relation to climbing than taking a plane to Petersgrat does to ski mountaineering. One Wengen guide was heard to declare that he could have dragged his grandmother up the network of fixed ropes … '

Even amongst experienced mountaineers there was a feeling that it was wrong to use expedition tactics in the Alps. I am convinced that the climb could not possibly have been completed by any other method that winter; it is quite possible that given the ten days of perfect weather that John had hoped for, they would have completed the climb as they had planned by conventional alpine methods, but even so the likelihood of the weather breaking before they reached the top would have been so great, that I do not think an alpine-type assault was, or would be, justified in winter.

Neither team planned the long-drawn-out assault that occurred – their requent returns to Scheidegg both for rest and supplies were forced on them by the circumstances of bad weather. I do not think that this action caused a particularly dangerous precedent in the history of alpine climbing; just because these methods were used on one climb, because they were expedient, does not mean that they are going to be used on every subsequent first winter ascent or new route done in the Alps – apart from anything else, it is much more enjoyable going straight on to a climb and getting up it.

Only a few people would deny that the Eiger Direct was a great line, whatever methods were used to climb it. To the people who climbed on it, it became more than just a climb; it was a place where twelve people of different nationalities came together and from initial distrust and competition built up a very real friendship and understanding under stress and extreme difficulties. This friendship had been forged before John's tragic death – the two teams would have reached the top together in unqualified victory but for the breaking of a rope.

More important from a personal point of view, perhaps, there is the solid balance of experience that has enabled me, and the others who survived, to go on to tackle other challenges in the mountains and, in my own case, along different paths of adventure journalism. Alongside, is the loss of a powerful personality and brilliant climber – one more name to be added to an ever-growing list of close friends who have died in the mountains, doing something they wanted above all to do, for reasons that none of us have fully succeeded in defining.

14   Sangay from the East

My backside had never been so sore. I shifted in the wooden saddle, but this merely altered the point of pain as the mule I was riding took each jerky step through the morass of mud that pretended to be a path. A trickle of rain ran down my back, unpleasantly chill for the tropics. There was water everywhere, weeping from the grey sky, pounding on the foliage, cascading from the ceiling of leaves above us; it rushed in a brown foaming torrent over the entanglement of dead branches and leaves that covered the floor of the forest.

A far cry from the North Wall of the Eiger in winter, it was difficult to believe that just six weeks earlier I had been sitting in my sleeping bag in a sub-zero temperature in the snow cave on the Death Bivouac. This was when I had first heard about Sangay. It was on the evening radio call, when Pete Gillman said, almost as an afterthought,

'Oh, by the way, John Anstey says, "Do you want to go and climb an active volcano in Ecuador? You'd be the photographer." '

I didn't even think. 'Sounds terrific. Yes, I would.'

It was largely a question of out of the fridge on to the hot plate – but apart from the fact that anywhere warm seemed attractive, this could also be my big break – another job with the *Telegraph* magazine.

The following six weeks passed in preparation for my next assignment whilst sitting it out in hospital, recovering from frostbite. I spent much of the time as a guinea-pig for a new method of treatment called hyperbaric oxygen, which entailed hours spent lying in a cylinder filled with two atmospheres of oxygen. You had to wear a special anti-static tunic, and were not allowed to take in with you even a book; apparently, in oxygen so pure and concentrated, even the slightest static electricity could have caused a fire that would have sent you up in a puff of smoke. As a result, I just lay there for hour upon hour, trying out patience as a potential guru – a role in which I failed miserably.

But at last I escaped and now, on the 16th May, a mere ten days after getting out of hospital, I was jogging through the jungles of Ecuador, bound for our volcano, when the mule in front came to a sudden halt and my own cannoned into it. Long ago I had resigned myself to the fact that I had no control over the beast – it went where it chose. Our way was barred by a fallen trunk, and one of the muleteers jumped into the mud, in an attempt to manhandle the mules over the barrier. Glancing back at Sebastian Snow, my companion on this adventure, I saw that his proofed anorak looked like blotting paper and a trickle of water, which was running down from the tip of his nose, passed his slightly pendulous lower lip. He looked peculiarly helpless, largely because his glasses were completely misted up and he was unable to see where he was going. He presented a very different picture from that of the dark-suited, smooth, old-Etonian to whom I had been introduced by John Anstey in London. This trip had been Sebastian's idea. One of a fast disappearing breed of gentlemen explorers, he had started his own career of adventure after leaving Eton by answering an advertisement in *The Times* to join an expedition to survey the true source of the Amazon. While wandering alone in the shadow of the Andes he had conceived the idea of following the Amazon all the way down to the sea, something that no one had ever done in its entirety. What made the adventure so attractive was the total lack of planning, combined with the sparseness of his knowledge of the problems involved and his relative lack of funds. Hiring a faithful Indian – Sancho Panza to his Quixote – he embarked upon a series of horrendous, yet slightly bizarre adventures in his journey to the Atlantic. This trip developed in him a taste for South American jungles, causing him to return time and time again to probe and explore, always in the manner of the Victorian amateur. By the time I met him, he had made another river trip, this time a north-to-south continental crossing up the Orinoco from the Caribbean, across the Casiquare link, a geographical phenomenon which joins the Orinoco to the Amazon, and then down one of the Amazon tributaries to link up with the River Plate and finish at Buenos Aires. He had made two attempts at this venture, the first ending in sickness, before eventually he completed his journey.

When I had met him over lunch in Quaglino's in early April, it was difficult to believe that he could possibly be a hardy jungle explorer: he was undoubtedly eccentric, probably neurotic and enjoyed making extravagant, and at times outrageous, statements, simply to watch the effects on his audience.

This was one of the first things I was to discover about the difference between going climbing with chosen companions, and carrying out a journalistic assignment. In the case of the latter, you go with whom your employer selects, and it is up to you to make the best of it. There was obviously going to be no shortage of adventure on this mission. Our objective was Sangay, a very remote volcano on the eastern edge of the Andes, overlooking the Amazon Basin. It was also high, 17,496 feet, and very active, with a reputation for having had as many as 400 eruptions in the course of a single day. As an objective, this was one of the factors which had endeared it to both Sebastian and John Anstey, since Anstey wanted to be sure of having truly spectacular photographs, and it promised to satisfy Sebastians unquenchable thirst for action which, at times, I felt was akin to a fanciful form of death wish.

In our venture, Sebastian was to be the jungle expert and writer, I the mountain guide and photographer. After only a week in Sebastian's company all my reservations about him vanished, leaving an easy relationship of mutual mockery, which hid a real affection. His affectations of neuroses, eccentricity and dyed-in-the-wool conservatism were little more than a shell concealing a whimsical sense of humour and a special organisational ability perfectly geared to the elaborate etiquette and principle of mañana (leave everything until tomorrow, in the absolute confidence that tomorrow will never arrive), which dominates all dealings in South America.

We had flown out to Quito via New York, Miami, and Bogota weighed down with 400 lb of excess baggage, which included a high altitude tent, ropes, climbing boots, and a special Boots first-aid kit. The trip had started on the right footing when I, having succeeded in leaving the ice axes in Miami Airport, with equal facility convinced Sebastian that it was his fault. Cables had criss-crossed, and eventually the missing axes had caught up with us. In Quito I had been even more impressed by my companion. He had a wealth of important contacts and our expedition had been organised in the course of a few days, mainly over endless cocktails and dinner parties. All the necessary permits, local food and other impedimenta materialised with an almost magical quality. Sebastian even succeeded in enlisting the help of a local climber, one Jorge Larrea, who worked in a bank and had climbed Chimborazzo with him some years before. He was to interpret and generally act as diplomat.

Without Jorge's services (neither of us spoke Spanish), as bargainer, and remembering all the things which both Sebastian and I invariably forgot, I do not think we should ever have come within a hundred miles of Sangay.

The volcano had had several previous ascents, and had claimed at least one life, but all of these had been from the west, where the volcano abuts on to the high grasslands of the Andean plateau. The approach from that direction is relatively straightforward; three days' march from the road-head over grass-clad foothills. This did not sound adventurous enough, so I hit upon the idea of tackling the volcano from the east – from the Amazon Basin. The nearest civilisation was the small town of Macas, on the banks of the Rio Upano, a tributary of the Amazon. It had an airstrip and although we could have flown in from Quito in a matter of hours, this, once again, would have destroyed the adventure. Why not go overland? – we should see so much more of the country and as a result get that much better story material.

And that was why we were jogging along on the backs of mules, through a tropical downpour in the middle of a seemingly pathless jungle, somewhere between the towns of Cuenca and Macas. Up to this point, the trip had been a magical kaleidoscope of colours, smells and zany experiences, ranging from the dinner parties in Quito, in modern apartments which might have belonged to the wealthy in any country in the world, to the earthy reality of our present situation.

Our journey started in Quito, its narrow streets filled with motor cars, neon signs, patient, inscrutable, poncho-clad Indians – a perfect Spanish colonial city, on which the trappings of modernity hung like fragile cobwebs ready to be brushed away. It is a city of churches with ornate cupolas and baroque columns, their interiors filled with gold and precious stones, a tribute to the rape and pillage of the Inca civilisation.

And then – the first stage of our Odyssey, the bus ride to Cuenca. Sebastian, still clad in dark suit and wearing his Old Etonian tie like a banner, presented a sharp contrast to myself, already scruffy in T-shirt and jeans. He was squeezed between me and a splendidly fat Indian lady nursing a small pig, surrounded by a cacophony of sound, of talk, of clucking hens, of the honk of the horn and the rattle of the engine. We were in the bus for twenty-three bone-shaking hours, as it bumped over paved roads, round hair-pin bends marked with little white crosses to commemorate the victims of accidents.

Cuenca was another old Spanish colonial town in Southern Ecuador, with less of the trappings of modernity than Quito. There was colour everywhere, with women washing clothes on the banks of the river, spreading a veritable coat of many colours over the grass to dry. The Indian market poured forth its noise, bustle and smells, guinea-pigs, fowl, turkeys, vegetables, cones of grain like dormant volcanoes, and people – women in wide sweeping flannel skirts of tangerine, purple and blue; heads shaded with panama hats; faces brown and impassive. I just wandered, absorbed, excited, stimulated by the challenge of transferring the atmosphere from reality to film. I'm not a natural tourist, have never enjoyed seeing a place or museum with the visit as an end-product in itself. But this was different. I was here with a purpose – to get a photographic record – and it was this very intention – the fact that I wanted to reproduce the pictures which were pressing on me, that made the impressions all the more important.

From Cuenca we took a taxi to the village of Gualaceo, one more step away from our familiar Western way of life – but only a step. We stayed at a *hosteleria* run by an enigmatic German – 'Martin Bormann without a shadow of a doubt,' Sebastian assured me. The hotel was at tourist standard, but the village itself could hardly have changed in the last 200 years – ever since the Conquistadors overran the country.

After Gualaceo the escalation into wilderness moved faster. A jeep over a muddy road to the road-head, an hour's bargaining with a group of dissolute, villainous-looking muleteers whose breaths stank of Aqua Diente, the local fire-water, and then we were on narrow paths, an up-and-down trip through banana plantations past small huts and through scrub, to the village of Limon, a collection of clapboard houses on either side of a dusty trail, that could have come straight out of any Western film. Sebastian had, by now, shed his dark suit, and he rode into town with the nonchalance of any gun-toting cowpoke.

We looked up the best saloon in town and found it at least moderately clean. It had bare-board rooms upstairs, and on the ground floor an open saloon with a miniature billiards table which seemed to provide the sole local pastime, and a fly-blown bar. We certainly had little chance of living it up on our *Daily Telegraph* expense accounts. Supper consisted of a few lumps of tough meat, mixed into a mash of overcooked rice, washed down with the local wine. Our muleteers had insisted on being paid the previous evening, and evidently, having enjoyed an all-night debauch, were even more drunk than they had been when we had hired them. Jorge, therefore, sacked them and then succeeded in finding a quiet, dour-looking Indian, who looked altogether more reliable.

Whilst planning our trip, no one in Quito had been very certain whether there was a road, or even a path, to Macas – no sane person would ever dream of going overland when there was a perfectly good plane service. Even at Cuenca, it had been impossible to get any reliable information, and in many ways this was the charm of our experience. That night we stopped at our first jivaria – home of a jungle Indian. The Indians whom we had met so far came, had originated, from the plateau. They had been exposed and in bondage to the original Spanish invader for nearly 400 years, and their lives, dress and customs were influenced accordingly. The Indians of the forest had had less direct contact and their lives had not changed much in the last thousand years. We came across the jivaria in the late evening, at a time when I was beginning to wonder just where we should spend the night. It was a single building, in a small clearing in the forest, with a high, steep-angled roof of thatch. The walls were merely vertical bamboo poles, close enough together to stop an intruder or a large animal, but sufficiently wide apart to allow the chickens and small pigs owned by the family to run in and out freely. There were no windows, and the doorway was simply a gap, barely wide enough to squeeze through. Inside, there was just the one big compartment, softly lit through the gaps between the bamboo walls. From the two supporting timbers of the roof hung the worldly possessions of the family – an old gun that looked as if it would be a greater danger to the man who fired it than to the object of his aim, a few pots and, somehow out of place, a transistor radio. The man of the house wore a tattered shirt and trousers and his wife was clad in a grubby long frock that trailed in the dust and mud – standard wear for all Indians at this time, imposed by the prudery of the local mission. The children, and there were six of them, ran about stark naked, showing off distended bellies and pathetically thin little legs and arms.

Yet there was a quiet dignity in their hospitality; we were strangers in the forest, and we were welcome. I am not sure whether they expected anything from us, but there seemed to be no bargaining. They even offered us some of their evening meal – a bowl of yucca – a root vegetable which seemed a cross between a potato and a parsnip, and less tasty than either!

Next day it was raining, with the torrential deluge that I have already described. In its own way it held a greater fascination than any experience on the Eiger and, in some ways, was even more frightening: I thought I understood mountains but felt lost and ill at ease in the mystery of the forest.

Three days later we reached Macas, a dusty, lost outpost of Western man, dominated by a huge clapboard church and criss-crossed with power lines for an electricity supply not yet connected to a generator. It boasted a few tired little saloons which were still to be modernised for the ubiquitous tourist.

We were a mere thirty-five miles from Sangay, could see it from the top of a bluff, which also performed the duty of a cemetery, high above the river Upano. At first sight, the volcano seemed unreal, like a Japanese painting, its symmetrical cone silhouetted against a copper sky, and a gentle plume of smoke drifting from its summit.

It was the last view of our objective that we were to have for seven days, for we were now in the rainy season and most days the skies wept and Sangay was hidden from view. We could take our mules no further and Sebastian, the fixer of the expedition, produced an introduction to the only European in Macas. He was a German baron, who promised to do his best to help with porters, and to find a guide for our trip.

'But it might be difficult,' he warned us. 'Everyone here is frightened of the volcano, and no one has ever been on its slopes.'

Apart from anything else, the inhabitants of Macas were settlers from the Andean plateau, agricultural pioneers trying to hack away the wilderness of the Amazon Basin. Most of them were ex-soldiers who had been given a plot of land in lieu of a gratuity, and had little more experience of virgin jungle than we ourselves. We had almost given up all hope of finding a guide to take us to the base of the volcano, when a small wiry old man, clad in a faded bush shirt, shorts and a pair of old gym-shoes, presented himself at our hotel. Through Jorge, he assured us that he knew the route as if it were his own back-garden. Eight years before he had guided an Austrian botanist up the Rio Volcan, a tributary of the Upano that flowed down from the base of Sangay. We were to set out the following day at dawn, and eventually left at three in the afternoon – a mere eight hours late which, by Macas standards, was the epitome of punctuality.

Altogether, we had six porters; they were well-built, cheerful lads. Like the Sherpas of Nepal they used a head-band for carrying their loads. One factor that worried me was that they were clad for the hot jungles around Macas, and I could not help wondering how they would fare once we reached the base of the volcano and started to gain altitude.

The approach had a spice of sleepy adventure to it, and this gained piquancy as we got closer to the mountain. Don Albino, our guide and mentor, assured us it would take only three days to reach the base of the volcano. We planned our provisioning accordingly. At first the way led along a footpath on the banks of the River Upano, through a hotch-potch of maize and banana plantations, virgin jungle and entanglements of undergrowth where the exhausted soil had allowed the jungle to encroach once again. Every now and then a Jivaro house would rear from rich vegetation and each night we stayed at one of them, always meeting with the same standard of dignified, slightly withdrawn, hospitality.

Then, after three days, we reached the last jivaria. Our porters were becoming nervous, and Don Albino was visibly losing confidence. He muttered about it being a long time since he had walked into the Rio Volcan; that the way had changed; of the unspeakable dangers that might lurk waiting for us. At last, he admitted frankly that he could not possibly guide us any further and we should have to find a local guide. He duly produced a Jivaro, whom he assured us had regularly been to the base of the volcano, and we set out on the last leg of our journey. We were now in real rain forest that had never been cleared and had the sepulchral look and gloom of a cathedral – but it was quite easy to walk through, there being little undergrowth. It also held an indefinable menace – the feeling that it stretched for ever, into the wild confines of the Amazon Basin. We followed our guide, whispering like so many tourists in the crypt of St Paul's, for two hours, walking through the forest until we came out once more into the open on the wide shingle beds that flanked either bank of the Upano River. We were just short of the tributary of the Rio Volcan, which flowed down into the Upano, at its confluence, over a series of shingle banks formed from black lava dust between high cliffs of gravel.

The sky was a leaden grey, and it had begun to rain as we trailed up the side of the river. Our porters looked singularly uncertain and unhappy in this strange environment. The rain already had a cool bite to it, and the porters' claims to be able to make themselves shelters from the boughs of trees began to ring somewhat hollow. They seemed to be just as helpless as any city dwellers confronted by the wilderness. We ended up by rigging a bivouac tent between a couple of trees for them, while the three of us retired to our two-man tent.

Next day we walked up the Rio Volcan, and as we walked the sides closed in, towering above us with an ever-closer proximity. There was no sign of the volcano; it was hidden in cloud, and I had the disturbing feeling of being in the middle of a vacuum, perhaps exaggerated by my own sensations of lethargy. Whether it was the altitude, a forest fever, or the result of my four weeks in hospital, I felt desperately ill and tired, yet was determined not to betray this to Jorge and Sebastian. At last we reached a point that seemed a dead end. The Rio Volcan spewed forth from a narrow gorge which would have been impossible to follow; our only hope seemed to be a steep gully, leading to the top of the cliffs and the upper jungle.

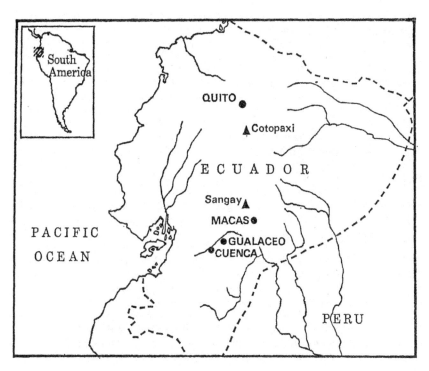

Ecuador: Sangay

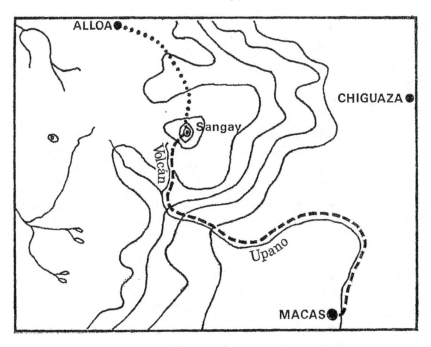

The route to Sangay

I retired to my sleeping bag that night, unable to control my shivering fit, worried that I might fail to complete this second, crucial, professional assignment. Our porters were crammed beneath the bivvy tent in a pile of humanity which at least enabled them to retain some warmth, for they did not even have woollen blankets to cover themselves at night but merely made do with a ragged cotton sheet.

To my relief, next morning, the fever had vanished, and I felt my strength renewed. Our Jivaro guides would go no further, but Don Albino, though obviously scared stiff, agreed to accompany us towards the base of the volcano. We were now gaining height fast, but every foot of the way had to be hacked from the impenetrable entanglement presented by the undergrowth. That day we advanced only a couple of miles. It had rained non-stop all day; our porters were cold and miserable and food was nearly exhausted. Sebastian was obviously enjoying the situation. He loved melodrama, and had a touch of the masochist in his make-up. I was sour and bad-tempered, worried about whether we should ever find our volcano, let alone climb it! And Jorge – patient, phlegmatic Jorge – who, I am sure, never ceased to be amazed by Sebastian and myself, did most of the cooking and somehow kept our porters going.

That evening, we stopped on the crest of an overgrown ridge; higher than the previous night's camp, it was also considerably colder. We had now issued all our spare clothing to the porters, but by this time everything was soaked and they had the greatest difficulty even in lighting a fire, the brushwood was so wet and rotten. Next morning, we were confronted with mutiny – Don Albino was the spokesman.

'The men are frightened and very cold,' he told Jorge. 'They want to go home. If we stay here any longer we shall all die.'

With promises of bonuses, Jorge persuaded them to stay for three more days at this camp, where they could, at least, find some firewood, help us to carry the tent to a high camp and then wait for us to return.

Reluctantly, Don Albino agreed and three of the youngest and fittest of our porters shouldered loads to help carry the gear to a point where we could, at least, see the volcano. The vegetation had now changed to a form of giant and leprous weed of huge umbrella-like leaves on soft fleshy stalks. It made me feel like a pygmy in a science-fiction film, and I half expected to be confronted, at any moment, with a giant sixty-foot high spider or a mammoth ant. We could have been on a set for Conan Doyle's Lost World – and it continued to rain as though it would never stop.

Our progress was slightly faster than the previous day; by dusk, we had emerged from the forest of Sachapalma, and had reached the grass-line – great tussocks of coarse, man-high grass, which were almost as impenetrable as barbed-wire entanglements. With some way still to go, it was obvious that we were going to need a higher camp. I persuaded Gabriel, the strongest of our porters, to stay with us. This meant cramming four into our two-man tent, while the other two returned to await our descent.

Just as dusk fell, all our efforts were rewarded. The clouds suddenly unrolled, and we were able to see Sangay, squat, foreshortened, towering over us. Even as we gazed, there was a dull, heavy rumble, accompanied by a great mushroom of ochre-brown smoke which welled up from near the summit. There was no glow, no pyrotechnics, just boiling, expanding cloud that was somehow more menacing than any amount of molten lava.

We settled down for a damp and very cramped night. The bottom of the tent was full of puddles and a strong sense of survival was needed to avoid getting one's sleeping bag soaked. I wriggled and manoeuvred throughout the night, in order to remain dry, while Sebastian, the eternal stoic, lay still and silent, in the middle of a large puddle.

I suspect I was the only one to appreciate fully how serious our position could become. We now had no more than two days' stock of food, and although we were only thirty-five miles from Macas, that thirty-five miles had already taken a week to cover. More to the point, if anything should happen to us, there was no one in Macas who could, or, for that matter would, come to our aid. In the flat light of dawn, I could gaze back over our path. It was just possible to discern the swathe in the forest, cut by the River Upano, but apart from that there was a matt carpet of dull green stretching to the far horizon. Above us was the volcano, with featureless lava rubble stretching up into an even ceiling of cloud. Suddenly, I realised how easily we could get lost. It had taken three days to cut our way through the upper jungle to reach this point. If we missed this narrow thread of a path on the way back down, we should have very little chance of cutting our way back to the Rio Volcan. We were on our own, and the responsibility for the party was mine.

But we needed to get closer to the base of the volcano, and so, leaving a trail of wands marked with some torn-up red flag, we waded through the chest-high grass, towards the top of the grass line. Now we were faced with another problem. There was no running water and all the liquid we had was the contents of a single water bottle. That night we camped immediately below a ridge of lava that stretched smoothly up towards the brow of the skyline. There could be no question of awaiting the perfect weather. We had no food or water, and there was some element of doubt as to whether our porters in the camp below would wait for us. I was not sure how high we were, but guessed our altitude to be about 10,000 feet – still 7,000 feet below the summit, a long climb by any standards.

That night I was on edge, hardly slept and, at midnight, poked my head out of the tent to see a sky, velvet black, studded with stars.

'Come on Sebastian, wake up; it's a perfect night.'

He groaned and rolled over. Even so, I got the primus lit, boiled the half-panful of water, which was all we had, made some coffee, and thrust it into his hand. Jorge was still dead to the world.

Not wanting to waste any more time, I ordered Sebastian to get ready as quickly as possible. I got dressed and started out, up the lava slope, where I could see deep patches of cloud silhouetted against the glitter of the stars. I aimed to get to the summit by dawn, hoping to get those precious photographs of our objective.

The angle was easy, about 20 degrees, but the surface was covered with a thin layer of lava pebbles, which skidded underfoot on a compact base of lava mud. Even so, with a focused drive to reach the top, I just plodded on through the dark, occasionally flashing my torch to get an idea of my immediate surroundings. And then the lava changed almost imperceptibly to ice – it was dusted with lava dirt, embedded with lava bombs, but it was ice nevertheless.

Just as I reached the start of the ice, the stars blurred and then vanished – the mountain was, once more, engulfed in cloud. There were no features – no way for the others to follow my trail. I began worrying about them and cursed myself for being so impatient in leaving them behind. I sat down to wait for them until an hour had gone and there was still no sign of them. Where the bloody hell can they be – what do they think they're doing?

I plunged back down in a towering rage; I had lost about 2,000 feet in height when I saw three shadowy figures emerging from the mist and gloom of the dawn.

'Where the bloody hell have you been?' I asked.

'I'm frightfully sorry, Chris – all my fault,' said Sebastian. 'I'm afraid I forgot the rope and had to go back for it. We were only ten minutes or so behind you when we started, but we'd been gone for an hour before I noticed it. Don't worry, I went all the way back for it.'

'You've wasted three bloody hours in doing so. Anyway, what's Gabriel doing with you?'

'I thought he'd like to come to have a look at the crater as well.'

'God almighty, do you think we're on a bloody holiday jaunt? There's some steep ice up there. Jorge, can you explain to him that it's too difficult for him and that he'll need crampons?'

Gabriel, looking a little relieved, turned back and I drove the rest of my team up the lava slope. It was like going up a giant slag-heap, and in the swirling mist it could have been somewhere in the smog of a South Wales coalfield. Then we came to the ice – time to put on crampons. Jorge and I had put ours on, but when I glanced over to Sebastian – he was trying to put them on back to front!

'I really am most frightfully sorry,' he said. 'I've never worn these things before.'

I strapped them to his feet, tied a loop in the middle of the rope and dropped it over his head, to attach to his waist. Jorge quietly tied on to the other end and we set out once again. The slope was not steep, but had anyone slipped it would have been impossible to stop, since the ice was too hard for the pick of an axe to act as a brake.

'I'm terribly sorry, Chris,' Sebastian was always very apologetic. 'I can't see a thing. My glasses are misted up.'

'Can't you take them off?'

'Well, no; that's even worse – blind as a bat without them.'

'Just follow the rope then – I'll tell you if there's anything to watch out for.'

At that point we reached a gaping crevasse, guarded by a superb portcullis of icicles. A narrow ice bridge led over it, and Sebastian felt his way across, tapping his axe to either side, as if he were a blind man. I began to feel a little like a guide-dog, as I sniffed my way up the slope, tugging at the leash, impatient to reach the top.

There seemed no end to it. We could have been in one of the circles of hell, destined to eke out eternity plodding ever upwards. The entire adventure had an unreal quality unlike any climb I had ever undertaken. The risk was there; I was a good deal more frightened than I had ever been on the fixed ropes of the Eiger Direct, but my fears were intangible, almost superstitious. I half expected the entire mountain to explode suddenly beneath my feet. And the lava bombs were real enough. It was like being at the end of a long skittle alley, as lumps of rock, some the size of a small table, came bounding from out of the mists, bouncing and ricocheting down the slope past us to disappear once again. You could almost imagine a group of old Inca gods swinging their bowls at us from somewhere near the top. There was no sound, no interruption – just the ting and clatter of the boulders bouncing past.

As we climbed higher we were able to guess their origin. We passed through a museum of lava bombs, hurled from the crater during former eruptions and now, each one isolated on its own icy plinth, raised in monument by the action of the sun melting the ice around each separate boulder. And then the ice beneath the rock had melted and down the monument had fallen, to roll and rattle to the foot of one of the highest slag heaps in the world.

A chill wind, just above freezing-point, was blowing thin sleet across the slope, but suddenly a warm blast of air, slightly sulphurous, mingled with the wind. Underfoot the ice vanished, to give way to a fine brown powder, hot to the touch. We could not see anything, but there was a smell of sulphur everywhere – a smell which tortured the back of the throat and sent us into paroxysms of coughing. The slope dropped away to our right, and we were struck by the heat, like the blast from the opened door of a furnace. We peered into the mist – but what was mist, and what was smoke? We couldn't tell. There was a hiss at our feet, and little wisps of steam jetted from a crevice stained green and yellow by the sulphurous fumes of the fumarole. We stumbled on.

Sebastian pointed up the slope, to where it seemed to rise in some kind of crest.

'Follow me,' he gasped. 'We must place the Union Jack on the summit.'

Although we had no Union Jack, we followed him dutifully. On taking a few uncertain steps, he collapsed, overcome by the fumes. I grabbed him and, with Jorge to help, dragged him back down the slope. Fortunately, after a couple of minutes, he regained consciousness and we were all able to stagger back the way we had come. The heads of our ice axes were stained a dull yellow-green, and I couldn't help wondering what effect the fumes had had on our lungs.

I trailed back down to the camp in the woods with mixed feelings – relief at getting away from this strange, unpredictable living beast of a mountain, but nevertheless filled with a sense of failure. My mission had been to get pictures – gaudy, lurid pictures of pluming red, hot lava fountains, and firework displays in the black night sky – but all I had managed to get were a few shots of Sebastian in the mist, looking like a bedraggled Outward Bound schoolboy in the mists of Wales or the Lakes. I found it impossible to transmit on to film the feeling of uncontrollable, unpredictable power that the heat, and the hiss of the fumes and the swirling clouds had imparted to all three of us. I could not reproduce my own fears. I did not even know what I had on film. I had just clicked the shutter release of the camera, in the midst of the grey gloom, uncomfortably aware of the all-pervasive grit and water which covered not only the lens, but also my hands and clothes.

I should have liked to have returned to the summit – to have sat it out until at last we had a fine, sunny day – but having no food, and with porters who could be held from flight no longer, we had no choice but to retreat.

15 Sangay from the West

Our adventures on Sangay were far from over. That night we got back to the camp in the woods, where our long-suffering but faithful porters were awaiting us. The following day we dropped back into the bottom of the gorge of the Volcan river, but by now it had rained almost non-stop for a week, and the entire bed of the gorge was filled with boiling brown waters.

'We'll have to wait for it to subside a bit and then make a dash for it,' I decided.

'But what if the rains don't let up?' asked Sebastian. 'I've known them to go on for weeks at a time.'

'Well, we'll then have to cut our way out, along the top of the gorge.'

'If we don't make it, I suppose we could always make a second Fawcett story,' said Sebastian. 'Do you think John Anstey'd send anyone out to find our bones? I'll keep a diary to the very end, with a last, loving message to Laetitia and the children.'

We sat it out, on a lava sprit at the end of the gorge, for another day. On the second morning, the level seemed to have dropped a little and we made a hurried descent of the gorge, fording a couple of torrents which had been little more than trickles on the way up. In the process, we very nearly lost Don Albino, who, frail as he was, let go of the rope I had taken across the torrent, and was on the point of being swept away into the main stream when Sebastian, with great presence of mind, and considerable courage, dived in and saved him. The Indians, indifferent to death, just looked on and, I suspect, would have let him drown.

This proved altogether too much for Don Albino, who sat down and told Jorge that he would go no further – we could leave him where he was and once he had rested he would continue the journey. I felt it impossible to abandon him, and ended up by carrying him, piggy-back fashion, down the river bank. He was little more than a skeleton held together by a few sinews and a bit of skin. At first he seemed to weigh nothing, but as the miles crept by, his weight increased, and at the end of the day I felt exhausted.

We had now reached the end of the Rio Volcan, where it joined the Upano. The gods were undoubtedly mocking us, for the weather had cleared, rewarding us with our first cloudless day since leaving Macas. Sangay, conical, serene, eternal, lay just ten miles up the valley down which we had fled the previous day. There was no question of returning, however, as we had to get more food before we could tackle the volcano once more. But determined to tackle it I was – I put it to Sebastian:

'Look, I know you've got a superb story – the trouble is, I haven't any pictures to back it up. My whole future depends on this story. Will you come back with me?'

'But how can you guarantee it won't be just the same, all over again?'

'There's no need to go in from this side again. We'll go in from the other side, where it should be a hell of a sight easier. If we take more food, we can sit it out until we get a good day. Do you mind?'

'My dear Christian, all I ask is a single hot bath in Quito, and I'll go to the ends of the earth to help you get your pictures.'

Sebastian, although a master of superlatives, really meant what he said, and so we trekked all the way back to Macas. On the last night, before reaching the town, we went to bed at dusk, as was our usual custom. We were told the next day that we had slept through the most spectacular eruption of Sangay in living memory. Had I only been awake, I could have photographed the perfect volcano firework display. Everything about Sangay seemed ill-fated.

We flew back to Quito, where we spent a week collecting food, sending for some money, and living it up in the aseptic luxury of the Intercontinental Hotel. There were letters from Wendy, full of love and her own adventures in the Lake District. She was, at last, beginning to gain confidence in her folk-singing – had sung at a folk festival and was full of plans for the future. I longed to get home to her, and dreaded the thought of going on to Peru to join the expedition to Alpamayo. I had had enough of adventure for the time being, and had become a homing bird. But first, I had to get my pictures on Sangay. From the west, it would be as if approaching a different mountain, on a different continent, for we would approach it from the High Andean Plateau: no jungle, no slimy forests of Sachapalma, just shoulder-high grass, spread over a switchback of sharp, knife-edge ridges, that guarded Sangay with an intricate network of ramparts, as if it were the citadel of an eighteenth-century fortress.

The road-head was at a hacienda called Alloa, set in an upland grassy valley which could have known little change in the past 300 years. One man owned the entire valley, and though theoretically the feudal system (with the Indians being treated as serfs) had been abolished, in practice the system remained. If the Indians wanted to stay in the valley, they had to work for the landowner on his terms – and these seemed fairly harsh. The homes of the Indians, resembling mouldering haystacks, were huts made from bunched grass, without windows, doors or chimneys. Each had a small patch of land for his own crops, and much of his pay was in kind – food and grain. For escape, he could go to the cities, but found little prospect of work, and a life which could be even harsher. At least on the hacienda some measure of security was provided, and the hardship of the life was made bearable by alcohol.

We arrived at the Hacienda Alloa on the second day of one of the many religious feasts which grace the Ecuadorian calendar. In the morning all the peasants went to church – a dark, windowless barn of a place, with none of the gold and glittering ornaments of the churches of Quito – just a stark wooden cross on a battered old table. But the room was packed to bursting, with an overflow standing around the threshold and the walls outside. There was a constant babble of voices, cries of children, as the priest celebrated Mass. At the end of the service they held a procession in two long parallel columns round the field immediately outside the church. One of these columns was formed by the major domo of the hacienda leading the menfolk, whilst his wife led the women in the other. There was something infinitely sad in the stoic, melancholy cast of their features, all of which seemed weakened and debauched by a life of hardship relieved only by alcohol and drugs.

At the end of the procession they all flocked to the village tavern, a bare mud hut and compound, which was soon packed with Indians – men, women and even children, all of whom proceeded to get more drunk than I have ever seen anyone before or since. The scene was Hogarthian – with a soldier lying flat in the gutter, blind to the world, his rifle beside him – a man offering his wife or lover a draught from his half-full bottle of Aqua Diente, in the middle of the street – a mother giving her eighteen-month babe a slug of the fire-water, to stop it crying.

The binge lasted three days, during which time I had no choice but to wait patiently until the porters we had been promised had recovered from their hangovers. When, eventually, they did, we set off on our journey, the first leg on horseback to an outlying ranch about fifteen miles from the foot of the mountain, followed by two days' march through the long, near-impenetrable grass, to the base of the volcano.

Away from the bottle, our porters proved wonderfully reliable – much stronger and more self-sufficient than our brave little bunch of lads from Macas, who were so much out of their element once in virgin forest. These men had spent their childhood and working lives wandering the sierra, in search of game or stray cattle. Dressed for the part, with broad, heavy felt hats, thick woollen ponchos and well-made boots, they knew how to make effective shelters by cutting the long grass and building little thatched huts – mini-replicas of their own hovels by the hacienda. They never complained of the incessant rain, nor of the heavy loads, nor the hard going through the pathless maze of grass-clad ridges.

Reaching the base of the volcano on the third day, we waited there for another couple of days, and then moved a camp up the side of the mountain, to an altitude of about 15,000 feet, on a shoulder immediately opposite a lava run.

It was a strange, rather frightening place. By day the lava blocks, which were pushed down the slope by the remorseless power of the volcano, looked like dull, black coke. But at night these glowed a rich cherry red as they rattled and rumbled down the slope. Every few hours there was an eruption from the main crater. We could not see anything, for the entire summit was wrapped in cloud. We could, however, feel the mountain tremble beneath us, and it was all too easy to imagine a great river of molten lava, poised somewhere out of sight, above us in the clouds, ready to sweep down and envelop us.

We had some trouble persuading the Indians to help carry our tent so high on the volcano, and when they left us there, they had shaken our hands with a fervour which seemed to imply that this was the last time they ever expected to see us. Having lived in the shadow of Sangay all their lives, they had a healthy and perhaps superstitious respect for the mountain. In the two nights and days that Sebastian and I spent high on its flanks, we began to share both their fears and their respect.

And then, at last, I had one clear day. I raced to the summit, tailed by Sebastian, and took my pictures, which had a peculiarly anticlimactic quality. Although the crater was vast, it was filled with a dense steam and you could see nothing – you could only hear a steady hiss from its depth – a hiss which, to my untutored ears, sounded exceptionally sinister. I spent an hour on the brink of that crater, hoping for a clearance – even half-hoping for an eruption – to get some truly spectacular photographs, yet at the same time fearful of my own prospects of survival in such an event.

An hour went by. Nothing happened, and with a sense of relief, feeling I had done my duty, I fled down the slope, back to our camp. Our Indians welcomed us as if we had returned from the halls of the dead, but still I wasn't happy. I was worried in case I had not succeeded in getting sufficiently dramatic photographs of the volcano. Paradoxically, on the day of our return to its base, the weather once again cleared into a series of perfect, cloudless days, when even the interior of the crater seemed free from steam. I had just persuaded Sebastian – ever loyal and patient – to return with me to the summit for yet another attempt to get the perfect definitive picture of a volcano. We were to go up first thing in the morning, and I was sorting out my gear for what would be our third ascent of the mountain, when an Indian came running into the camp.

The moment I saw him I knew there was something terribly wrong. He had a message addressed to me. I dreaded opening it – fearing something might have happened to Wendy. I had an instant, appalling sense of relief that it was not Wendy – although it was Conrad. He had been killed in an accident. It was like a physical blow, instantaneous, believable and real – dreadful in its finality. I collapsed on to the ground and cried, with the Indians standing silent, sympathetic around me. Sebastian, holding my shoulder, gave me all the sympathy and strength that he could.

I did my best to pull myself together, knowing that I had to get home without delay. The accident had occurred over a week before, and the fact that I learned of the tragedy as soon as I did was entirely due to an old climbing friend, Simon Clark, who was now working in Ecuador. We had met in Quito on our way out, and later he had seen a mention of the accident in *The Times*. *The Daily Telegraph* had already cabled to the British Embassy, but there was no way in which they could get the news to me, since they had only a vague idea of our whereabouts. Simon knew even less than them, but immediately made inquiries about our route into Sangay. He drove to the Hacienda Alloa, and would have carried the message in person but for the fact that he had vital business commitments. He sent an Indian with a note to tell me of the tragedy, and I shall always be grateful to him for his efforts. He left a Land Rover with a driver to take me to Quito, and this must have saved Wendy from several days' unmitigated hell in our loss, compounded as it was by my own absence on the other side of the earth.

I started back that afternoon, knowing that I could not sleep until I reached home. Our Indians, whose own lives are full of death, held a silent compassion that I shall never forget. We walked through the dusk, and as night fell I looked back at Sangay, that dark conical silhouette, against a star-encrusted sky – a flaming red snake of molten lava coiling down its slopes. Even in my grief I was aware of the intense beauty and peace of the scene. I walked and walked, drugged by fatigue, yet telling myself over and over again that I should never feel and see Conrad again.

They had horses waiting for us at the outlying station and we rode on through the night, over the hairpin path which led to Alloa, reaching it at dawn. I shook hands with the Indians – their leader, a fine, grizzled old man, crying as he waved his farewell – and we drove on through the dusty little town of Riobamba, past Cotopaxi, snow-capped, conical and pink in the early morning sun, and into Quito. There, I was taken to some friends of Simon who were infinitely kind, and we held to that tight brittle edge of small talk that enables one to keep grief private. Then the plane to New York; long hours of waiting for the connection, longing for Wendy, keeping going till we could hold each other close, worrying about whether she was all right. And Heathrow, Immigration, baggage collection, Customs, then Wendy broke through and we just clung and clung together, isolated from the world in the totality of our grief and love for each other.

Wendy had been staying with Mary Stewart, and Conrad had gone playing with Mary's four children. At the bottom of the field abutting the garden was a stream. Normally it was little more than a trickle, but there had been a cloudburst. Conrad, ever independent and adventurous, had strayed from the others and must have fallen into the swollen waters. Wendy herself had found him. It was one of those one-in-a-million chances that you can never guard against. Mary's and countless other children had played by the banks of the stream all their lives, and then, for some unknown reason, by some chance, this had happened.

Now we have two fine children, and time, and the love of our children, has eased our grief, but it will always be with us in a closed quarter of our minds. There will always be the nagging questions; the asking of what Conrad might have done with his life – how he would have developed. He had a rare quality of gentleness tempered with intrepid independence. His was a happy, intense little life, lasting only two-and-a-half years, without any of the sorrows and disillusion that inevitably accompany the joys and challenges of a life which is allowed to follow its complete course.

Wendy had endured a hell that I could never know; for the fact that the news was a week old, that the accident had occurred so far away, meant that I had known only thirty-six hours of solitary grief compared with the long days of Wendy's suffering. Her parents and a host of wonderful friends had been a tower of strength to her, but neither of us felt whole without the other. Together we could admit our sorrow and Wendy was able to release, slowly, some part of the pain of our loss.

16   The Old Man of Hoy

'Life goes on' is an over-used, but very true, cliché. Even in the depth of our grief, Wendy and I knew a joy in each other. Desperately, we wanted and needed another child. Wendy quickly became pregnant again and was due to give birth in the early spring of 1968. Various assignments and climbs followed, some close on the heels of our tragedy and my own return from Ecuador.

Some weeks after my return, Tom Patey, always compassionate, phoned to tempt Wendy and me up to the Isle of Hoy in the Orkneys. He made a climb the excuse, but I suspect that as much as anything he intended to get us away from our immediate environment. The bait was the Old May of Hoy. 'The finest rock pinnacle in the British Isles,' Tom assured me. 'It's 300 feet high, as slender as Nelson's Column, sheer on every side, and unclimbed. It'd make a great story.' I couldn't resist it, though Wendy decided she would rather stay in Haywards Heath with her parents for the few days I hoped the climb would take.

I caught the sleeper up to Inverness, where Tom met me at the station for the drive to Thurso in the far north of Scotland. It is a wonderful drive, up the eastern seaboard of the Highlands and then over the bleak heathered flats of Caithness, with thunder clouds like Spanish galleons sailing over-head, the hills of Ben Klibreck and even Ben Hope in the far west, etched clear in rain-washed air. Tom was full of legends of the Old May of Hoy — of obscure scandals he was happy to offer my journalistic pen, gathered from some of the colourful characters who lived in self-imposed exile amongst the Western Isles.

The remainder of the team were awaiting us at Thurso: Rusty Baillie, his wife Pat, their baby, a dog and an impressive pile of ropes and ironmongery. Rusty was to be the technical expert, I the photographer and Tom the stage manager of our venture.

In order to reach Hoy, I had to survive a sea-sick voyage to Stromness, well described as the Venice of the North, followed by a shorter, less painful trip in a specially chartered fishing boat to Hoy. A bumpy journey in one of the island's few cars (and only taxi) then took us to Rackwick Bay, where a collection of single-storeyed crofts clung to a wind-swept shore. The Old Man of Hoy was the other side of the hill that rose in an easy sweep from behind the youth hostel, the former school-house of the dying community. Setting out to view our objective that same evening, we walked over the short, springy turf,

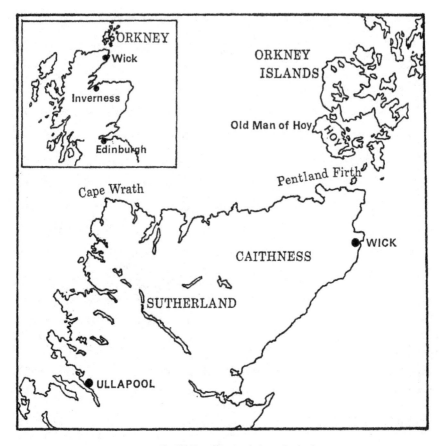

The Old Man of Hoy in relation to Scotland

while skuas wheeled and dived over us, their great wings and hooked beaks posing a tangible threat.

We came to a bluff, and there in front of us was the top of the Old Man of Hoy, truncated by the cliff top. It was square-cut, obviously slender, and yet gave little idea of just how tall it was until we reached the brow of the cliff, and could look down and across at the most remarkable monolith and summit in the British Isles. It could have been a fairy-tale tower, 450-feet high, with a grassy top that seemed little larger than a billiard-table.

'Looks bloody loose to me,' I commented. 'That sandstone'll just crumble away as you climb it. The whole issue could come toppling down.'

'Och, no. Where's your spirit of adventure? Those are no words from Bonington of the Eiger,' replied Tom. 'I can see I'll have to start amending some of the verses in your song.'

'That crack should go,' said Rusty, ever practical. 'Just the right size for bongs.'

We returned to the youth hostel, where Pat had already prepared the supper, and settled down to a long night of Patey songs, accompanied by malt whisky.

It was eleven the next morning before we were ready to set out, and we scrambled down to the foot of the Old Man. We saw that it was linked to the island by a neck of piled boulders, probably a natural arch which had collapsed hundreds or thousands of years earlier. From its base, the Old Man was slightly daunting, and had, undoubtedly, reached a stage of advanced senile decay. Indeed, it was difficult to understand how it had succeeded in standing against the buffeting of the storms of the Pentland Firth all these years. To the seaward side, a series of pendulous folds of wafer-like sandstone overlapped each other, like a whole series of double chins. No hope there. The landward side offered more scope – here, there was a series of steps leading up to a small ledge, and Tom started up this. Climbing solo, as was his wont, he got to about twenty feet above the ground, and in pulling up on to a seemingly sound step, pulled out a shelf-sized block. He retired to the ground and we made another perambulation round the Old Man – no one keen to commit himself to any one line. I had defined my own position very firmly, having cast myself as the photographer – a role reinforced by the battery of cameras I had slung round my neck.

We returned to the landward side of the Old Man.

'I think you should go up there,' I suggested. 'It's the only place where you can get started; and I can get some good pictures from the side. It'll look fantastic!'

Tom, this time armed with a rope, returned to the fray, stepping cautiously up the rickety staircase that led to a platform about eighty feet up. Beyond this, the line seemed to peter out. To the right, facing into land, the pillar leaned into a steady overhang, jutting out at least twenty feet from the wave-washed base. On the seaward side of the corner, the rock was sheer, featureless and repulsively yellow, a sure sign of bad rock. The only hope seemed to be a crack that probed through the overhangs.

'That's the line,' Rusty announced firmly, as he arranged himself in iron-mongery, bing-bongs, and all the other appendages of the modern technical climber. Patey regarded these preparations with a philosophical patience, whilst I hovered around, changing lenses and trying out different angles. At last, Rusty, ape-like with his long, strongly muscled arms and crinkly ginger hair, swung on to the platform and lowered himself round the corner to get into the overhanging crack. I retired to the cliff side opposite to take pictures, and Tom smoked endless cigarettes, or searched through his rucksack in search of sustenance, preparatory to the long wait.

Tom had little faith in ropes, and no enthusiasm at all for rope management, being a great believer in the old school of climbing which laid down a maxim that the leader should not fall. He relaxed, therefore, noting Rusty's slow progress and the frequent tap of his peg-hammer, which indicated that he was using artificial aids and was, as a result, most unlikely to fall. They had no verbal communication because of the crash of the sea and were out of sight of each other. From my own perch on the side of the cliff, I had a seagull's-eye view of both climbers – Rusty spread-eagled over the crack, Tom dreaming in the sun – each in his own little world. The crack was overhanging, its side covered in a fine grit that was like a million ball-bearings. Rusty, emboldened by a slight easing of the angle, and a few rounded holds, moved up without the security of a piton. A foot-hold crumbled, his feet skidded off the rock, his fingers slipped on the powdery surface of the holds and he was left jammed solely by his shoulders in the chimney. Down below, happily oblivious of the drama round the corner, Tom was lighting up a cigarette. Rusty slid back to his last piton, secured the rope and abseiled back down.

The following morning we returned to the fray, thrusting Rusty into the battle once more, so that Tom could day-dream on the belay ledge and I could take my pictures. Rusty took six hours to lead the pitch, clearing away the loose sand, hammering in his bongs, till at last he was standing on a small ledge just above the overhanging chimney. It was time for action – I was going to have to do some climbing.

I scrambled down the cliff front, to the foot of the stack.

'You don't need a rope,' Tom shouted over the crash of the breaking seas. 'This first pitch is a piece of duff.'

I started up. It was the first time I had actually done any rock climbing since I had been on the Eiger Direct – months before, in the winter. Although it was easy, I was frightened of the looseness of the rock, of the seas smashing into the base of the stack to one side, of the hard ground below. Poking my head over a flat step, I suddenly confronted a small, very indignant fulmar chick – a little bundle of down with a yellow beak. It squawked a couple of times and then, with unnerving accuracy, ejected from its mouth a gob of foul, slimy sick, that landed squarely between my eyes. The shock very nearly toppled me over, and I cursed the chick for its insolence yet somehow, at the same time, feeling a certain respect for its courage. I stepped carefully over it to reach Tom sitting on his perch. He was sharing it with another fulmar chick, but was astute enough to position himself just out of range of the gobs of vomit which the angry little bird ejected at him at regular intervals. The mother bird swooped and dived, just out of range, indignant at this invasion of her privacy.

'You might as well get all the pegs out,' said Tom. 'You're the expert in technical climbing, and I'm sure you'd do it a lot quicker than I would.'

'Wish I could,' I replied; 'but remember I've got to get the pictures. I'll jumar up, just above you, and photograph you as you climb up, and take all the pegs. It'll look fantastic. Just think of it – you'll be immortalised.'

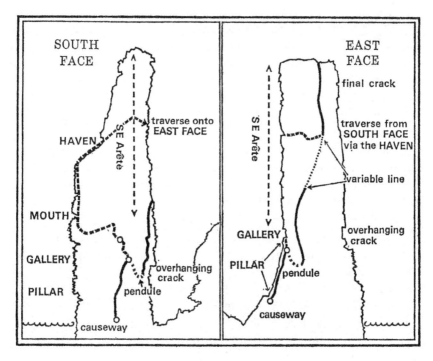

The Old Man of Hoy: routes

And so Tom, grumbling, followed up behind Rusty, while I swung out on the rope Rusty had dropped from above, and jumared up past him, photographing his struggles with étrier, pitons and rope. Tom's forte was fast, free climbing with the very minimum of clutter of modern aids. He was totally unmechanical, delightfully unmethodical, and could guarantee getting any rope system into an inextricable tangle. Two sweating and cursing hours later we were all on a small ledge about 150 feet above sea level. But the day was already nearly spent.

'We could bivouac,' suggested Rusty. 'It's only a few hours of darkness.'

'I don't mind – what do you think, Tom?'

'You must be mad – a hundred and fifty feet off the deck, with a good bed and a bottle of whisky half an hour's walk away! I'm off down. I'll happily give you a call in the morning.'

The flesh is weak, and the determination of Rusty and myself quickly waned at the prospect of spending a night sitting on a small ledge while Tom was back in his bed. We all retreated to Rackwick Bay, returning to the third day of our siege next morning. The climbing was taking longer than the North Wall of the Eiger!

We made an early start and it was now agreed that Tom should take over the lead, since the next section was peculiarly suited to his special talents. The angle had eased slightly to less than vertical, but the rock had softened to a consistency that was little firmer than hardened mud. There were no cracks for pitons, something that didn't really matter, since Tom could rarely be bothered to use them, and the rock was covered in a light mould. He swarmed up with reassuring speed, and a mere two hours later we were all assembled below the final pitch to the top – a splendid clear-cut open corner.

'It's my turn to have a lead,' I stated firmly, and started up. In some ways it was both the pleasantest and the easiest pitch on the entire climb. The rock had suddenly become firm and reassuring to the touch, there were big holds, and in a matter of minutes I was standing on the top of the Old Man of Hoy. We raised a cairn on the summit, lit a bonfire, and then waved to the solitary spectator standing on the cliff top opposite.

It had been an idyllic three days, far removed from the normal British climbing scene, yet having its own peculiar charm. The climb had given all the satisfaction of having reached a virgin summit as spectacular as any of the Chamonix Aiguilles.

A year later we returned, in very different circumstances, to take part in the BBC live broadcast of a multiple ascent of the Old Man. It was to be by far their most ambitious venture in this field, involving six climbers making three different routes up the Old Man. Two climbing camera-teams were used, and tons of equipment, and gantries had to be erected on the cliffs opposite, and even on the stack itself.

It was like a military operation, with an army assault craft carrying all the gear, together with a large tractor, into Rackwick Bay, whilst a platoon of the Scots Guards coped with the catering and the shifting of the gear. This was the advance guard for a whole host of BBC personnel to put on the climbing spectacular.

Joe Brown and Ian McNaught-Davis were to make a new route on the South Face of the Old Man, while Peter Crew and Dougal Haston, representatives of the new generation of technical climbers, were going to hammer their way up the South-East Arête. Tom Patey and I, the traditionalists, were to repeat our original route. We were to be the one sure factor in the proceedings, since the others were to attempt new routes on sight and, as a result, their speed of progress or even their success, could not be guaranteed.

The invasion of Hoy took place about ten days before the broadcast, but the BBC, ever careful of their budget, did not want more of the stars around than was absolutely necessary, and so Ian McNaught-Davis, Tom Patey and I were due to arrive only a few days before the transmission. In the meantime, we decided to snatch a couple of days' climbing in the North-West Highlands, near Tom's home, before joining the big circus. We could be sure of an interesting time with the Patey. Mac picked me up at Carlisle on a Friday evening, and we drove through the night to Ullapool, Patey's eyrie, where Tom ran one of the biggest medical practices, in terms of area-cover, in the whole of Britain. We arrived there, bleary-eyed, in time for breakfast, and Tom was already full of plans – almost before we had managed to get across the threshold.

'I thought we might polish off the Stack of Handa,' Tom suggested. 'It's not as spectacular as the Old Man of Hoy, but no one's actually climbed it, though I've heard that an intrepid egg collector managed to get there at the beginning of the century by having a rope trailed across the top.'

Having eaten a leisurely breakfast, we drove to Tarbet, a tiny hamlet that nestles at the bottom of a valley cradled between craggy, heather-clad hills. The far western seaboard of North-West Scotland has a special, wild beauty of its own. The mountains are isolated and very, very ancient in geological terms, well worn and hoary, standing in their solitude like hermits who have sought the wilderness. Tarbet was a row of little two-storeyed houses at the end of a narrow, single-track road, ending in the sea with a single jetty. It was a sheltered spot, guarded to landward by the low hills, and to the seaward side by the rolling bulk of Handa Island, which was uninhabited and preserved as a bird sanctuary.

'The stack's the other side,' Tom told us. 'We'll get out there by boat.' We called on Donald MacLeod, the Handa boatman responsible for taking parties of bird watchers out to the island. The bulk of his income, however, came from lobster fishing in the treacherous seas around Handa. Tragically, only two years later, he and his son, Christopher, were to be lost at sea, one wild, wintry day.

'Och, Christopher'll take you out to Handa,' he told us. 'You'll be wanting to climb the stack, will you? I don't think you'll be doing that – it's sheer on every side, and there's nowhere to land.'

But Tom was not a man to be put off by any warning. We embarked in the MacLeod's boat, a solidly built rowing boat, powered by an outboard motor. Even so, it seemed very puny for anyone to think of using it to venture out on the open sea in the winter storms. As we chugged round the point of land which sheltered Tarbet, even on this comparatively calm day, the boat quickly began bucking in the swell which perpetually sweeps down through the Minch.

On we sailed, around the Isle of Handa, past the teeth of reefs marked white by the swirl of the seas, and on which sat a host of gulls, which took off, plummeting and diving as we passed them. The cliffs began to build in height: sheer, dark sandstone, dropping straight into the sea, every ledge stained white from the excreta of the thousands of gulls which made Handa their home. And then – the stack itself; at first it seemed to merge with the cliffs of the main island, for it was very unlike the Old Man of Hoy. This was no shapely obelisk, but a massive keep, standing clean-cut from the sea, filling a small bay formed by the line of the main cliffs. It might have been part of the island itself, but on closer inspection, you could see that there was a gash between island and stack, a narrow passage-way filled with foaming seas and flanked by sheer cliffs. At its bottom it was around twenty feet wide.

'Do you want to go through the gap?' asked Christopher.

I would have declined, happily. I have always been nervous of the sea, but the Patey was made of sterner stuff. Aye, let's have a look; we might be able to find somewhere to get a footing on the thing.'

And so we swung through the gorge, white waters swirling to either side, and the walls black, dripping with water, stained with white streaks, stretching up, threatening, and obviously unassailable.

We cruised round the stack, trying to find a chink in its defences. The gulls seemed to pose the greatest problem. Even if we managed to make a landing, every ledge, every possible hold, was filled with slippery, stinking excreta.

'You'll never get up that,' I pronounced.

'Ah, but you'll never achieve anything if you don't have a try,' replied Patey, the true pioneer. 'Do you think you could land us on that little ledge over there?'

'I'll have a go,' said Christopher, as game and adventurous in his own medium – the sea – as we could ever be on the rocks.

We edged our way into the base of the stack, rocking crazily as we came in close. Patey took a prodigious leap on to a seaweed-covered rock, scrabbled in the weed with the waves lapping at his feet, and then pulled up on to a narrow ledge, just above the water-line. A fulmar ejected a stream of vomit at him, a dozen others went into the attack, but Patey was not to be deterred.

'Come on across – it's great over here, I think there might be a line we could get up just over to the right.'

I'm afraid Mac and I were made from a weaker mould, and so declined the invitation. Tom returned to the boat, but certainly was not prepared to admit defeat.

'If we can't climb it, we'd better try putting a rope across it,' he suggested, and we were duly landed on the island to walk over the close-cropped, springy turf, to the top of the cliff overlooking the stack of Handa. Soon we had three 150-foot ropes tied together, and by taking either end and dragging them on along the cliffs flanking the stack, we were able to drape them over its flat summit. Anchoring the rope to a couple of large boulders, we were all set to go or, to be more accurate, we were all set for Tom to go – for Mac and I had already made our own personal decisions that under no circumstances were we prepared to trust ourselves to such a dubious lifeline. The stack is about 200 feet high, and the gap between it and the cliff-top, over which we had draped the rope, was at least fifty feet. It was all set for the perfect Tyrolean traverse, as Tom launched forth, clipped on to the rope with a karabiner, with a jumar clamp to use as a handle in order to pull himself across. Inevitably, he got the ropes into a tangle, and by the time he reached the mid-point, he had tied himself into a nearly inextricable knot.

'Are you going to stay there all night, Tom?'

'We'll come back for you after the broadcast, if you like.'

Tom muttered and cursed, eventually disentangled himself on his high trapeze and slowly pulled himself across to the stack of Handa, to become the second man ever to stand on its summit. One couldn't help wondering how that fisherman of former times had reached this point – had he used a thick old hawser; had he just pulled himself across hand over hand?

Tom let out a yodel on the summit and tried to entice us across – alas, to no avail – and then he returned to solid land. So ended a delightful little adventure – one of the hundred I had with Tom. There was always that light-hearted, carefree quality about anything you did with Tom – however serious the undertaking might have been. Perhaps it was due to his total lack of competitiveness, the sheer, boundless scale of his search for adventure for its own joyous sake. Tragically, he was killed abseiling from one of the stacks he so enjoyed discovering. In his death I, and all his many other friends, lost a source and inspiration to discovery that we shall never be able to replace.

Lagging behind the others as we walked back to the boat, I sat and gazed over the strip of waters that separated Handa from the mainland. In a way the land was an extension of the sea, a wild, stormy sea, petrified into stillness, the white caps, tips of rocks jutting through the heather, and peat hags of the foothills – the oft-repeated gleam of waters and the mountains – Suilven, Canisp, Quinag, jutting like rocky islands out of the storm-wracked seas. At that moment, I loved the hills and the sea and the sky, almost dreaded the next day when we were to go on to Hoy, with all the hurly-burly of the preparation for the big happening, the climbers and all the other people involved. I shrank from it as I had often done as a small boy when invited to a children's party, shy and a little frightened by exposure to so many people, yet knowing full well that, once involved, I should lose these inhibitions and enjoy myself.

And so to Hoy; the big circus – and it was tremendous fun. Dougal Haston and Pete Crew were hammering their way up the South-East Arête. It was obviously going to take such a long time that it was essential they got at least part-way up it before the start of the actual broadcast. Hamish MacInnes was in his element, as one of the climbing cameramen and consultant engineer for the erection of all the platforms needed for the big live-cameras and the complex set of pulleys required for lowering them into place. Joe Brown, relaxed as ever, had climbed the Old Man by our original route at the start of the proceedings, taking only an hour on the steep overhanging crack where Rusty had spent more than eight!

'It's not too difficult,' he reassured me. 'You can climb it free all the way.'

One of the features of the programme was that we were going to try to make the climb as spontaneous as possible by not rehearsing every move. As far as

Joe was concerned, his climb would be a genuine new route. It was essential, however, that I should be able to guarantee climbing quickly on our route, so that if the other two parties became stuck for any reason, the cameras would be able to swing on to Patey and me, in the assurance that we, at least, should be showing some signs of action.

I was determined, therefore, to rehearse that long, overhanging crack. The fact that Joe found it easy did nothing to reassure me. I had no illusions about our disparate rock-climbing abilities – what he found easy, I might find bloody desperate!

Happily, in this case I did not. Secure in the knowledge that Joe had climbed it free, I approached the crack aggressively and to my amazement, in spite of its bristling overhangs, the holds slotted into place, so that I managed to get to the top in about half an hour. It was truly wonderful, sensational climbing.

I was less happy about my final role in the spectacular. Someone – I'm not sure who – had had the brainwave that the broadcast should end with an abseil, all the way down from the top of the Old Man of Hoy to the ground – 450 feet, in a single plunge, for the top actually overhung the bottom.

Coming in late to the meeting at which this was discussed turned out to be a definite mistake, for the team had, in my absence, voted me into the job.

'But the descendeur'll get so hot that the rope might melt if I stop on the way down,' I protested.

'Simple,' said Joe. 'Don't stop.'

'But what if I do? – it could jam or something.'

'It's all right, Chris,' said Hamish. 'I've got just the thing – a special friction brake which will absorb the heat, and won't melt the rope.'

He produced a slightly Heath Robinson-looking device, made of alloy, with an asbestos cam built into it. This, he assured me, would absorb all the heat. I was not convinced.

'Have you tried it out?'

'Och aye. I did a two-hundred foot free abseil on it the other day.'

'But this is four-hundred and fifty feet!'

'Won't make much difference. Give it a try, anyway.'

'I don't want to do it more than once – I'll wait for the actual thing.' In fact, I did try it on a 150-foot abseil from part-way up the Old Man. By the time I got to the end of the rope, there was a frightening smell of burning nylon. I was not reassured.

The day of the broadcast arrived. The action was to be spread over the two days of the Whitsun holiday, with a bivouac thrown in for good measure. In addition, we had a spectacular pendule by Tom Patey, as he swung out from the base of the overhanging rock, to jumar up the rope to join me at the top of the pitch, accompanied by the racy repartee of MacNaught-Davis and even an attack by the odd fulmar. It was good climbing, in spite of the element of circus, and it undoubtedly made superb television. There were crises, when radios wouldn't work, when one of the climbing camera teams very nearly failed to get their gear into position in time, until finally, right at the end, when all six climbers had managed to finish their three separate routes on schedule and preparations were being made for the grand finale in the sunset – with Bonington abseiling into fame from the top of the Old Man of Hoy – my nerve failed!

'Would you do it, Joe?'

'No.'

'All I've got to do is jam a bit of clothing in the descendeur, and I'll melt the bloody rope. Could I have a top rope?'

'No good. You'll spin for certain, and the two ropes'll wind round each other. You'll be jammed up for certain that way.'

'I'm bloody well not going to do it!'

'Just think of your public,' said Tom. 'Seven million viewers are waiting for you. You can't let them down – anyway, think of the immortality you'll win.'

'Not much good to me if it's posthumous,' I replied.

'Only ten minutes to go,' said practical Joe. 'I know what, we'll lower you down a rope that's been secured at the bottom. That'll stop you spinning and it might even look better, because they can put it at an angle and you'll be silhouetted against the sky.'

And that was how it was done. I was lowered from the summit by the others, rather like an Admiral in a bo'suns chair, slightly apprehensive at first, and then, when it worked, I felt superbly, wonderfully elated, drifting down, talking away into the microphone of my radio, in spectacular circumstances but at no risk to myself.

Two days later, the camera platforms had been stripped down and the Old Man of Hoy was left to its regular inhabitants – the fulmars, puffins and cormorants who lived on its flanks. Climbers have often criticised these live climbing broadcasts on the grounds of the simplification, the popularisation and some of the cheating which must inevitably accompany them to make them technically possible. Whatever the rights and wrongs, these broadcasts are tremendously exciting for those who take part, and they do give the non-climber the best opportunity of seeing and feeling through the eyes and experience of others. The challenge of communication is very much in the hands of each climber taking part, for while the cameras are on him, not only can he show how to climb a stretch of rock, he can also impart his own particular feelings and even his own peculiar philosophy. A problem the BBC have is trying to find new climbs and new ways of presenting them; spurred on, perhaps, by a need for each broadcast to outdo the last, making each one much bigger, different or more exciting.

I suspect that the Old Man of Hoy broadcast will never be superseded as the perfect live broadcast. It had every ingredient – a perfect, very obvious summit, a scale which was also perfect, since the climbers clinging to the tower were dwarfed by its size, yet were not totally lost in its immensity. In the group of six climbers, our personalities jelled particularly well – Joe, silent, laconic, supremely competent; Mac, extrovert, clowning happily and stepping into the breach whenever the commentary seemed to be dying; Pete and Dougal, both somewhat terse, workmanlike, practical – the modern climbers; Tom, the very antithesis, laughing quietly at the entire circus, poking gentle fun at my own earnest professionalism.

At the end of the broadcast, after a magnificent victory binge in Stromness, we all scattered our different ways: Mac back to London and his high-pressure business life; Dougal to Leysin and his climbing school; and Tom back to the mainland to search out another sea-stack. I couldn't help envying him, for in my relative success as a photojournalist I had lost a great deal of freedom, was getting trapped into the very rat-race from which I had wanted to escape in 1962. But it was, at least, a self-sought race — one by which I couldn't help being enthralled, as I was sent on an ever-widening variety of assignments, learning more and more about my craft as a writer and photographer.

17 Eskimoes

I knew I should ask Joanacee to stop the dogs so that I could take some pictures, but could not bring myself to do so. I was so cold.

The sun had dropped below the low line of hills to the south-west, but the sky was still red; tattered streamers of steam, rising from an open lead in the distance, were coloured a fiery crimson; the smooth surface of the ice around us was broken by petrified eruptions of ice blocks. A low pressure-ridge, like a neglected piece of dry stone walling, stretched into the distance and the shadows beneath a sprouting tumescence of ice were deep green.

The sledge pulled round the headland and the view was gone, but for the rest of the journey I was racked with guilt that I had not recorded those few moments. I sat hunched on the back of the sledge behind Joanacee, wriggled my toes, rubbed my fingers, but could not rid them of the cold that bit into them. The cold now crept through the double thickness of my caribou-skin parka, played gently up and down my back. We had been travelling since dawn, and had had little to eat; our bodies were running out of the fuel needed to combat the intense cold of minus 40 degrees Fahrenheit.

In front, the eleven dogs were trotting effortlessly, each one of them hauling on its own lead, all of which were clipped into the main lead only a few feet in front of the komatic or sledge. It was about twenty feet long, and eighteen inches wide, with our equipment, fuel and food covered by the caribou skins, securely strapped to it. Joanacee crouched in front, ever watchful, with his deadly twenty-foot-long sealskin whip trailing behind. A flick of the wrist and it snaked forward, cracking at the hind legs of a dog who had lagged behind the others.

Only a week earlier I had been saying goodbye to Wendy in our Lakeland cottage, then four days ago I had been sitting in an ultra-modern office in Ottawa, discussing with an official of the Canadian Department of Northern Affairs the problem of the Eskimoes' adjustment to modern society. Now I was sitting on the back of a komatic, near the head of Cumberland Sound in Baffin Island, just a few miles south of the Arctic Circle.

'Plenty of people have done stories of the far north in the summer,' John Anstey, editor of the *Daily Telegraph* magazine, had told me before I set off. 'I want you to go hunting with the Eskimoes in midwinter. See what their lives are like today and how they are adapting to change.'

This time I was to take on the job of both writer and photographer. I had flown to Canada at the beginning of February, and then on from Montreal to Frobisher Bay, the administrative capital of Baffin Island, en route for Pangnirtung. Here I was going to spend three weeks hunting with the Eskimoes, at the same time collecting my story. On getting out of the plane at Frobisher Bay the place seemed totally hostile to man – it was dominated by machines. The cold hit us as if it were a solid wall as we hurried from the plane across a few yards of iced tarmac to the entrance of a building. From the reception hangar, I was taken by car to the Federal building – a vast, barn-like edifice comprising government offices, social centre, store rooms, repair shops and accommodation for all the unmarried personnel posted to this outpost of so-called civilisation. It appeared there were some people who never left the building throughout the winter, and I could well believe it, for there was no reason for them to do so – outside was a bitterly hostile world, with an icy wind blowing clouds of snow past neat rows of prefab huts, the homes of the Eskimoes. The lucky ones were employed about the station as drivers while those less fortunate were cleaners. The vast majority, however, had no employment at all, and just lived on Welfare – an aimless existence, spiced by alcohol when they could lay their hands on it. I was glad to escape from the claustrophobic confines of Frobisher Bay.

A big single-engined Otter aircraft took me to Pangnirtung, our route leading us over a sea of low rolling hills, flecked with the black of exposed rocks. It was a bleak, empty, inhospitable place and seemed as foreign to man as the surface of the moon. Yet in these hills roamed small herds of caribou nibbling the moss and lichen hidden by the shallow covering of snow. Then we came to the sea; tentacles of ice-cold water writhed into the coastline; the sea-ice stretched white and featureless into Cumberland Sound, then darkened towards the floe edge; grey mist covered the black waters and mountains jutted above the mist on the other side of the Sound. We were approaching Pangnirtung, flying up a long fiord with hills towering on either side. On first sight from the air the settlement looked like a handful of tiny matchbox houses that a child had scattered carelessly over a white carpet. The plane landed on the ice of the fiord and taxied to the group of people waiting for us.

Jim Cummings, the manager of the Hudson Bay Company store, was amongst them. He had agreed to arrange my hunting trip and to look after me while I was in Pangnirtung. A quiet, stockily built man, he gave the impression of being quite shy, but lingering under what first appeared to be an abrupt manner was an impish sense of humour and considerable kindness. He was a bachelor, as are many of the Hudson Bay Company managers, for they spend long periods in isolated communities where there are few, if any, European women. Rightly or wrongly, the Hudson Bay Company do not encourage mixed marriages with the Eskimoes, though many managers, I am sure, have taken Eskimo girls as mistresses. Jim, however, was courting one of the school teachers, an attractive, strong-minded Scots lass, whom he has since married.

He showed me to his home, a single-storeyed, double-skinned building, heated by a magnificent oil stove. It was deliciously warm inside, and had a humanity about it that the Federal building in Frobisher Bay had lacked.

'What exactly do you want to do?' he asked.

'Have a good look at Pangnirtung, and then go hunting with the Eskimoes,' I replied.

'Well, looking at Pangnirtung won't take long,' said Jim. 'It's what you can see – a collection of prefabs, a few of the old Eskimo tents, the hospital and the school. As for hunting, there are not many Eskimoes that bother any longer. What do you want to hunt, anyway?'

'Caribou, if possible,' I said. 'That's what the editor wants.'

'I suppose I could find a couple of lads who'd take you,' he said. 'Do you want to go by Skidoo, or dog-team?'

'Dog-team, definitely; it's more romantic – I want to make it as original as possible.'

'Well, even that has problems; there aren't many decent teams left. The best hunters can afford Skidoos, and the ones who aren't so good don't keep their dogs in good condition. It's easier for them to hang around the settlement and live on Welfare. Still, I think I should be able to find something for you.'

Next day he introduced me to two young Eskimoes, Joanacee and Levi. They owned a dog-team each, and Jim assured me that they were reliable. Our food preparations for the ten-day trip were simple. Jim made a massive stew in a ten-gallon pan, poured it out on a plastic sheet in an unheated store-shed and, next morning, broke up the frozen mass with a hammer, packing all the lumps in a couple of sacks. These, a bagful of sugar and a bag of tea were our rations.

We left Pangnirtung that morning and all day our two komatics skirted the coast of Cumberland Sound, running over the flat sea-ice, past bare rocky islands and the occasional stranded iceberg. Every three hours or so we stopped and the dogs immediately curled up in the snow, or rolled ecstatically on their backs before settling down.

Joanacee lit the petrol stove and started to melt some snow. While it was melting, they sorted out the leads of the dogs, which had become plaited together during the run as the dogs had changed their positions. Once the snow had melted, the two Eskimoes turned over the komatics, and iced the steel runners, taking water into their mouths, and letting it run out in a steady stream over the metal. Once this was done we had some tea and hard tack biscuits to eat. Levi produced a hunk of raw, frozen meat, chopped pieces off it and popped them into his mouth. 'Tuctu,' he muttered. It was the meat of the caribou.

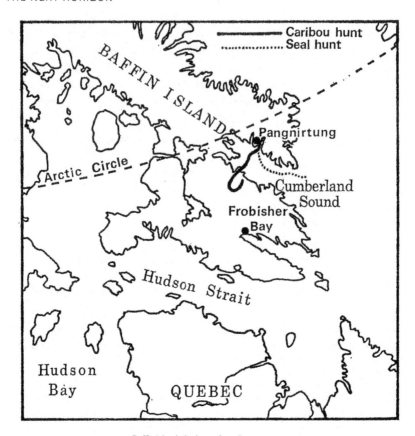

Baffin Island: the hunts from Pangnirtung

While the Eskimoes worked I felt extraordinarily helpless; they were so sure and quick in everything they did – I was so slow; the cold had a numbing effect, making even thought difficult. I quickly decided to allow myself to be mollycoddled by our two guides and to concentrate just on getting pictures. I was already having problems. The metal of the camera was so cold that if it touched my cheek as I held it to my eye, I received a cold burn. As soon as I brought the eyepiece anywhere near the warmth of my body, it misted and froze over, so that I could see nothing. Worst of all, though, the film was so brittle in the cold that it snapped at the least excuse. I tried to warm the camera inside my parka, but felt the heat drain out of my already chilled body, into this lump of metal, which had a temperature of around minus thirty.

Our first day brought us to Bon Accord, an Eskimo hunting camp near the head of Cumberland Sound. We reached it in the dark, for we had only eight hours' daylight at this time of year. I was glad to stumble into the warm tent, leaving the Eskimoes to feed the dogs. This was Levi's home, where he lived with his parents and four brothers and sisters. It was warmed and lighted by three seal-oil lamps, long wicks glimmering on the edge of an open dish of melted seal blubber.

We left in the dawn, the sun, a heavy red orb, hanging above the horizon. This tiny settlement felt like the furthest outpost of the world; five snow-covered tents clung to a rocky headland, surrounded by a waste of ice. The Eskimoes rounded up the dogs and packed the sledges; in a mad scamper we raced across the chaotic jumble of reef ice that bordered the land.

We picked our way through an archipelago of islands jutting through the ice. A biting wind whispered from the north, freezing my face, building long icicles on my beard and moustache, and yet I now felt I could contend with the cold, felt intoxicated by the empty desolation yet utter beauty of this world of ice and snow and granite, rich brown in the rays of the sun.

We stopped early that day on a small island. Levi and Joanacee immediately started probing the snow for a suitable site for our igloo; they were looking for a drift of hard, compact snow. Once they found one, they cut out the blocks for the snow house, and then built it up in a continuous round spiral. In just over an hour the igloo was completed, but there was still work to do. They shouldered their axes, and walked over to a pile of stones; the dogs, unleashed from the sledge, followed them, gathering around in tense expectancy, as the two Eskimoes levered off the stones to reveal a cache of frozen seal. The dogs lunged forward, but a lazy flick of the whip followed them and quickly drove them back, and they waited impatiently until the seal had been chopped into small pieces. Then they tore into the scattered meat, snapping at each other for choice bits, devouring it with the savagery of the wolves they were originally bred from. All our belongings were put either inside the snow house or on top of it, out of reach of the dogs, who would have a try at eating almost anything, including their own harnesses.

It was dark when, at last, we crawled through the low entrance and settled down for the night. In comparison with the cold outside, the igloo felt more comfortable than the most luxurious of hotels. The floor was covered with caribou skins, the cooker was roaring, making the air warm and heavy with fumes. Melt water crept down the walls; where it dripped between blocks, Joanacee made bridges of toilet paper. For supper we broke off some lumps of the stew we had pre-cooked in Pangnirtung, and as an appetiser we ate raw frozen caribou – no meal had ever tasted more delicious.

It was difficult getting to know my two companions – for the first day or two I even found it hard to link their names with their faces. The main trouble was that we could not speak a word of each other's language. Levi and Joanacee were both in their late twenties; like most Eskimoes they smiled a great deal, never became flustered, and yet I felt they never gave much of themselves away. During the journey I came to like and respect them, but I could never discuss anything with them or learn what they really felt about me, themselves or the life they led. Even so, we established a relationship that I found pleasantly restful. They were eager to teach me their language and we spent many an hour repeating Eskimo words – a whole string of gutturals that I found almost impossible to remember, one word from the next.

It took two more days to reach the area where we could hope to find caribou, first up a long fjord that plunged into the land, low craggy hills on either side, and then into the land itself, up through a winding defile, where the dogs laboured hard under the whip, sliding on smooth ice, catching their traces on upthrust rocks. I have never been anywhere so desolate; the snow-covered land was like the swell of a frozen ocean, bare rocks replacing windswept spume. It was difficult to imagine how anything could live in such surroundings and yet we could see the tracks and droppings of caribou. Beneath the shallow covering of snow was the moss they lived on.

We built an igloo in the middle of this waste and on the following day started the hunt, travelling in a huge circle round our base. I could not help wondering how my two guides would find their way back, it was all so featureless. It was bitterly cold, for we were now forty miles inland – the temperature was probably minus fifty degrees Fahrenheit.

The two komatics were several hundred yards apart, at times out of sight of each other. After we had been travelling a couple of hours the dogs picked up a scent and broke into a fast run, letting out excited yelps. Joanacee stood up and, balancing easily on the bucking sled, peered into the glare of the snow; but the dogs slowed down, the scent was dead.

We had another false alarm and eventually Joanacee turned to me apologetically and confessed, 'Tuctu no more,' and he waved at the hills to show that they had gone away. We got back to the igloo late that evening, finding it with unerring precision. The next morning we discovered that our fuel can had been leaking and that we had practically none left. We had no choice but to return to Pangnirtung.

Back in the settlement I felt I had seen only one aspect of Eskimo hunting; I wanted to go out again, to hunt seal, this time by Skidoo instead of dog team. I was recommended to approach an Eskimo called Owalook who was one of the best hunters in Pangnirtung and could therefore afford to run a Skidoo. He could also speak some English, having spent nine years in a mental hospital in South Canada. I could not help wondering about his background, but was reassured on meeting him. His manner inspired confidence; he was quite short but powerfully built with the battered features of a professional boxer, but in his case, the wind and cold had been his antagonist. There was a strength and kindness in his face that was offset by a twinkle of humour in his eyes. He was forty-seven years old, already a grandfather, with five children of his own.

Behind him he had a lifetime of narrow escapes; and in 1947 he had been caught on a small floe that broke away from the pack in a violent storm. He had no shelter or spare clothes, only a baby seal for food, yet he managed to survive for nineteen storm-racked days before the floe ran aground, fortunately only a day's march from his home, then at Bon Accord.

On our trip to the floe edge, I quickly saw the advantages of the modern form of transport. We raced across the ice at about thirty miles an hour; the komatic, to which I clung, yawed from side to side behind the Skidoo, bucking over every ridge in the ice. We could see the floe edge from a distance. At first it was like a solid wall, stretching across the entire horizon, but as we came closer, the wall disintegrated into a thin grey mist, rising from the open water. Ice merged imperceptibly with dark waters that seemed vicious in the cold.

Owalook stopped the Skidoo about twenty feet from the floe edge and, taking a boat-hook and his rifle, walked forward probing the ice. Close to the edge he halted and began scraping the hook from side to side with a steady rhythmic motion. A few minutes passed and a small dark blob appeared in the water and then vanished. Owalook dropped the hook, sat down on the ice, raised his rifle and waited. The blob appeared again. It was three hundred yards out, and barely discernible as the head of a seal. The rifle cracked; there was a flurry of water. 'Dead,' announced Owalook.

It had all happened so quickly and smoothly that I hardly realised what had happened, could not conceive that anyone could shoot so accurately, even with telescopic sights. Owalook had already unfastened the small, flat-bottomed dory tied on to the back of the komatic. He pushed it gingerly to the edge of the ice, rocked it once or twice to break the thin skin between him and the water, and pushed out.

Soon he was back with the seal in tow – it twitched a little and its brains flowed in a dark stream over the ice. I felt slightly sick, and walked away, but then felt ashamed and forced myself to return. I had not been watching someone killing for sport; this was Owalook's sole means of livelihood.

To me, the saddest thing of all is that Owalook is part of a dying breed. One cannot afford to be sentimental about quaint old ways involving a great deal of hardship, malnutrition and disease, but on the other hand the impact of an industrialised society on a simple, so-called primitive people can be terribly destructive. Today, the Eskimoes are fed and housed and clothed – even educated, but in a stereotyped way that has little relevance to their cultural background.

In 1965, Pangnirtung had a population of 412 Eskimoes and thirty-four whites. Today, in 1973, this will be considerably higher. Only five years before there had been just a few Eskimo families living in tents around the mission station, Hudson Bay Company store, and Mounted Police post. Forty-five years before the fjord had been empty. This gives some idea of the rate of change in the last few years.

For thousands of years the Eskimoes had succeeded in living around Cumberland Sound and along the length of the Arctic coast and its islands, in one of the harshest environments in the world, hunting with bone-tipped harpoons and arrows, living in snow-houses or tents of caribou skin, surviving without the aid of either metals or wood, dependent entirely upon the flesh, fat and bones of the animal life of the Arctic sea and land.

During these years they evolved methods of Arctic survival that have never been improved upon – with all the resources of modern technology, there is no better temporary shelter than the igloo or snow-house, the traditional garments of caribou skin are warmer than any modern-designed polar suits. The Eskimo lived in small, self-sufficient groups of either one or several families. The Camp Boss, or Leader, was the best hunter of the group, and each person had his own role: the short-sighted or cross-eyed would be delegated menial tasks; the women did the cooking and made the clothes, but within that group everyone had a fair share of its produce.

Baffin Island was first visited by a European in 1576, when Martin Frobisher was seeking gold and the North-west Passage reached its southern coast. But the European had little influence on the Eskimo's way of life until the mid-nineteenth century when they came in increasing numbers to hunt whale, and even established whaling stations in Cumberland Sound. They also began trading with the Eskimo, giving him metal cooking-pots, guns, canvas and duffel material, in return for his skins. He acquired a taste for some southern foods, adding tea and sugar and flour to his menu of meat. Today, this is still his basic diet, although he is rapidly being introduced to other imported foods. When the whaling died down at the end of the nineteenth century, the Hudson Bay Company traders took over, establishing permanent posts throughout the Arctic.

Although the Eskimo became increasingly dependent upon these imported goods, he did not radically change his way of life. He still lived in small groups in the best hunting areas; still lived off the land. His life was undoubtedly a hard one and if he was improvident, or unlucky, his family could starve. He was also a prey to diseases, particularly those carried by the Europeans. Epidemics of polio or measles attacked complete communities. Chest troubles caused a heavy toll.

The establishment of a permanent trading post at Pangnirtung, followed by a Mission hospital and Mounted Police post, still had little effect on the life of the Eskimo. The site had been chosen for its good anchorage and position as a centre for trading to the camps scattered around Cumberland Sound. There was no reason for Eskimoes to settle there, as it was a long way from all the hunting grounds.

And then, in the late fifties, the Canadian Government suddenly became aware of the Eskimo population; before this they had been happy to leave the welfare and administration of the far north to the Mounted Police, its economy to the Hudson Bay Company, and its education to the church; but now the Department of Northern Affairs began to take an increasingly active interest in the northern coastline of Canada and developed a strong sense of responsibility towards its population of 12,000 Eskimoes, trying to bring them a standard of living and availability of opportunity comparable with that of the people living in southern Canada.

One of the most important facets of the government's programme was education. Until the Eskimo could read and write English, and eventually compete on an equal footing with other Canadians, there seemed little hope for his future development. Even today, very few adults can speak a word of English, and the children, who have been to school for some years, barely have a working command of the language.

A school was opened in Pangnirtung in 1960: in 1968 it had five teachers and over a hundred pupils. The opening of the school naturally attracted the Eskimoes to Pangnirtung from their camps around Cumberland Sound. There were other reasons, too, all of which had a cumulative effect, for as the population of Pangnirtung increased, so did the amenities: Saturday-night Bingo, the movies; a coffee bar for teenagers, complete with juke box; an enlarged Hudson Bay Company store as well equipped as any of our own supermarkets.

The government had just launched a housing programme with the intention of renting prefabs of one to four rooms to all the Eskimoes on the basis of the individual's family size and income. The houses were undoubtedly more comfortable and convenient than the double-skinned tents in which the Eskimoes had lived up to this period, but aesthetically they were hideously ugly-little boxes littering the foreshore of Pangnirtung Sound.

There had been a wonderful peace and strange beauty in the tented camp at Bon Accord, one of the last family camps to survive. There was no Bingo or Saturday-night movie, but the family who lived there appeared to have a peace of mind which was lacking in Pangnirtung.

As I climbed into the Otter and took off on my journey back to England, I couldn't help feeling sad that a people who had survived so successfully and proudly in so harsh an environment were slipping into the role of the aimless unemployed, with full bellies, synthetic entertainment, yet with no real purpose or place in a modern technological world.

I should have liked to return home, for I was worried about Wendy, now getting close to the date when she was due to give birth, but I had another assignment in central Canada to do a story on a newly-opened oil field. My trip to Baffin Island had been the closest I had come to straight journalism, where I had to do more than just have an adventure and record it. I had been fascinated by the lives of the Eskimoes and had felt a deep sympathy with them.

The Athabaska Oil Sands were different. I was confused by the massive machinery, the economics of the operation, and felt nothing in common with the managers and operatives of the concern. At the end of a week of talking to people and taking pictures of this symbol of modern industrialisation dropped in the middle of the featureless, trackless forests of mid-Canada, I still had very little idea of what kind of story I could possibly write. In fact, I never did write one.

And then, back home to England, to write up my Eskimo story, to be with Wendy once more, now in the final stages of her pregnancy. Daniel was born by a caesarean operation on the 25 April 1967; an agonising gap in our lives had been filled, but at Bank End Cottage, beautiful though it was, we were constantly reminded of Conrad's short life. We did not take the decision consciously, but I think we needed to make a move to break away from these reminders. We bought a house in Cockermouth early that summer, but even as we bought it I was beginning to feel restless in the Lake District. The idyllic, easy-going days of Woodland were for ever finished. I was getting more and more journalistic work, more lectures, and this meant long, awkward drives out of the Lake District to wherever I happened to be going. I began to feel isolated, both from the society of other photographers and writers and from the main climbing stream. By this time a strong climbing community had formed in Wales, based around Llanberis, but in the Lakes there was no such development. There was a fair number of local climbers, but these were scattered over a wide area.

Another factor was that although I had been climbing round the Lake District for five years and had by no means exhausted all the climbs in that area I had begun to tire of Lakeland hills and was looking farther afield.

I wanted to move to London, feeling that now my career was developing into that of a photojournalist and since all the magazines had their offices in London, this was the place where I should also be. Wendy, on the other hand, loved the Lake District, had built a circle of close and loyal friends and had grown roots much deeper and more lasting than I ever could. With real justification she felt that since I was away from home so much, in the main doing things which I thoroughly enjoyed, she should have a strong say in where we lived.

These two, differing ambitions caused the greatest strain our relationship has had, before or since. I was determined to move; she wasn't at all sure whether it was even in my best interests to do so, but she knew she could not budge me from my view. We spent several very unhappy weekends, hunting for a possible home in London. Starting in Hampstead, where I had been brought up, we breezed into an estate office and asked for houses at around what we considered to be a reasonable figure. The receptionist raised a polite eyebrow, and assured us they had nothing at less than double that figure. Eventually we found our financial level which took us to an area where we trailed round a series of slightly grotty terrace houses, deafened by the sound of traffic, becoming suddenly aware of the smell of petrol fumes. We fled from London and headed for home.

On the way back we stayed with Nick Estcourt, who had recently moved from London to work as a computer programmer with Ferranti in Manchester. He and his wife Carolyn lived in a flat at Alderley Edge which, after London, seemed delightfully clean and quiet – the perfect compromise. Already we had plenty of friends in the Manchester area – we could get back to the Lake District comparatively easily and, living on the outskirts of Manchester, there was not the same feeling of claustrophobia which London seemed to generate in me almost as badly as in Wendy.

Less than a year after we had bought our house in Cockermouth, we started hunting for a house on the southern side of Manchester, and as we hunted the tempo of my own career seemed to grow ever faster. It was spring, 1968, and I had been asked to accompany Nicholas Monsarrat to Hunza as photographer, while he wrote a profile on this obscure little kingdom in the heart of the Himalaya. And later that summer I was due to join an expedition to attempt the first-ever descent of the Blue Nile – again as writer and photographer. But first I was to visit Hunza.

18   The Valley of the Hunza

Hunza is an emerald in a setting of browns, greys and dazzling white, an oasis in the heart of a mountain desert of soaring ice peaks and sun-blasted rock. They say its inhabitants live to ages of anything up to 130 and that they are descended from the soldiers of Alexander the Great.

Nicholas Monsarrat and I were trying to find out how far reality lived up to legend. In London this remote Himalayan valley had seemed almost too accessible: VC10 to Karachi, a connection to Rawalpindi and the next morning a local plane to Ghilgit in the heart of the mountains. A tourist brochure assured us that there was a jeep road through spectacular scenery into Hunza itself, and it seemed we could be there within forty-eight hours of leaving London.

I should have been disappointed if this had proved true. Our first delay was in Rawalpindi where we waited for three days in the anonymous cloying luxury of the Hotel Intercontinental, while storm clouds scurried over the foothills to the immediate north. The plane could only fly to Ghilgit in perfect conditions.

Monsarrat and I must have made an unlikely looking pair. He, urbane, charming when he wanted to be, yet with a caustic wit that could lash out unexpectedly, had come equipped with dinner jacket and clothes for every social occasion. I had two rucksacks full of boots, ropes and climbing gear.

The flight from Rawalpindi to Ghilgit must be one of the most impressive in the world. The twin-engined Fokker Friendship ridge-hops over the tree-covered tentacles of the great peaks – one second the plane is barely clawing its way over a ridge and the next it is suspended over the abyss of a deep-cut valley, brown waters swirling far below. The gigantic mass of Nanga Parbat towers over the plane with its complex of icefalls, snow fields and rocky buttresses.

Approaching Ghilgit the plane dives through narrow valleys, giving the impression of driving flat out along a narrow country lane. We overshot the runway once, caught a glimpse of mud-roofed houses and upturned faces, seemed to fly straight for the rock wall of the valley, banked at the last minute and touched down at Ghilgit airport. The following day an air force plane crashed on its way out to Rawalpindi with the loss of twenty-two lives, a grim reminder of the dangers of flying among high mountains.

Ghilgit itself is a dusty garrison town, surrounded by bleak rocky hills, but the bazaar has a feeling of Kipling's North-west Frontier, of being the threshold of something more strange and exciting. Jeeps jostle with pedestrians and donkeys, bearded holy men stride through the teeming streets, and the shops, like open-ended boxes, are crammed with brightly coloured trashy goods. It is a world of men, and the few women in sight are heavily veiled by the hideous burkha. The muezzin calls the faithful to prayer over the loudspeaker, harsh and metallic. Here is an uneasy, at times ugly, marriage between progress and tradition.

We spent the night in the rest house and the next morning were ready to start the final stage of our journey by jeep to Hunza. Our party had now grown. The Pakistan Press Information Department had put at our disposal one of their officials, a Mr Mir. At times one felt he had the role of an 'Intourist' guide, deflecting us from anything that might not show Pakistan at its best. At Ghilgit we were joined by another guide from Hunza, who had with him his seven-year-old son. With the driver and his mate, six of us, with all our baggage, were crammed into the back of the jeep.

At first the road ran up a wide flat valley – weeping grey clouds clinging to its rocky flanks, the road, a dirt strip marked by cairns of stone; and then the valley began to narrow, the road crept up its side, wound in and out through tottering pinnacles of rock, clung to precarious slopes of scree. The jeep was now permanently in bottom gear; each meeting with an oncoming vehicle became a battle of wills between the drivers as to who should go back to the nearest parking place. The road was like a switchback gone mad, as it bucked from valley floor, over spurs, round re-entrants and down again. And as the rain fell, water rushed down every gully, eating away the road, carrying little avalanches of stones that built up into drifts across it. I have never known a journey like it. I was perched on the outside of the jeep and seemed to overhang the creaming torrent hundreds of feet below. The jeep snarled and skidded on the loose stones and mud, brushed the precarious outer wall, teetered past giant bites that had been eaten from the road.

After forty miles, with another twenty-five to go, we were finally brought to a halt: the entire road had been swept away. We spent the night in the rest house at the nearest village. There were no amenities and the only available food was a few hard-boiled eggs and leathery chuppaties, which we ate under the assembled gaze of the inhabitants. I could see Nicholas Monsarrat's sense of humour beginning to wear a little thin, and that night he began to mutter about returning to London to meet his publishers' deadline on a new novel he had just finished. By morning, his mind was made up – he was determined to return; Mr Mir was eager to volunteer his services as escort – his winkle-picker shoes and sharp city suit were hardly suitable for a trek into the lost valley of Hunza.

I decided to walk on into Hunza. Apart from anything else, I have always preferred being on foot to being in a vehicle. In a jeep one is separated from the people of the land, not only by the speed of one's passing, but also by the barriers set up by one's relative affluence. The rain still poured down, but I had a feeling of freedom as I plodded on with my interpreter, his son and an elderly mail-runner who volunteered to carry my gear.

That night we reached the village of Hindi – we were on Hunza territory for the first time. Hindi is a tiny oasis of green clinging to the arid rocks and sand of the gorge. Houses like little mud boxes are scattered among a mosaic of terraced fields and irrigation channels. Everywhere are trees, straight rows of poplar, clumps of apricot, little jungles of lavender.

We stopped at the rest house, a mud hut with a gaping square in the roof to let the smoke out and the rain in; there was no sign of beds or food but we just sat and waited. You have got to be patient in a place like Hunza; things move slowly but eventually something happens.

One of the village elders arrived and made a courtly little speech which was translated to me:

> Just as the sun has been hidden by the clouds for over ten days, so the British have left Pakistan for many years. I am very glad to welcome you, a Briton, back to Hunza.

He then produced a rather dirty cloth full of dried apricots and apples. I had barely recovered from my last attack of dysentery, but did not see how I could refuse, so shoving my fears into the background, I tucked into the dried fruit. Another long pause and we were invited to supper.

Our host, Ali Murad Khan, was seventy but looked fifty, and lived near the edge of the cultivated area. We picked our way along narrow paths by the side of irrigation channels to his house. It was typical of a moderately prosperous Hunza home, flat roofed with two storeys; the lower one, a dark dungeon, they live in during the winter, while the upper storey is for summer. There are no windows and all the light comes from a hole in the roof.

Ali Murad Khan owns two small fields, twenty sheep, two cows and an ox. He, like all Hunza people, is almost entirely self-sufficient – has to be, for there is practically no money coming in to buy food, furniture or clothing. From his farm he gets fruit in season, apricots, grapes, apples, peaches and mulberries; he owns a few poplar trees for timber and some lavender for firewood. He also grows wheat and potatoes. His clothing comes from the wool of his sheep.

He apologised to me that this was the lean season; they were waiting for their fruit and wheat to ripen. There was little food to be purchased from the shops in the bazaar, and what there was, was expensive. The only income that Ali Murad Khan had was from selling cloth woven from the wool of his sheep and from making Hunza wine from his grapes. Although they are Muslims, the people of Hunza take a liberal view on the subject of drinking. His eldest son, who lived with him, had a pension of fifteen rupees a month from serving for fifteen years in the army. No family in Hunza could survive without sending some members down into Pakistan to earn a living either in the army or as servants or porters, thus bringing some hard cash back into the valley. In many instances men spent ten months of the year in the lowlands, leaving wives and families to look after their farms.

That night Ali Murad Khan brought out some mutton that had been hung in the cellar for the past three months; the spices barely disguised its pungent flavour. We sat on the floor round the big communal pot and, using bits of chupatti as a spoon, shovelled meat, gravy and curried vegetables into our mouths. For the first time in the week I had been in Pakistan I began to feel part of the land and people in a way that I would never have done if Monsarrat, or any other European, had been with me. The two wives sat in the background, waiting for us to finish, for they could not eat in front of a stranger.

Next morning we finished our walk into the valley of Hunza; another six miles up the gorge, and we came round a low spur that had barred our view. Suddenly the valley opened out into a great basin, about eight miles long and four wide, paved in brilliant green, yet dominated by stark rocky sides that stretched up into ramparts of snow-clad peaks.

This oasis in the midst of a mountain desert is entirely dependent on glacier melt water, which is channelled into irrigation canals by a complex system of channels and sluices, and shared out amongst the separate villages and then amongst the individual fields in strict rotation. A wide stony river splits the valley in two, dividing the State of Hunza from Nagir. At the end of it, you can just see the Mir of Hunza's palaces. His old one is a white painted eyrie, perched high on a crag, while the new, in grey granite, nestles below.

There are many theories about the origins of the people of Hunza. That afternoon, walking through the valley, I couldn't help noticing how many of the inhabitants had fair skins, blue eyes and blond hair. Hunza is on the old caravan route between the interior of Asia and the Indus Valley, one of the most important trade routes of the old world, and an area where there must have been a constant intermingling of peoples. Besides the theory that the Hunzas are descended from soldiers of Alexander the Great, there is one the Mir suggested to me: that they originally came from a place called Hunz in the Caucasus, and were driven into their present home during the reign of Tamerlane. Their language, Brushaki, bears no relation to either the Indian or Iranian language families.

The women of Hunza do not hide under the burkha, like most of the women of South Pakistan, and by Muslim standards they have a great deal of freedom. They wear an attractive embroidered pill-box hat, held in place by a scarf, brightly coloured tunic and baggy trousers. The girls are deliciously pretty, but there is one snag: under no circumstances would they allow

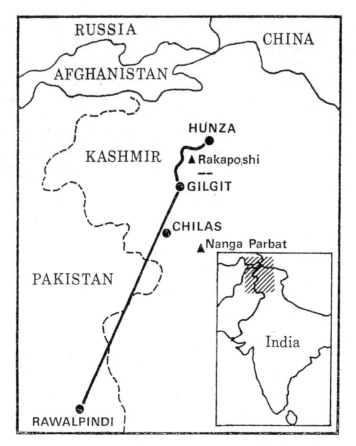

Kashmir: the route to Hunza

themselves to be photographed. My guide told me that this had not always been the case, but a Brazilian film company had made a film in Hunza some years before and had then inserted into it a childbirth sequence shot somewhere else. This had so incensed the sensibilities of the ladies of Hunza that they had spurned all forms of photography ever since.

That night, and for the next ten days, I stayed at the Hunza Hotel; it was hardly four-star, except for the prices. A pot of tea cost two rupees (approximately eight pence) and a vegetable curry, the standard meal, was seven rupees. I had a bare, but clean, room furnished with a bed and a small table, with a commode next door.

Each day I explored the valley, took pictures and talked to as many people as I could. At times I could not help being painfully aware that I was in a place that was on the threshold of becoming a tourist resort, when every form of goodwill becomes a marketable commodity.

Certainly, no Alpine valley could compare with Hunza for sheer, devastating beauty – it is the contrast more than anything else, green upon arid brown all capped with white. To the south-west, Rakaposhi, a huge complex of writhing snow ridges and hanging glaciers; to the north, the soaring wall of the Passu peaks that jumps 16,000 feet to a turreted ridge of ice and rock spires. To the east, more mountains, glaciers, rock and snow.

On my first morning I attended the Court of the Mir of Hunza; it was an informal affair. At ten o'clock, the Mir, an absolute monarch with complete control over the internal affairs of his 20,000 people, walks from his palace to the Durbah, a courtyard with a verandah down two sides. The Mir sits on a small rostrum, and his Court, in strict order of precedence, squat on carpets in two lines on either side of him.

The Court consists of the headman and elders of Hunza; they are appointed by the Mir, but he is careful to choose men who are respected by the villagers. They meet every day and spend an hour or so hearing disputes, giving judgement or just gossiping. This is Parliament, High Court and Cabinet, all rolled into one. There is no civil service, taxation, army, or even police force.

Anyone can walk into the court without appointment, and state his grievance. On this particular morning there was one case. The servant of a villager called Dadu complained that he had not been paid his wages. On the other hand, Dadu claimed that the boy had stolen a goat worth 120 rupees and had drunk his entire stock of wine. Everyone had a say in the case, sometimes everyone speaking at the same time, but eventually the Mir raised his hand and pronounced judgement.

'If Dadu makes an oath on the Koran in the presence of his headman, I am quite sure he will be telling the truth. It is therefore only fair that you lose your salary. Do you agree to this?'

The boy agreed and the case was closed.

There is little violence in Hunza. The only murder committed in recent years was two years before, when Nadir Aman, a farmer, had a dispute over the position of a poplar tree in one of his fields. By custom, trees cannot be closer than fourteen yards to another man's field. Nadir Aman was told by the village elders to cut down the tree, but he took no notice. His neighbour finally cut it down himself and, in a rage, Nadir Aman went to his house and shot him. At court, the Mir had sentenced him to be banished from Hunza, the most serious punishment possible, for there is no death penalty or prison.

That afternoon I had tea with the Mir. A short, fairly portly man, he looks rather like an English country squire, favours tweeds and visits Europe every year.

'I always stay at the Savoy in London. I don't like those modern hotels where you do everything over the telephone; it's so impersonal and the service is so bad,' he told me. 'This is a very happy country; there are no rich or very poor. Money can bring many problems and here in Hunza there is very little. I still pay all my servants in kind, with food or cloth. People grow their own produce; if someone is building a new house, everyone gives a hand. There is no question of payment, for they all help each other and eventually it balances out.

'A few years ago the Pakistan Government started their system of basic democracy to give villagers more say in their affairs. I offered it to them here in Hunza, but the elders turned it down. We already have a democracy.'

As I explored Hunza, I felt he was right. What other state exists without police force or prison?

It was certainly difficult to tell rich from poor. When I went to see Zafarulla Beg, who has the reputation for being the wisest man in Hunza, I found him working with a pick and shovel, alongside his servant; and yet he is headman of Hindi, a fairly big landowner and eighty years of age. As he showed me round his orchards, he was giving me a hand over walls, rather than the reverse.

He is also respected for being a skilful physician. Until comparatively recently, there were no medical facilities in Hunza, and even today there is only a small hospital run by a medical orderly without a doctor, but it is rarely used and the people prefer their own home cures. They make concoctions of herbs for illness and set simple fractures or dislocations. I saw Zafarulla Beg at work on one of his servants, a man who had dislocated his foot. He strapped it to a split piece of wood and then tapped in a wedge, which forced the dislocated joint back into place. It looked very painful, but effective.

The Hunzas have a reputation for longevity, but on this score they do not seem to be in the same class as the inhabitants of the Caucasus, who also claim they live to ages up to 130 years. The oldest man in Hunza is said to be 106 years old, and I was able to talk to the 102-year-old grandfather of my guide. He still does a little farming and showed no sign of senility. It wasn't so much the great age of the people of Hunza that impressed me, but rather the vigour and obvious happiness of the old people.

This might partly be accounted for by the balance of their diet which is frugal, yet highly nutritious. They eat meat only on special occasions, and the staple diet is wheat chuppatis with potatoes or vegetables, washed down by sour milk. In season, there is any amount of fruit, and they dry all the surplus for consumption during the remainder of the year. In addition, the family is still a strong unit, and the old are both respected and cared for. The elders of the village have a tranquillity and pride that one seldom sees amongst old people in the West.

During the day there is always a rattle of tin drums and the squeal of whistles played by the children. At weddings, house-moving and religious festivals, the men perform their traditional dances. This is still very much part of their lives and not just a money-earner for the benefit of the tourists.

One night I was invited to a prayer evening and feast at the home of Ghullam

Mohammed. There were eight of us altogether, seated round the floor of his living room. Most of them had come straight from the fields where they had been working all day. Jan Mohammed, the priest of the Jamal Khana, their place of worship, was dressed just the same as everyone else; he received no salary, and earned his living by teaching the girls of the village and running a small farm.

That night he conducted the prayers and singing. His face was cadaverous, with a huge beak of a nose jutting from it. He needed a shave, and his bare feet were none too clean, but when he sang in a strong grating voice that pulsated with rhythm and an unbelievable happiness, it hit deep into one's emotions. They all joined in for the choruses, and I was told they were singing love songs to the prophet and ballads of their own religious experience. It made the best folk-singing in Britain sound a bit insipid.

Hunza is a place of sounds, of water hurrying through irrigation channels, a donkey braying in the night, children crying or the muezzin calling the faithful to prayer from the palace roof – there is no loudspeaker system and his voice merges with the grandeur of surrounding mountains and the peace of the evening.

That night I met my first tourists; the road from the outside world had at last been opened. They were very disappointed that I was not Nicholas Monsarrat – 'He must be such a gorgeous man.' They boiled and sterilised all their water, even when it had already been boiled once by the cook – 'You just can't trust anything out here.' They grumbled, probably with good cause, about the amount they had been charged for sightseeing.

I couldn't help resenting their presence, and everything that tourism stands for. One has an instinctive and selfish longing to preserve places that are strange and picturesque, but beyond that, Hunza seemed a tranquil and contented island in the midst of a sea of violence, corruption and poverty. A new road has been built into the valley that links it with China. This might bring in some industry and hotels, but with it must inevitably come all the other attributes of a more sophisticated society – crime, graft, political strife, a police force and prisons.

There is no answer to the problem, and anyway there is very little anyone can do about it. Progress is a runaway monster whom no one seems able to control.

19　The Blue Nile

From a distance it had seemed a harmless shimmer on the river, but now we were looking straight down a steep chute into a boiling pit of white water.

'Straighten out the boat,' shouted Chris Edwards.

But it was too late – three paddles could do nothing against such a current. We smashed on to a rock and scraped down with the water piling round us. It all happened so quickly that I cannot remember any sequence of events; there was no sense of direction or time – just an angry, foaming wall of white, towering above us. Then I was in the water. I had a glimpse of the boat only a few feet away before being dragged under.

It was like being in a washing machine. No sooner did I reach the surface than I was pulled back again. I was not particularly frightened – I had not even swallowed much water but I realised I was drowning. My body, limbs, muscles seemed to have lost their own identity and to have become an integral part of the water around me. Thoughts swam sluggishly in a brown void – a feeling of guilt at having betrayed Wendy, and then one of curiosity. 'What will it be like when I'm dead?'

Then, with equal suddenness the water released me and I found myself being swept towards some rocks just below the fall. I couldn't swim properly as the trousers of my rubber wetsuit had been dragged down round my ankles, pinioning my legs: but somehow I managed to reach a rock and drag myself out of the river.

Up to that moment, I don't think that I, or any other member of the Great Abbai Expedition, fully appreciated just how savage and powerful the Blue Nile can be. It was a turning point in the expedition. Before the accident, it had been possible to be light-hearted and to enjoy the exhilaration of plunging through racing white water, but after it we just plugged on doggedly, trying hard to complete the job we had started.

The previous day, nine of us in three Avon Redshank inflatable boats had pushed off from the bank at the start of the Blue Nile – or Great Abbai as it is called locally – where it flows out of Lake Tana. It was difficult to believe that this was one of the most dangerous, and least known, rivers in the world, for the current was almost imperceptible, flowing in a wide stream between tossing plumes of papyrus. Heron and egret flew low across the water, and a hippo sank out of sight as the front boat glided past.

It is called the Blue Nile, but its waters are a muddy brown flood that hurtles through 500 miles of unexplored gorge to the deserts of Sudan and Egypt. It seemed incredible that at a time when almost every natural feature on earth had been conquered and explored, one so accessible and important to the history of man had succeeded in retaining its secrets.

The source of the river is easy enough to reach; it lies in a swamp in the Highlands of Ethiopia, a small spring that nurtures a stream flowing into Lake Tana. The expedition had already completed the lower and easier section of the river from the Shafartak Road Bridge to the Sudanese frontier, and was now about to attempt the first-ever descent of the completely unknown part of the Blue Nile. For its first twenty miles the river flows through gently undulating farmland, until it drops 150 feet sheer over the Tississat Falls and plunges with ever-increasing violence through twenty miles of gorge to the Portuguese Bridge. From there, the river was completely unknown as far as the Shafartak Road Bridge, 120 miles further on.

We were members of one section of the seventy-strong Great Abbai Expedition, and as we set off down-river, other groups were moving into position on the bank to give us support. Our three boats were called *Faith*, *Hope* and *Charity*: Captain Roger Chapman, leader of the 'white water' team, had made extensive modifications to the boats, having the bottoms strengthened and inserting inflated football bladders into the sides, so that they could not sink. He had decided to do without engines, since there was too great a risk of the propellers being smashed against rocks in the shallow rapids. So we were to depend on paddles for power and steerage.

I was sailing in *Charity*, with Corporal Ian McLeod and Lieutenant Chris Edwards. Edwards played rugger for the Army and was a powerful 6ft 7m. McLeod was lean, even emaciated, yet probably the toughest and most experienced member of the expedition. He had served with the crack Special Air Service regiment in jungle and desert, and was used to working in small parties under exacting conditions. *Hope* was crewed by Lieutenant Jim Masters (at forty-two years old, the oldest member of the party), Staff Sergeant John Huckstep and John Fletcher, who owned a garage at Tewkesbury and specialised in renovating vintage cars. The third boat, *Faith*, was crewed by Roger Chapman, Alastair Newman, a lecturer in physics at the Royal Military Academy, Sandhurst, and Corporal Peter O'Mahoney, who admitted to being worried by the water but volunteered to come because we needed an experienced wireless operator.

Our gentle introduction to the Blue Nile did not last long. Imperceptibly the speed of the current increased and a distant roar heralded the first cataract. We were swept round a bend and could see a cloud of spray in front. I had a sagging feeling as we were drawn towards it. It was barely possible to steer and we were spun, helpless, against the rocky bank. Somehow we straightened up before hitting the chute of racing water that led into the cataract. Walls of white water lunged above us and around us, smashed into us with a solid force. There was now no time for fear, just an intense excitement. It was like skiing and surfing and fast driving all rolled into one – a roller coaster ride down an avalanche of white water. We were all shouting as we smashed through the last wave.

That night we set up camp in a meadow near the river. We were full of confidence and talked of reaching the Tississat Falls in the following two days. Next day we started by pushing the boats through an archipelago of tree-covered islands – rather like the Everglades in Florida, with spiky palms overhead and dank undergrowth blocking the stream bed. It was midday before we reached the open channel, where the current raced wide and shallow over a series of cataracts, each one more dangerous than the last. There was no chance of making a foot reconnaissance, for the banks were covered by dense scrub and tentacles of marsh. We had to press on and hope for the best. In one of the cataracts the crew of *Hope* were flipped out of their boat by a wave. Jim Masters was dragged underwater and only got back to the surface by inflating his life jacket. As we paused on the bank to repair the bottoms of the boats, he sat very quiet and tense, slightly away from us. At that stage we could not conceive what he had experienced nor fully understand why he was so badly shaken.

As we set off again we were joking about it being '*Charity*'s turn next'. For a short distance we roped the boats down the bank, but it was a slow process and we were becoming impatient. We could hardly see the next fall – it was just a shimmer of water in the distance, but we decided to take it: Roger Chapman went first and vanished from sight with a frightening suddenness. There was a long pause and then we saw the green miniflare which was the signal to follow. We let *Hope* go a few yards in front and followed immediately. They managed to get through without tipping over, but were carried, barely in control, over several more cataracts, before pulling into the bank.

We were the unlucky ones, and capsized. I don't think there was any question of greater or less skill; it was simply a form of Russian roulette, with us and our boats helpless playthings of the river. Once I escaped the grasp of the undertow and had reached a rock, I was able to see Chris Edwards bobbing down in the main stream, a few yards from me. He had had the same treatment, but had been hurled out into faster water and was now being dashed, helpless, over the sharp volcanic rocks. His wet-suit trousers had been dragged down over his ankles so that he could not swim, and his legs were completely unprotected. On the brink of a huge cataract he managed to hold on to a rock just below the surface.

'I'd lost all control by that time,' he said. 'It took a good five minutes just getting a grip of myself. I kept on repeating the number written on my life-jacket. It was all I could do to hold on to the rock and I knew that if I was swept

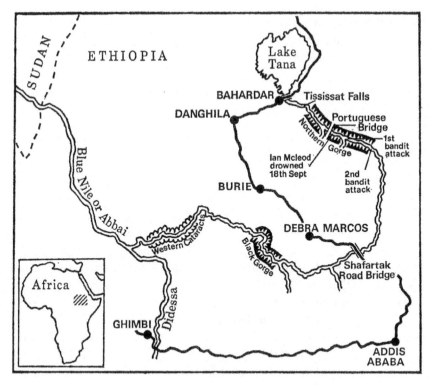

The Blue Nile area

over I'd almost certainly have had it.'

Meanwhile, Ian McLeod had managed to get back on to the upturned boat and was floating downstream. For a few moments the boat paused in an eddy and I even thought I might be able to reach him. I abandoned the dubious safety of my rock and dived into the river, but before I had gained more than a couple of yards the boat was clutched by the current and whipped out of sight. McLeod did his best to steer the boat into the side with a paddle, but he was helpless against the force of the water and was swept down over several cataracts, past *Faith* which had now reached the bank, to the brink of the worst fall we had yet encountered. McLeod described this as 'a smooth brown chute that went straight into a great pit of boiling water'.

He told us that he never thought he would survive. He just clung to the straps on the bottom of the boat and went right under. Fortunately, as he felt himself being torn from it, he was swept into the bushes at the side of the river. He grabbed them, but was unable to hold the boat, and had to let it go.

Roger Chapman had managed to stop *Faith* just beyond the cataract where we had capsized, and had swum out with a rope in an attempt to 'field' *Charity* as it swept past. I was now able to swim across to him and grabbed the rope, but we still had to rescue Chris Edwards. We could hear him shouting for help, a desperate, raucous quality in his voice. Knowing we could not afford to make a mistake, slowly and methodically Peter O'Mahoney and I let the boat out on a line from a tree on the bank, so that Roger and Alastair Newman could reach Edwards.

There just was not enough rope, and the boat was still twenty feet from him, so they threw a line, but it missed and the boat pivoted away. It was all we could do to pull it back against the force of the current so that they could try again.

This time they tied a paddle to the end of the line and it reached him, but he was unable to move as his leg was trapped in a crevice in the rock. Alastair Newman went over the side, fighting his way across to him: from a distance it was like a terrifying slow-motion ballet. Although the water was only around their knees, it threatened to dash both of them down the cataract with its unbelievable force. Eventually, they both got into the boat and we dragged them back to the tree. We were now presented with the problem of getting to the other side of the river in a leaking boat which was weighed down by five men.

We bottomed on every cataract, had to jump out in the swirling water to push the boats free, then on the last one I was dragged away and found myself once again swimming for my life. My nerves were so deadened that I barely noticed it, allowing myself to be swept through the turbulence till I could wait for the boat to pick me up. It was almost dark when finally we reached the bank, and then we found a thunderstorm crashing over our heads.

We had lost our boat, had nearly lost our lives, and even the next morning we were still stunned by the accident, but most of us were determined to continue. Chris Edwards was obviously going to be out of action for some time and John Huckstep decided that he had had enough.

The boat was quickly discovered by the Beaver aircraft which had been flown out from England to support the expedition, and I went out to retrieve it with several members of the shore support party. Twenty-four hours later the shock of my near-escape really hit me, and manifested itself mainly in a sense of horror at letting down my family. I had learned to accept the risks involved in mountaineering, but the risks I was taking now seemed so totally uncontrollable. I went to Roger Chapman and told him that I did not think I could go on any longer.

The entire venture was now on the brink of failure, and Roger Chapman, realising that a thorough reconnaissance was vital, decided to leave the 'white water' party for three days to make a foot reconnaissance of the river below the northern gorge while the rest of the party roped the boats down the Tississat Falls. I agreed to help in this and, working with Ian McLeod and Alastair Newman, I slowly rediscovered my confidence and peace of mind.

We edged the boats through narrow channels, often dragging them over waterlogged grass in order to avoid the worst of the falls. Even so, the river was always ready to pounce on a single mistake. John Fletcher nearly lost his life when he was dragged under as they lowered his boat down a fall.

I could not help wondering and worrying about my decision to pull out and that of the other married members of the expedition who had decided to press on. John Fletcher had a simple philosophy – 'I came out here realising that I was doing something dangerous and that I might be killed. I told my wife of the risks involved and she accepted it.' I thought of Jim Masters, happily married for twenty years, with three children; he was obviously unhappy about going on, but his sense of loyalty to the expedition was so great that he persevered.

Roger Chapman now decided to reduce his team to six men in two boats: Ian McLeod, Richard Snailham (a lecturer from Sandhurst) and himself in one; and Jim Masters, John Fletcher and Alastair Newman in the other. As a result of his reconnaissance, he decided to portage the boats from the Tississat Falls to a point about a mile beyond. I was to follow the bank on foot.

The river had now assumed a new character, racing through a single channel between tree-clad banks. Stretches of choppy, fast water alternated with boiling cataracts. As I watched the members of the 'white water' team arrive at each cataract I could not help noticing a tension which was getting close to nervous exhaustion.

'The river's alive with power,' Ian McLeod said. 'It seems to be sucking us down the whole time and you can't stop the boats filling up with water.' Once the boats were full it was impossible to manoeuvre them and it took a good 500 yards to get into the bank.

After about twelve miles the river plunges into a sheer-sided gorge. This was one of the most frightening sights I have ever seen; the entire volume of water pouring over the Tississat Falls is compressed through a gap no more than fifteen feet wide, into a cauldron of bubbling, effervescent water. Even if they had carried the boats beyond this point, the next six miles of gorge seemed unjustifiably dangerous, for it would have been impossible to stop the boats before reaching the numerous cataracts boiling at its bottom. Roger Chapman, therefore, decided to send the boats down by themselves to be picked up by a party already in position at the Portuguese Bridge, while the two crews walked round the top.

It is one of those tragic ironies that Ian McLeod lost his life while taking the safest course. We had nearly finished our march to the Portuguese Bridge and had to cross the River Abaya, a miniature Blue Nile, at the bottom of a deep gorge. It was only thirty feet wide, but he was snatched away from us with such speed that there was nothing we could do. Alastair Newman had swum across first and McLeod followed, after tying on a safety-line. He nearly reached the other bank when he seemed to lose his strength and was swept back into the centre. As the rope came tight it pulled him under. We gave him more slack and although he came back to the surface he was now being swept rapidly downstream. The next moment the rope ran out. Someone shouted 'Free the rope' – at that split second it seemed the only way to prevent McLeod from being dragged under. At the same time Roger Chapman, with considerable heroism, dived in in an effort to save him, even managing to drag him to the side on the brink of a cataract. But McLeod was snatched out of his arms by the force of the water. We never saw him again.

We were stunned with a terrible feeling of helpless guilt that we had managed to do so little to save him. It seemed callous just to carry on with the expedition, yet there was no other course. Captain John Blashford-Snell, leader of the expedition, was waiting at the Portuguese Bridge to take command of the final phase, through the 120 miles of completely unexplored gorge, down to the Shafartak Bridge. Air reconnaissance had shown that the cataracts were not quite as savage as they had been higher up, but that there was a large number of crocodiles. He had, therefore, decided to reinforce the two Redshanks with two inflatable army recce boats, powered by 9½ horsepower engines.

By now I had decided to return to the water for this phase, since it was impossible to cover the story from the bank, but I dreaded going back to the boats. The two Redshanks released at the start of the gorge had reached the Portuguese Bridge, only to be swept past. As a result, two new boats which had not been modified with inflated football bladders, were brought in. They were named *Deane-Drummond* and *Crookenden*, after two British generals who were supporting the expedition.

The attitude of the local villagers was a further complication. The people of the Gojjam province, particularly those living on the brink of the gorge, had a long record of warlike independence. They had been fighting with Government forces over a new tax law. Their chiefs, having taken exception to our invasion of the river, had tried to force us to withdraw, even threatening violence if we did not comply. A band of thirty local chiefs and retainers, all armed with Italian rifles captured during the war, gathered on the 300-year-old stone bridge over the Abbai, offering us a rising crescendo of threats. However, they left guards with us at night to ensure that no other band would attack us. Eventually, the police chief from the neighbouring town of Mota persuaded them to allow us to continue on our way down the river, and we set off on the final leg of our journey on the morning of the 20th September.

A belt of creaming waves stretched across the river only a few hundred yards below the bridge. The two recce boats went first, one of them helmed by Sub-Lieutenant Jo Ruston with John Blashford-Snell, and the other helmed by John Fletcher with Colin Chapman, a twenty-four-year-old zoologist, who was hoping to make a crocodile survey. Their job was to protect us against crocodiles and come to our assistance if anything went wrong. Our boat, with Alastair Newman and a newcomer to the river, Lieutenant Garth Brocksop, was the last to go. It was like waiting to go into a boxing ring for a fight which you were convinced you would lose. I had a queasy feeling in my stomach, and could not take my eyes off the tumbling waves in the distance. And then the green flare went up and it was time to start.

The water was never as bad as it had been above the Tississat Falls, but it was like going down a liquid Cresta Run, never sure what was round the next bend and barely able to stop. There was no more exhilaration, just a nagging fear and taut concentration, as we spun the boats out of the way of the boulders, or edged round the worst of the waves.

Now the river began to take on a new character, hurrying in a solid smooth stream between sheer rock walls. It was at last possible to relax and marvel at the rock architecture around us. Slender towers jutted hundreds of feet out of the river bed, while huge natural arches spanned its tributaries. We stopped that night in an idyllic campsite by the tree-covered banks of a side stream. The walls of the gorge towered 150 feet above us.

We were intrigued by two caves in the sheer cliff opposite, which had obviously been inhabited at one time. Next morning, we succeeded in climbing to them from the boat, and discovered a number of broken pots and old grain silos well covered in bat dung. We were all excited by the discovery as we packed up camp. I was drinking a cup of coffee when John ran into the camp and shouted: 'Hurry up, it's time we got out of here.' At the same time, there was a sudden, high-pitched keening from above, followed by a volley of rifle fire. We were completely taken by surprise, finding it impossible to believe that people were actually trying to kill us.

After our experience at the Portuguese Bridge, my first reaction was that perhaps they just wanted to warn us off. John Blashford-Snell ran out with the loud-hailer, shouting 'Ternasterling, Ternasterling', the conventional form of greeting, but one of the men on the cliff opposite replied by firing at him. I can remember running out myself, trying to wave to them, and then noticing a rifle pointing straight at me.

While some of us tried appeasement, others loaded the boats, racing out from cover with handfuls of gear and hurling them in. We were still arguing in the shelter of the trees about what we should do, but no one recommended firing back at this stage. One party wanted to make a break for it; the other, of which I was one, felt we should stay put and try to reason with our attackers, or call up support on the wireless. The deciding factor was a huge rock, the size of a kitchen table, that came hurtling down from above.

'Gentlemen, someone has got to make a decision,' said John Blashford-Snell, in a remarkably cool voice. 'When I say go, run for the boats.'

The next thing I remember is pushing our boats through the shallows. Glancing up, the whole sky seemed full of rocks; bullets spurted in the water around us. We were gathering speed in the main current when I suddenly felt a violent blow on my back and was hurled across the boat. I had been hit by a rock.

John Blashford-Snell and Colin Chapman had now got out their revolvers and were giving us covering fire. Fortunately, only a few of our attackers were armed with rifles. At John's third shot, one of the attackers seemed to be hurled backwards – it was almost certainly a hit. His fire might well have saved or lives, for it seemed a miracle that none of us or our boats was hit by a bullet. If an inflated side had been punctured, it would have been fatal for the entire crew.

At last out of range of their fire, we were now worried in case the entire country might have been raised against us; we watched every bluff overlooking the river with apprehension. Whenever we saw anyone on the bank we waved a friendly 'Ternasterling', but kept our weapons at the ready. Fortunately we could easily outstrip anyone following us on the bank, and that afternoon we covered about twenty miles. We even found *Charity*, snagged in some trees at the side of the river.

At the end of that day we stopped on an island just off the Gojjam shore. At 1.30 a.m. Roger Chapman decided to make sure the boats were moored securely. Casually shining his torch at the water's edge, he picked out a group of men. Automatically, he called out 'Ternasterling', but they replied by firing at him; he returned their fire immediately and ran back to the camp. I remember waking to the high-pitched war-whoops of our attackers. I had been worried the previous night about the boats, thinking that if the bandits did manage to release them we should have little chance of survival.

Putting on my boots, I started down towards the boats. It was a confusion of gun flashes and shouting. John Blashford-Snell was a magnificent sight, wearing his pith helmet, firing mini-flares and taking pot shots at a bandit.

Then, as suddenly as the noise had started, there was silence – just an occasional rustle from the bank showed that our attackers were still there. We packed up the camp in the dark and withdrew to the boats. We stayed there for a couple of hours, hoping to wait until the dawn before descending the river, but at 3.30 a.m. the bugle blared, almost certainly heralding another attack. John Blashford-Snell was worried about our shortage of ammunition and gave the order to cast off.

We drifted into the main stream in complete silence – it was an eerie experience, for we were able to see only the sheen of water and the dark silhouette of the banks. Then we heard the thunder of a cataract ahead, tried to pull into the bank, but were helpless in the current. Suddenly, we were in white water; we climbed a huge wave, came down the other side and were through, but the other two boats behind were less lucky. 'We seemed to stand on end,' Roger Chapman told me afterwards. 'I jammed my leg under the thwart and somehow managed to stay in the boat, but the other two were thrown out.

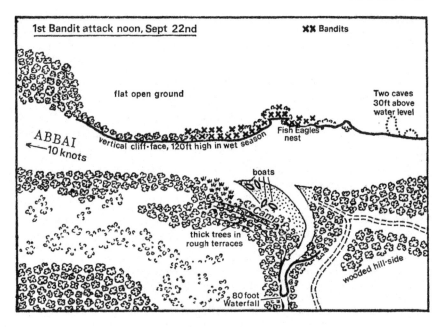

The Blue Nile: the first attack

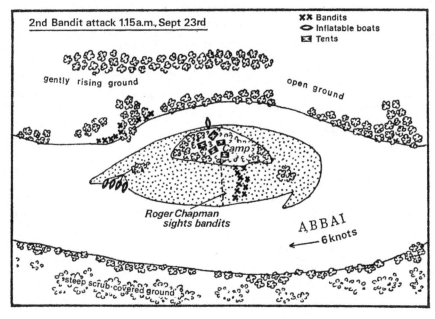

The Blue Nile: the second attack

I immediately realised that if I couldn't grab them we should never find them in the dark. They came to the surface just alongside the boat, and I dragged them in.'

Meanwhile, Jo Ruston's boat, which had us in tow, was sinking: the air valve had developed a fault and the front compartment was completely deflated. He had no choice but to release us and we drifted away in the dark. It was a good half-mile before we managed to pull on to a sandbank in the middle of the river. We sat there until dawn, feeling very lonely and vulnerable.

The drama never seemed to end. John Fletcher had damaged the propeller of his boat immediately after being thrown out in the cataract. As soon as they reached a sandbank he got out his tool kit to change propellers while the party waited for the dawn. A few minutes later he walked over to Roger Chapman.

'A terrible thing's happened. I've lost the nut holding the propeller,' he whispered.

The outboard motor was essential for our escape and they tried fixing it with a bent nail, but that was no good. Then, as a last resort they mixed some Araldite glue and stuck it back on the shaft, but the glue needed at least an hour to stick and by now it was beginning to get light. John Blashford-Snell waited as long as he dared before giving the order to move. John Fletcher tied a polythene bag round the propeller in an effort to keep the glue dry, and the boats were pushed off and drifted down the river.

The only noise was the gurgling of smooth, fast-flowing water. The wan light of the dawn coloured the fluted rocks and pinnacles on either side of the gorge a subtle brown. In contrast to the night's violence it was unbelievably beautiful. And we swept on down the river – it was all so peaceful, yet full of lurking threats. We began to see more crocodiles, but they seemed a small threat compared with our human attackers. The crocodiles just scrambled into the river and vanished without trace.

At nine that morning, we reached the assault boat commanded by Captain John Wilsey, which had struggled up river to meet us and escort us for the last leg of our journey. Our progress was now like a triumphal procession as the assault boat, flying the Ethiopian flag and the Union Jack, towed us for the last fifty miles down to the Shafartak Bridge.

We finished our 500-mile journey at 4.30 p.m. on 25th September. Our Beaver aircraft dived low over us and a small welcoming party waved from the bank. As we pulled the boats ashore we drank champagne, yet felt rather sad and maudlin. I think we had all come too close to death and were too aware of Ian McLeod's absence. We had succeeded in descending the Blue Nile, but no one could ever claim to have conquered it – too often we had been helpless in its grip.

20   Annapurna: Preparation

The Blue Nile marked a boundary in my life. We had found a house in Bowdon, Cheshire, just before I had set out for the Blue Nile and Wendy was left with all the worry and hard work entailed in the removal, together with undoubted sadness at leaving the Lake District. We had lived there for five years and she, especially, had come to love the area where we had known carefree happiness, had met day-to-day worries and in which we had experienced a total, over-whelming grief. It was she, not I, who needed the real courage while I was away on the Blue Nile.

I came back to find a sharp knife had been cut through a section of our lives. For a time we were in limbo, for the house we had bought in Bowdon was still in the hands of the builders. We had snatched it in desperation, only a few weeks before my departure. It was an ugly, old Edwardian semi-detached in a cul-de-sac on the flat top of one of the few hills in that part of Cheshire – on top of a hill, but there was no view – we were surrounded by other houses. Although it was very different from Bank End Cottage, or even our house in Cockermouth, I was glad to be living in Bowdon; there were plenty of climbing friends around; also plenty of climbing within reasonable range, of a greater variety than is available in the Lake District – the Peak District, North Wales, Bristol and the Avon Gorge just down the motorway. I could get out climbing once a week in the evening, and become again a weekend climber, going off to Wales or the Lakes.

For a period of three months, while we waited for the builders to complete alterations to our house, we stayed with Nick and Carolyn Estcourt, still in their two-bedroomed flat in Alderley Edge. We arrived intending to stay for a few days and by some miracle we did not get on each other's nerves, even though this time was extended so considerably – certainly this was a fine test of compatibility for any expedition. And it was here that the Annapurna South Face Expedition was conceived, or rather, was evolved, for it started out as something far less ambitious before it took its final shape.

Nick, Martin Boysen and I had been discussing expeditions for the past couple of years with little progress. That October we decided that come what may we should go on an expedition in 1970, but suitable objectives were limit-ed. At that time all the mountains of Nepal and most of the better ranges in Pakistan and India were closed to climbers for political reasons, mainly the result of tension on the Tibetan border. It was possible to climb in the Hindu Kush in Afghanistan, and in the outlying peaks of the Karakoram in Pakistan, but I found these unattractive, for they seemed overshadowed by the true Himalayan giants. We considered Alaska, where there are still hundreds of unclimbed walls and the mountains are even more empty and desolate than those in the Himalaya, though of course very much lower.

I had known Martin for about eight years. One of Britain's finest rock-climbers, at ground level his limbs seem uncoordinated, but once poised on a stretch of rock he drifts up effortlessly, a smoothly functioning climbing-machine. He is like a huge intelligent sloth, conditioned to a vertical environment. We had climbed together extensively in this country, but never in the Alps or farther ranges. For a brilliant climber he was remarkably uncompetitive, secure perhaps in his own natural ability and too lazy to enter into the rat-race that can dominate some aspects of British climbing. Even so, some of his new routes in Wales and Scotland are among the most difficult and dangerous ever put up in this country; he went on to climb at a very high standard in the Alps, making several first ascents and first British ascents.

Nick, on the other hand, was not a natural climber. Wiry, yet powerfully built, quite highly strung, very competitive, he had forced himself to a high standard of climbing. In some ways he had the traditional middle-class background of the pre-war climbers, and for that matter most of the Everest expeditions right up to the successful one of 1953. He was introduced to climbing by his father in the Alps, while still at school, and he gained a very broad mountaineering background in alpine climbing. Whilst at Cambridge he became President of the University Mountaineering Club, and also took part in an expedition to Arctic Greenland, his only experience of climbing outside Europe. He was sufficiently devoted to climbing to try to bend a conventional career in engineering to fit in with his sport, but finding engineering somewhat tying abandoned it for computers. Living in Alderley Edge, near Manchester, he was able to combine his new career with plenty of climbing.

As the fourth member of our team we chose Dougal Haston, whom Martin also knew well. Then, the news arrived – Nepal was allowing in climbers for the first time in four years. Immediately we forgot about Alaska and started to consider possible objectives. There were several unclimbed peaks of below 24,000 feet, which to me seemed unattractive, since they would have given me a lesser experience than I had received on my two previous expeditions to Annapurna II and Nuptse. The thought of a major face climb, however, did catch our enthusiasm – taut excitement and technical difficulty tempered with the slow snow-plodding that can turn Himalayan climbing into a featureless treadmill.

Then I remembered seeing a photograph of the South Face of Annapurna which had been sent to Jimmy Roberts.

'Lets go for that,' I suggested, with very little idea then of what 'that' entailed. The others, in their innocence, agreed. Another British expedition, to Machapuchare, immediately opposite the South Face of Annapurna, had included Jimmy Roberts and it was here that he had first seen the face. Having written to him, I telephoned two of the other members of that expedition.

'South Face?' said David Cox, a lecturer in Modern History at University College, Oxford. 'I don't remember much about it; looked huge; yes, there were a lot of avalanches coming down it, but I think they were going down the runnels.'

Roger Chorley, a London accountant, was even more discouraging. 'Going for the South Face of Annapurna?' in a voice of mild disbelief. 'It's swept by avalanches the whole time.' By this time I had begun to think of other objectives, then Jimmy Roberts' letter arrived:

'The South Face of Annapurna is an exciting prospect – more difficult than Everest, although the approach problems are easier. Certainly it will be very difficult indeed, and although I am not an oxygen fan, it seems to me that the exertion of the severe climbing at over 24,000 feet may demand oxygen.' I felt encouraged.

Then, a few days later, I received a colour slide of the face from David Cox. We projected it on to the wall of my living room – a six-foot picture – and gazed and gazed – first excited and then frightened.

'There's a line all right,' Martin said, 'but it's bloody big.'

It was. I had never seen a mountain photograph giving such an impression of huge size and steepness. It was like four different Alpine faces piled one on top of the other – but what a line! Hard, uncompromising, positive all the way up. A squat snow ridge, like the buttress of a Gothic cathedral, leaned against the lower part of the wall. That was the start all right; perhaps it would be possible to bypass it, sneaking along the glacier at its foot – but what about avalanche risk? The buttress led to an ice arête which was obviously a genuine knife-edge. I had climbed something like this on Nuptse – in places we had been able to look straight through holes in the ridge a hundred feet below its crest. That had been frightening, but this would be worse. The knife-edge died below a band of ice cliffs.

'I wonder how stable they are?' asked Nick. I wondered too, and, with only partial confidence, traced a line through them leading to a rock wall.

'Must be at least a thousand feet.'

'But where the hell does it start? It could be twenty-three thousand. Do you fancy hard rock-climbing at that altitude?'

'Yes, but look at that groove.' It split the crest of the ridge, a huge gash, inviting, but undoubtedly more difficult and sustained than anything previously climbed at that altitude.

The rock band ended with what seemed to be a shoulder of snow leading to the summit.

'But the picture must be foreshortened. That could be a long way below the top.'

Looking at some transparencies I had taken from Annapurna II in 1960, we saw that the top of the rock band was at around three-quarter height; there was another 3,000 feet to the top of a steep snow arête, with a rocky crest on which to finish.

Sobered by what we had seen, realising that this was something bigger and more difficult than anything that had ever been tackled before, we flashed a picture of the South Face of Nuptse. It was completely dwarfed by the huge South Face of Annapurna.

In spite of everything, I felt confident that with the right team we had a good chance of climbing it; that my own mountaineering background had perhaps built up towards this attempt. In a Himalayan environment we would use the techniques developed on the ascent of the Eiger Direct; in addition I had a yardstick of comparison from climbing the South Face of Nuptse, although that had been considerably more straightforward than Annapurna's South Face. I had been to a height of 25,850 feet on Nuptse unaided by oxygen, but I had experience in the use of it from Annapurna II, and understood the tremendous difference it can make to one's climbing potential.

Although attracted to the idea of a small, compact, four-man expedition uncluttered by the paraphernalia and complications of a larger expedition, it was obvious that the South Face of Annapurna would require a larger party. Six men also seemed insufficient and we went up to eight.

The next problem was the selection of the team from the numerous leading climbers of Britain. They would have to be the men who could climb at a very high standard on rock and ice, with plenty of endurance, and an ability to subordinate their own personal ambitions to the good of the expedition as a whole. Most important of all, they would have to get on together. Many top-class climbers, having a touch of the prima donna in their make-up, are often self-centred and are essentially individualists; in some ways the best expedition man is the steady plodder. On the South Face of Annapurna we were going to need a high proportion of hard lead climbers who would be able to take over the exacting front position as others slowed up and tired.

One can never be sure of anyone's individual performance in the Himalaya, since people acclimatise to altitude at different rates and some never acclimatise at all. The safest bet, therefore, is to take out climbers who have already proved themselves at altitude, but because of the ban on climbing in Nepal and Pakistan in the late sixties, there was a distinct shortage of top-standard alpinists with Himalayan experience.

I approached Ian Clough first. I had done some of my best climbing with him and quite apart from being a capable mountaineer he was also the kindest and least selfish partner I had known. Certainly the perfect expedition man, he had very little personal ambition, but was always ready to do his best for the project as a whole.

Then I asked twenty-eight-year-old Mick Burke and, thirdly, Don Whillans. In some ways, Don was the most obvious choice of all, yet the one about whom I had the most doubts. Although certainly the finest all-round mountaineer that Britain had produced since the war, in the previous years he had allowed himself to slip into poor physical condition. He had lost interest in British rock-climbing, and even the Alps, preferring to go on expeditions to the farther ranges of the world. In spite of a strained relationship, which was ever-present, I had done some of my best climbing with him, each of us irritating the other, yet at the same time complementing each other's weak points.

Up to that time Don had had an unlucky streak, having been three times to the Himalaya, each time performing magnificently but never reaching the top. On his first expedition to the Karakoram in 1957 he spent eight weeks above 23,000 feet and struggled to within 150 feet of the summit of Masherbrum but was forced to retreat when his companion collapsed. On his next expedition, to Trivor, another twenty-five thousander, he worked himself into the ground getting the party into position for the final assault, and as a result was unable himself to get to the top.

On Gaurishankar once again he was unlucky. After considerable trouble in finding a route to the foot of the mountain the expedition was then forced to make its way round the peak on to the Tibetan flanks to get a feasible route to the top. Its communications were over-extended and it was finally forced to turn back.

Whilst most of the team I had invited so far were comparatively inexperienced, Don's particular qualities seemed ideally suited to the problem, but I was worried in case he had let himself slide too far into bad condition to function well on the mountain.

I suggested we had a weekend climbing together, without telling him of my plans. We were going up to Scotland one Friday night and, arriving at his house at about 10.30 p.m., I found he was out but would be back in half an hour. At 2.30 a.m. he returned, having downed eleven pints of beer, and we set off straightaway, with me in a slightly self-righteous bad temper. We arrived at Glencoe and the following day set out with Tom Patey to make the first ascent of the Great Gully of Ardgour. On the walk up to the climb Don lagged far behind, taking his time and in the gully he was happy to stay at the back, accepting a rope on all the difficult pitches. Then, on the last pitch, an evil chimney lined with ice and just too wide for comfortable bridging, he said, 'I think I'll have a try at this. It's about my turn to go out in front.'

There was an icy wind blasting straight up the chimney; it was so wide he was almost doing the splits on the way up, and its top was blocked by ice-sheathed boulders which you had to swing on. Don went up incredibly quickly and smoothly without bothering to protect himself with running belays. Both Tom and I had a struggle when it was our turn to follow. It was then that I made up my mind and that evening invited him to join the expedition. He looked at the photograph I showed him and commented, 'It'll be hard, but it should go all right. I'll come.' He was the obvious person to be deputy leader, and I promptly offered him this position.

So far I had selected people with whom I had climbed in difficult circumstances and knew deeply, who knew me and knew each other. This seemed the soundest basis for a tight-knit group – all with weaknesses and strengths, knowing each other well enough to accept them, and having in the past put ourselves and our relationships to the test of physical and mental stress. But now the choice of an eighth member of the team was influenced by finance.

'Couldn't you get an American? It would make my job a lot easier in the States,' asked George Greenfield, our agent, rather wistfully.

Not having any personal knowledge of any American who would be suitable, I had doubts, but we needed the money so I agreed finally. Various names came to mind, but one climber in particular interested me, and this was Tom Frost. Both Don and Dougal knew and spoke well of him.

Tom is a partner in a mountain hardware factory and is one of America's outstanding rock-climbers. The rock walls of Yosemite in California present some of the smoothest and most compact mountain faces in the world. To climb these, Tom and a few others have developed new equipment and techniques and had since adapted these ideas to tackle even bigger problems throughout the breadth of the American continents. The approach has influenced climbers everywhere. His reply to my letter of invitation was characteristic:

'I have just returned from Alaska where we succeeded in struggling up the tourist route on Mount McKinley. As a result of this experience I am somewhat confident in being able to ascend to 20,000 feet and on the basis of this credential hereby agree to come to Annapurna with you and will even attempt to climb.'

In fact, Tom had already been to the Himalaya and had climbed Kantega, a peak of 22,340 feet. He had also put up new routes in the Cordillera Blanca and the Alps. On learning that he was a practising Mormon, a faith which forbids strong drink, gambling, smoking, bad language, tea and coffee, I wondered how he would get on with us. Tom turned out to be not only a good Mormon, but also a splendidly tolerant one.

The party, now numbering eight, was certainly the strongest that had ever been assembled in Britain to tackle a Himalayan peak. In addition to the hard climbers it became evident we should need some men who would be prepared to concentrate on the more mundane but essential tasks of keeping open the lower part of the mountain and supervising the flow of supplies.

Mike Thompson, one of my oldest friends, was not a brilliant high-standard climber, but had an easy, equable temperament coupled with single-minded individualism. He was ideally suited to the support role I offered.

We also needed a doctor; someone capable of reaching the upper part of a mountain yet content to remain in a support role. It is no use having the doctor out in front. Dave Lambert, a thirty-year-old registrar at a hospital in Newcastle, had heard of the expedition from a friend, and telephoned me. He called to see me the following weekend and I found him bouncy, talkative, and full of enthusiasm. He was even prepared to pay his own way to come on the expedition. Having climbed in the Alps, he was a competent all-rounder without being an ace climber and I invited him on the spot.

Having the right equipment and food flowing up the mountain, in the right order, would be one of the requisites for success and some kind of Base Camp Manager would be essential. Possibly an older, experienced mountaineer would have taken on this job, but he might well have had too many preconceived ideas. A member of the 1953 Everest Expedition, Lt-Col. Charles Wylie, a serving officer in the army, at my request, recommended Kelvin Kent, a Captain in the Gurkha Signals, then stationed in Hong Kong. Not only did he speak fluent Nepali, he was a wireless expert and had a sound practical knowledge of the logistic planning required on the mountain. An assault on a Himalayan peak is comparable with fighting a war – logistics and planning are the key to success. No matter how tough or courageous the men out in front, unless they are supplied with food and equipment they quickly come to a grinding halt.

It has been said that the ideal age for the Himalayan climber is around the mid-thirties and in this case we were slightly below, for the average age of our party was just over thirty. But at twenty-five I had acclimatised quite satisfactorily on my first trip to the Himalaya, and Don Whillans was only twenty-three on Masherbrum where he put up an outstanding performance.

Our team now numbered eleven climbers. We planned to supplement our numbers with six Sherpas – a small figure for an expedition of this size, but with the face so steep, it seemed unlikely that we should be able to use them for more than the lower slopes.

We had succeeded in selling our story to ITN and Thames Television and hoped to get away with taking a single cameraman/director, but understandably they insisted on our taking a complete film team of cameraman, sound recordist, reporter-director from Thames and finally, since this was a joint venture, a representative from ITN to look after their interests.

I was worried about taking such a large self-contained group along, since an expedition imposes a strain on personal relationships at the best of times and a group reporting on us, yet remaining uninvolved, could have increased this danger still further. However, we needed the money and after meeting

John Edwards, the Thames Television director, and Alan Hankinson, the ITN representative, I felt reassured. John was a fast-talking extrovert who would obviously fit happily into any group. Alan had a slightly whimsical, yet diffident air, not at all the kind of person you would expect to find in television. He had an unconsummated passion for mountaineering and seemed to be looking forward to our trip for its own sake.

And so the total strength of the party would number twenty-one. On top of this we should have mail-runners, cook-boys and perhaps some local porters – more people than I had ever been responsible for in the past – twelve men and three tanks having been my biggest command in the army.

We considered the ways of sending our gear, having decided that the entire team could fly out to India. We chose the sea route but found the only reliable schedules are those of passenger liners. The only liner going out to India at the right time would be sailing too early for us to have ready the enormous amount of gear we should need. The only other possibility was a cargo ship and I booked the gear on to one sailing from Liverpool on the 23rd January. We were barely ready in time and many items we had had specially designed were still not finished.

Two days before sailing date I had a phone-call from the shipping agents: 'I'm afraid your boat has gone into dry-dock with engine trouble. It won't be ready to sail for another three weeks.'

'Isn't there another boat going out?' I asked.

'I'll try,' the shipping agent said, 'but I very much doubt it.'

I was on tenterhooks for the next twenty-four hours. We had quite enough against us on the mountain without this kind of delay. Then next day there was good news; he had found another boat which was sailing from London on the 23rd, the same date as the original boat.

A frantic dash to the docks to get all the gear loaded in time; more worries that there might be a dock strike or any of the dozen delays that seem to affect cargo ships, but it sailed on time – first stop Bombay.

I felt we had overcome the biggest problem of all. Nothing very much could now go wrong. Don and Dave would meet the ship in Bombay and have an uncomfortable trip across India on the backs of lorries, and we should be ready to tackle our mountain.

21 Annapurna: the Climb

As it happened our troubles were far from over. The boat carrying our five tons of gear – everything from kippers to bottles of oxygen – broke down in Cape Town, eventually arriving in Bombay a full month late. Fortunately, the RAF had flown out the absolutely vital equipment – radios, medical kit, together with enough clothing, ice axes, pitons and ropes to enable us to get started. We borrowed food from the British Army Expedition to the north side of Annapurna, and Jimmy Roberts lent us tents, ropes and sleeping bags left over from previous expeditions.

Don and Mike left Pokhara on the 16th March; there was little point in Don waiting in Bombay for the gear to arrive, as planned. There would be a month's delay, and I wanted him on the mountain. I asked Ian, therefore, if he would undertake the grim job of shepherding the gear through Customs when it arrived, and then across India. I decided to fly out to Bombay in order to help to smooth Ian's way, before going on with the rest of the team.

The setback with our equipment was then overshadowed by reassuring news from Don, who met us in a narrow gorge leading to the foot of the South Face.

'It looks even steeper than the photographs,' he said, 'but after I sat and looked at it for a couple of hours it seemed to fall back a bit. It's going to be hard, but it will go all right.'

And so our Base Camp was established, with such a magnificent view that for days afterwards our people tended to stop what they were doing, and stare and stare at the whole gigantic wall of the South Face. Big avalanches were coming down Annapurna on either side of our chosen route, but it seemed that none was crossing the line we planned to go up; the more we studied our route, the more we liked it.

In many ways the South Face of Annapurna was super Alpine – presenting both the problems and the atmosphere I had known in 1966 during the ascent of the Eiger Direct. On Annapurna our Kleine Scheidegg was Base Camp, situated on a grassy meadow beside the lateral moraine of the South Annapurna Glacier, with the South Face a mere three miles away framed by a ridge of Annapurna South on one side and the moraine on the other. All we needed were the trippers' telescopes and a better crop of tourists to be in business; but we did have a steady stream of visitors: a stray brigadier, hippies, climbers, earnest German tourists, Peace Corps people, and so on. The trickle that might well become a flood in years to come.

And then the way we tackled the South Face; once again very similar to the methods used on the winter ascent of the Eiger Direct. A continuous line of fixed ropes, climbers dashing back to base for a rest; a Base Camp that was in a different world from the face, with its TV team, a few girl visitors who had stayed; radio communications with the outside world.

Closer up, Annapurna looked by no means simple. Our way lay across the glacier and up a rognon, a sort of island of rocks round which the glacier flowed on either side. Here we established Camp I at 16,000 feet, pushing on towards Camp II at 17,500 feet at the foot of a protective, overhanging rock cliff. To reach this point involved a couple of 'objective dangers' – risks which have to be accepted if you climb in the Himalaya. These were both fields of séracs, areas where the slowly moving glacier passes over obstacles and breaks up into a series of ice ridges and pinnacles. From time to time the pinnacles collapse, usually without warning. The séracs, however, are passed in only a minute or two, and the risk is normally considered acceptable. It was on the higher of these two areas, weeks later, that Ian's luck ran out.

Don and Dougal reached the site of Camp III at 20,100 feet, halfway up the ice ridge, and with Base Camp growing every day and supplies flowing up the mountain, we could hardly believe the ease with which we had already climbed 6,000 feet of the South Face in nine days. Our complacency was short-lived.

It took a back-breaking, lung-bursting month to climb the next thousand feet, and we all agreed that it was as hard as anything we had ever done, with very little to show for each day's trail-blazing. This entailed climbing down to Camp IV at the end of each day, it being impossible to bivouac anywhere on the ridge, then a wearying climb up the fixed ropes to begin work again the next day. With this kind of leap-frog climbing, we estimated that we climbed thirty Annapurnas before finally reaching the top!

My overall plan was to have a pair out in front at any one time, forcing the route, with the rest of the team distributed between the camps below, ferrying up the mountain. Once the front pair tired I pulled them back for a rest at Base Camp before going back to the mountain; they would do some ferrying and then go once more to the front. We were already short of manpower in the lower camps, but we were able to recruit six of the best local porters for the carry from Base Camp to Camp I which, though across a glacier, was comparatively easy. These local Nepalese porters made a tremendous contribution to our eventual success.

Although frequent rests at Base Camp helped to keep members of the team climbing at a reasonable level of performance over the course of the expedition, it imposed a heavy strain on our available manpower. A pair resting at Base Camp would take three days to get back up to Camp III, four to Camp IV,

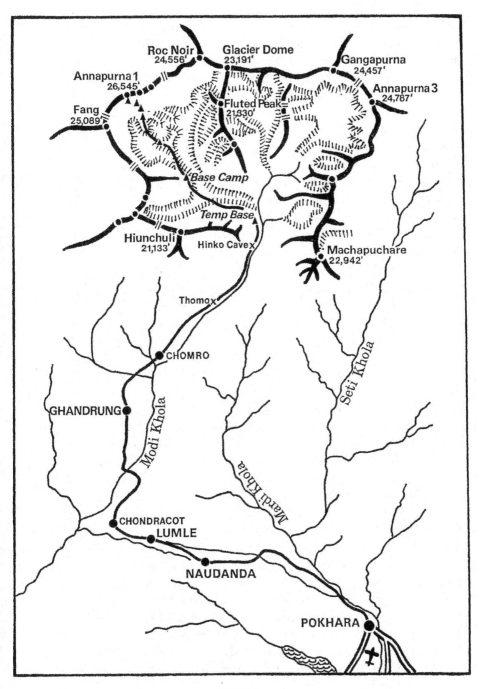

Annapurna

and so on. These were unproductive carries, for the climbers would probably have a fair amount of their personal gear with them, and therefore would be unable to carry much food or climbing gear while shifting from one camp to another. The most efficient system is to keep changes of camp down to the minimum, but this pays little heed to the psychological factor of the monotony of carrying day after day over the same stretch on a mountain, or the fact that the climbers out in front quickly burnt themselves out, so great was the physical and mental strain of tackling high-standard climbing at altitude.

Dougal and I finished the last pitch of the ice ridge in a snowstorm. Having run out of rope we cut steps in hard snow to the top of the ridge, propelled by curiosity about what we would find on top. The angle ahead of us did not seem too bad, was certainly easier than it had seemed in the binoculars from far below, but this inviting view did not extend very far. At the limit of vision, looming out of the snowstorm, was an ice cliff, about 200 feet high which seemingly cut off all further progress.

Although it is possible to climb ice cliffs, it is a slow, laborious job, screwing in ice-screws every few feet. In addition, an ice cliff at that altitude had never before been attempted and time before the monsoon was due was running short. The seeming impassability of the ice cliff was an unpleasant discovery, since we knew that above it was the 2,000-foot vertical rock band which we had decided all along would be the most difficult of the obstacles on the South Face.

Mick Burke led this part of the climb, from the start of the Rock Band. The method he used to fix rope in place was to climb on a 500-foot reel of nine-millimetre perlon, running out long pitches of up to 200 feet, then pulling the rope through till it was tight back to his second man, Tom Frost, fastening it off and letting Tom jumar up the rope behind him. In this way he was running out the fixed rope and climbing at the same time.

In three days they ran out 1,200 feet of rope, as much, in fact, as Boysen and Estcourt could keep ferrying to them. Eventually they took a rest from the face, when Burke dropped down to the dump at the top of the ice ridge to collect a load and Frost spent a day digging out the tent. We were now beginning to feel the strain of trying to keep open our communications. Ian Clough had been forced back for a rest but was now on his way back up the mountain. I was held down at Base Camp with an attack of pleurisy. Everyone on the face was badly run-down. We had already been using our local Gurkha porters, equipped with a variety of spare clothes and footwear, for the carry from Base Camp to Camp I. Some of these local porters were now doing the carry from Camps I to II, a fine achievement considering that they had never before been on a glacier. Various visitors to Base Camp also lent a hand. Two of them, Frank Johnson and Robin Terry, arrived on the 21st April and stayed for the rest of the expedition, ferrying loads as high as Camp IV. In doing this they gave us invaluable help. One of the TV team, Alan Hankinson, also rendered sterling service, carrying loads up to Camp III. This freed our Sherpas for work higher up the mountain and they were now keeping open the route from both Camps II to III, and III to IV; the latter run was considerably steeper than anything they had previously tackled.

On the evening of the 13 May, Tom and Mick were still at Camp V, immediately below the Rock Band at a height of 22,750 feet; Martin, Nick and Mike were in Camp IV, halfway up the ice ridge and Don and Dougal were at Camp III, on their way back up the mountain after a rest at Base Camp. Dave was with four Sherpas also at Camp III, having carried loads to Camp IV, while Ian, also on his way up, was at Camp I. From Base Camp, where I had not completely recovered from my attack of pleurisy, I opened up the wireless link.

'You're loud and clear, Chris,' replied Nick, at IV.

'How did things go today, Nick?'

'Not too bad. I was shattered from yesterday and took a rest, but Martin and Mike went up to V. Mike only reached the ice cliff, though, and was so buggered he had to turn back.'

'Don and Dougal will be moving up tomorrow,' I said.

'We're aware of that.'

'Well, I want them to move straight through to V, and go into the lead. Mick and Tom can then go down to the col at the end of the ridge to pick up loads while you three carry on up the col. Don and Dougal, being fresh, should be able to push on up the Rock Band that much more quickly! Hello, Camp V – did you hear that?'

It was Mick, at Camp V, who replied. 'I got that, Chris.' Then: 'As a matter of fact, I think you've got the wrong end of the stick, Chris. It's a lot easier going out in front than it is carrying. I don't see any point at all in Don and Dougal coming up here – it would be much better if they did some carrying first from IV to V. We've been above Base Camp for twenty-eight days. If we had to go back to carrying now we'd have to go all the way back down for a rest. We're just too knackered to carry.'

The argument went on. The crux of it was that I had originally agreed for climbers to take turns in leading out in front and in theory it was now the turn of Martin and Nick. Having been supporting Tom and Mick for a week, they had done the punishing carry from IV to V, a task so strenuous as to be almost impossible to do two days running. You needed a rest day in between, and at altitude you don't get back your reserves of strength – you are deteriorating the whole time – even when resting.

Nick admitted that he was going badly, although Martin was still climbing very strongly. On the other hand, I felt that Don and Dougal were the strongest pair and climbed superbly as a team.

'It's not that we mind Don and Dougal going through,' Nick said, 'but I don't think you have any concept of what it's like up here. Gear is piling up at IV much faster than we can shift it up the mountain. It'd be much better if we could concentrate for a few days on stockpiling Camp V before pushing Don and Dougal forward.'

I could see his point, but we were running out of time. I compromised. 'Let Don and Dougal do one carry and no more. Is that clear, Mick?' With Mick's agreement, the argument seemed settled, but then Don came on the air with the effect of a small nuclear weapon. 'I agree with everything you've said. Dougal and I left Camp V a week ago. It isn't even consolidated and progress towards Camp VI has been so poor it's had me and Dougal depressed all the way up the mountain. I don't know what Mick thinks he's playing at, but time's short and we want to get the route pushed out. Unless they can establish VI or at least find a way, they should make way for someone else.'

It was the closest we came to acrimonious argument during the entire expedition. I did my best to smooth it out, then closed down for the evening. As always, there was something to be said for both points of view.

Tom told me later that they were both so furious that Mick suggested taking all their rope and running it out next morning – just to show Don. They did, and this resulted in the most impressive push of the entire climb, with Tom and Mick reaching the Flat Iron, a spur of rock halfway up the Rock Band and very similar to the famous landmark in the middle of the North Wall of the Eiger. In getting this far, however, the two men burnt themselves out and the following morning they insisted on coming down for a rest. Mike, the great load carrier of the expedition, was also in a bad way, having collapsed just below Camp V but having recovered sufficiently to stagger back.

This meant that we were losing people from the front faster than I could replace them so I set out from Base Camp, still feeling run down after four days' rest. Meeting Mick Burke on his way down from Camp I, I reassured him when he said, 'Don't think we've come down out of spite – we just couldn't have gone on any longer.'

Mick had done magnificently, for together with Tom Frost he had spent longer above Base Camp than anyone else. I met Tom at Camp II the same day, when he told me: 'I think you have destroyed the spirit of this expedition by pushing Don and Dougal in front, out of their turn. It was a real stab in the back for Nick and Martin.'

Although I tried to explain equably that expediency on a big climb must sometimes overrule the principle of fair shares for all, privately I was appalled at how badly the people out in front seemed to have taken my decision.

There was trouble at Camp V, a grim spot in the direct path of all the powder-snow avalanches which poured off the Rock Band whenever it snowed. Don, Dougal, Martin and Nick were all there when, during the night, one tent was crushed by the build-up of snow. Martin and Nick could have been suffocated but for a small gap left at the top of the entrance. Nick was badly shaken by this experience; Martin, suddenly becoming sick, was forced to return to Base Camp.

With our strength running out fast, I pushed straight up to Camp V, Don and Dougal moving up to Camp VI with Nick carrying some rope for them. Unfortunately Dougal dropped the rucksack containing his down clothing, sleeping bag and food and, although Don tried to persuade him to sit out the night there with the stove going, Dougal, realising how cold it would be, returned to Camp V. It was about midday when Dougal returned and Don, who had by this time been without food for more than twenty-four hours, insisted on being fed before pushing on. Then they picked up a rope Nick had dumped about 400 feet below the Camp with the result that in the little time left they could do no more than round the corner of a buttress just above the tent, and look into a tantalising gully that seemed to lead all the way up to the top of the Rock Band.

Nick and I remained at Camp V.

At night most of us drugged ourselves with sleeping-pills. I found that two of them merely knocked me out from about 7 p.m. when we usually settled down for the night, there being nothing else to do, till two in the morning. From then on I used to doze intermittently, waiting for the dawn.

Most of our camps caught the early morning sun, but our Whillans Box at Camp V was tucked into the bergschrund below the Rock Band. A huge curl of ice, frighteningly reminiscent of the sword of Damocles, guarded us from spindrift avalanches, above – if it collapsed at least we should know nothing about it. After every snowfall it was necessary to dig the Box out; the reason why tents were useless was that the build-up of powder snow simply crushed them.

The interior of the Box was a nightmare rectangle, six-feet-four inches long, four-feet wide and four-feet high, with green, dreary walls, no windows and a zip entrance at one end which had to be kept closed most of the time to keep out the clouds of snow. The walls and ceiling were encrusted with ice which only melted when we were cooking on our gas-stove. Drips from the roof would then soak our sleeping bags – there was no way of drying them out.

Obviously there was no water at Camp V – just snow, which had to be melted. It takes about ten panfuls of powder snow and about an hour of cooking to produce one pan of lukewarm water. Mike Thompson, who had organised our food, had been determined to produce an interesting high-altitude diet. In the event it was a little too original. He had cut out such mundane ingredients as tea and coffee, replacing them with a variety of fruit drink cubes, all of which became equally detestable after a few weeks. We had a choice of hot cola, orange or grapefruit for the breakfast brew, followed by a tin of mixed grill or perhaps some kippers or herrings in white sauce. If you could face it there was then Pumpernickel – thin black wafers of compressed rye bread – a cheese spread and those little containers of jam such as you get on airliners. The jam was acceptable, but the Pumpernickel had too strong a flavour for altitude and we all longed for plain biscuits. The favourite breakfast food for all of us was instant porridge.

Cooking breakfast took about three hours – a single brew required more than an hour and you needed at least two brews before starting out: you are meant to drink seven pints a day at altitude to avoid dehydration.

As the Box is only big enough to take two people lying side by side, you cook breakfast without getting out of your sleeping bag. If you are untidy, as most of us were, the interior of the Box quickly becomes a sordid mess.

It is 5 a.m., the start of another day. Nick is still flat out, buried in his sleeping bag, only his nose sticking out. I light the stove, fill the pan with snow from immediately outside the door, being careful to take it from the right-hand side as we relieve ourselves during the night on the left (there is no question of going out of the tent – you just open up a corner of the entrance and shoot).

By the time we have cooked breakfast it is nearly nine o'clock. I delay departure, putting off the grim moment of climbing out of a warm sleeping bag to face another day of discomfort and hard graft. Ten o'clock – if I am to do that carry to Camp VII cannot stall any longer. Harness on, then the struggle to fit crampons on to boots – metal so cold that it sticks to your skin; straps frozen solid like wire hawsers. It takes fifteen minutes to put them on.

I dug out a 500-foot length of rope, and, with a walky-talky radio and a few Gaz cylinders, my load was around thirty-five pounds. This did not seem too heavy at first, but having carried it a few hundred feet I began to feel like a very weary Atlas carrying the world on my shoulders.

The route to Camp VI seemed endless. At that altitude it took an hour to cover fifty feet, slowly and laboriously. The last length of rope up on the Flat Iron was the most strenuous of all, taking two hours of lung-bursting effort to reach the top. From there, the crest of the Flat Iron curved in a sickle of snow for about 400 feet – an easy-going plod at ground level, but here, an agonising struggle. The tent was just visible at the top of the ridge – a tiny patch of blue, perched on a minute ledge.

Resting five minutes between each step, it was 5.30 that evening before I reached the top camp, and eight o'clock in the gathering dark before I returned to Camp V, where a worried Nick reheated some supper for me. That night I gulped down a concoction of powdered soup, tinned meat and sweetcorn, followed by Christmas pudding. Mike had collected our food just after Christmas and Christmas puddings were going cheap; so we had them cold, fried and even stewed!

Exhausted, the next day Nick and I stayed in the tent. It was a savage day with a bitter gusting wind and frequent snow showers. In spite of even worse weather at Camp VI Don and Dougal set out to force the route to the top of the Rock Band and managed to make 400 feet of progress.

It was the 22 May. Nick and I hoped to make the carry to Camp VI with the tent and camp kit which Dougal and Don hoped to pitch above the Rock Band. We decided to use oxygen sets to make the journey a little easier, in spite of the heavier load we should have to carry. Nick set off first, but I caught up with him at the top of the first fixed rope – he was hanging on it like a landed fish on a line.

'Sorry, Chris,' he said, 'I just won't make it. The oxygen doesn't seem to make any difference, even at full flow. I'll just have to go down.'

There it was. Both he and Martin had burnt themselves out in support of the front pairs and in doing this they had sacrificed all hope of going to the top. It also meant we had lost another load carrier, and everything we were trying to carry up to Camp VI that day was of vital importance. I took the food bag from Nick, adding it to the length of rope I was already carrying. With the oxygen set my load weighed forty pounds.

But the oxygen certainly made a difference. On reaching the last desperate jumar pitch up on to the top of the Flat Iron, I switched to maximum flow. I could feel the extra energy coursing through my body, and managed to climb this stretch in about half an hour, compared with the two hours I had taken without oxygen.

On reaching the tent Don and Dougal told me they had reached the top of the Rock Band that day. They had run out nearly a thousand feet of rope and had reached a point 200 feet below the top of the gully. It was on steep soft snow, but they had been so keen to get that precious view of the top that they had pressed on unroped.

Don said: 'It got us out on top of the Mini Rock Band and it looks a piece of duff to the top. Have you got the tent? We'll be able to establish Camp VII tomorrow.'

I had to confess I had brought up a rope in place of the tent, which Nick had taken down with him. Dougal suggested my moving up to Camp VI the next day, when I brought up the tent – I could then go with them to Camp VII and make the bid for the summit. Ian was due to come up to Camp V that evening and would be able to help make a good carry up to VI, so I accepted immediately.

That night I returned to Camp V full of optimism but was dashed to find it empty. It had been fine on the upper part of the mountain but had not stopped snowing all day on the lower. Ian had been unable to force his way up to Camp V because of the weight of new snow. Camp V was a macabre place to be alone, and the following morning, loaded with the tent, food, cine-camera and my own spare clothing I set off at about ten o'clock. I managed to get a hundred feet above the camp before I realised that I could never carry a load of at least sixty pounds all the way to Camp VI. It seemed to weigh tons.

Returning in complete despair, I felt tired and finished. There seemed no chance now of going to the summit with Don and Dougal and I even wondered whether I had the strength left to make another carry up to Camp VI. Feeling utterly helpless, I sat down and cried, then, ashamed of my weakness, shouted at the ice walls surrounding me, 'Get a grip on yourself, you bloody idiot.'

Leaving my personal gear behind, it was midday when I left Camp V with the tent and food, and I reached the top Camp at six. Ian was waiting for me when I returned to Camp V and I don't think I have ever been so glad to see anyone. I had been dreading another night by myself.

Once again on the radio we adjusted our plans. It was agreed that the following day, Don and Dougal should establish Camp VII, stay there that night and then make a bid for the summit. Ian and I were to move up to Camp VI and Mick and Tom from Camp IV to V. In this way we should be able to make three successive bids on successive days.

It seemed in the bag, though with the weather blowing even harder than usual that morning, Don wondered whether to play it safe and stay at Camp VI for the day. Yet he, like the rest of us, was impatient to finish the climb.

He decided to leave for the top of the Rock Band, while we at Camp V also had our doubts, but set out all the same.

That morning I had bad diarrhoea, an unpleasant complaint at altitude, and felt very weak – Ian and I only got away from the camp at eleven o'clock. Clouds of spindrift were blasting across the Face, blinding us with their violence, making movement almost impossible. Halfway up I had an irrepressible urge to relieve myself – I was in the middle of a gully swept by powder-snow avalanches. This was a tricky and exceedingly unpleasant operation. I was dangling on the fixed rope, and somehow I had to remove my harness, tie a makeshift one to my chest and bare my backside to the icy blast. And at that point a powder-snow avalanche came pouring down, filling my trousers, infiltrating up my back.

Eventually Ian and I reached Camp VI at five o'clock that afternoon, to find the tent semi-collapsed by the build-up of powder snow, and barely big enough for the two of us. Five minutes later we heard a shout from above – Don and Dougal had been forced to retreat through the most appalling weather conditions we had encountered. Their clothes were encased in ice and Don was sporting a pair of magnificently drooping moustachios formed of pure ice. They had hoped to pitch their tent on what had seemed to be an easy-angled slope just beyond the top of the fixed rope but, not only was it much steeper than it looked: when they tried to dig a platform they quickly came to hard ice.

There were now four of us in a two-man tent. I have had more than a hundred bivouacs in the mountains, but that night was the most uncomfortable of all, though Ian was the worst off, spending the night uncomplainingly crouched in a corner.

Next morning the weather was even worse, leaving no choice but for Ian and me to retreat to Camp IV to keep the fitter pair, Don and Dougal, supplied with food. For the next two days it snowed non-stop and we wondered whether the monsoon had arrived and if, so close to success, we were now to be cheated. Don and Dougal had told us that morning that they hoped to establish Camp VII, but it seemed unlikely in the face of the appalling weather conditions.

I opened up the radio at five o'clock and Dougal came on.

'Hello, Dougal, this is Chris at IV. Did you manage to get out of the tent today?'

'Aye, we've got some good news for you. We reached the top.'

Don told me the story the following day. They had reached the top of the fixed ropes but unable to find a suitable place for a campsite they plodded on up through the soft snow on the ridge. They had not bothered to put the rope on, and were not using oxygen, finding that in spite of the very strong wind, the climbing was quite easy It was twelve o'clock before they found a suitable site for Camp VII but by then they were just below the final headwall of the ridge and the summit seemed very close. As there was no point in having a top camp so high, they just kept plodding.

The climbing became more difficult, up steep snow-covered rocks, the last fifty feet vertical with big flat holds. Don said:

'Generally, I had done hardly any leading at all up to this point, but I felt completely confident, and it never occurred to me to use the rope.'

Once over the top of the ridge the wind immediately dropped and they found that the north side of the mountain was quite warm and pleasant with sun breaking through clouds. While waiting for Dougal to follow, Don looked around for the anchor point for the rope they would need to get back down.

The summit itself was a real knife-edge and there was not much to see from the top. The northern slope dropped away into the cloud, a great boulder field part-concealed by snow. The only tops visible were the other two summits of Annapurna; everything else, including the entire South Face, was blanketed in cloud.

Don said: 'We stayed there for about ten minutes. At this stage we didn't feel much in the way of elation – it was difficult to believe it was all over and anyway we still had to get back down.'

We had nearly completed our clearance of the mountain. Mick Burke and Tom Frost, forced back by the extreme cold, were now on their way down from the top Camp after their attempt to reach the summit as a second ascent of the South Face. We had been desperately worried about this attempt, since we knew that none of us had the strength to go to their help if they got into any kind of trouble. On the other hand, it seemed only fair and right that I should let them go – not only because their plea to go to the top had been so strong, but because they had their own right to taste the ultimate satisfaction of standing on top of that mountain to which they had given so much while making our successful ascent possible. Nevertheless, until the news came that they had turned back and were on their way down, I had spent twenty-four hours of sheer agony. I had a tremendous sense of relief – nothing could possibly go wrong now.

I had been waiting at Camp III for this news, with Mike Thompson, Ian Clough and Dave Lambert, and so I set off down, back to Base Camp, to start wading through the mass of paperwork which the end of the expedition, and our success, inevitably entailed. The following morning, while sitting typing out the report of the successful end of our venture, I could hear Kelvin giving out the news over the radio. Suddenly there was a pounding of footsteps and Mike Thompson, panting, hurrying, came dashing up to the tent with the cry, 'Chris – where is he – where is he? Something terrible's happened!' His voice was raucous, frightening, and immediately I knew – we all knew – that some ghastly tragedy had occurred. Rushing out of the tent I found Mike leaning over his ice axe, having just collapsed on to the ground. I remember going down on one knee and holding his shoulders while he sobbed out the story of what had happened.

> They were on the way down – Mike, Dave Lambert and Ian – and had reached the last possible dangerous section of our climb – the line of séracs which we had to pass under. It was an area which we had always known to be dangerous, but we had accepted the risk because we were only in this danger area for a few minutes. Mike described hearing a sudden, tremendous rumble from above. He looked back and saw this great tower of ice crashing down. Ian was just in front of Mike, who turned round and, with a split-second decision, ran back into the line of the avalanche. As he dived under the low wall to the sérac which was immediately above them, the ice avalanche came crashing over them. Mike just remembered lying there in complete darkness as the ice thundered down, convinced that he was going to die, and cursing the bitter futility of it. Then it all stopped and there was complete silence.

He found himself covered over in ice crystals as he pulled himself out to look for Ian. But Ian had not got back in time – he had been caught in the full force of the avalanche and had been swept down to his death. Down below, there had been a group of Sherpas coming back to pick up some loads from

Camp II. Miraculously they had not been engulfed by the avalanche, and for a few minutes they all stood stunned with the shock, before starting to hunt through the debris. They finally found Ian's body – he must have been killed outright.

And so, suddenly, in that moment of joyous victory, this tragedy had struck us. We had lost a close friend and one of the kindest, least personally motivated people that I have ever known. Ian spent much of his time repairing fixed ropes or giving the Sherpas that little bit of help and instruction. I think he was genuinely loved by the Sherpas and he was certainly the one person in the team for whom no one ever had a bad word. It seemed bitterly ironic that the person in the team who was, perhaps, the most safety-conscious should have been caught out by this cruel act of fate.

We took Ian's body down to Base Camp and we buried him in sight of the mountain he had given so much to climb. It was Tukte Sherpa, our cook, who suggested the burial place. We had been looking round for a suitable place – a place which would be above any floods, and where Ian's body could rest securely and safely. Tukte pointed to a little knoll, immediately below a rocky slab where Ian had spent many of his rest periods, teaching the Sherpas the various techniques they would need for their safety on the mountain. Tukte said, 'This would be a good place for him to lie.' We dug the grave and all the Sherpas – even the porters who had come up to help carry our gear – were scattered all over the hillside, picking the short blue alpine flowers to make wreaths. And then we carried Ian's body up to the grave. Standing there at its foot, I tried to say something that was remotely adequate, and at the same time to control my own emotion; and all I could say was, 'He was a fine mountaineer and a very safe one – but most important of all, he was the kindest, the most unselfish and, I think, the most universally-liked person that I have ever known.'

After this Tom Frost said a short Mormon prayer, while I think most of us were either crying or doing our best to hold back the tears.

Inevitably, the question arises – 'Was it worth it?' Was a successful climb worth a man's life – especially a man who was a close friend, who left a wife and a young child? But this is a question which has got to be faced and answered by all of us who climb, or base our lives round the mountains, because Ian's accident could have happened to any member of the team – could happen to any one of us, anywhere in our climbing lives – in Britain – in the Alps or the further ranges of the earth. This was brought home even more forcibly, because just before Ian's tragic death, we had received the news that Tom Patey, one of my closest friends, and certainly the richest, most wonderful personality that the mountains had produced since the war, had died in one of those inexplicable abseiling accidents – in this case on a sea-stack on the north coast of Scotland. His tragedy and that of his wife Betty, and his children, was as great as that of Ian, and all of us who go climbing must realise that we, also, could be killed by an accident over which we seem to have very little control. It is a cruel and difficult responsibility, particularly when we have wives and children whom we love. But once the mountains have bitten into us, we know, and the wives who love us know, that we could never give them up. All we can do is to try to be as careful as we possibly can, and pray that luck will remain with us.

22 What Next?

The grass of the lower moraines was a lush green and alpine flowers in pink, white and purple could be glimpsed from amongst their long blades. The rock was warm to the touch, the air balmy; and we were walking away from Annapurna, whose South Face had held the focus of our strength, effort and expectation for these last eight weeks. There was a strange mixture of exultation and sorrow; an exultation born from the closeness of unity that we, as an expedition, had achieved, and sorrow at the death of Ian Clough, a death which seemed the more cruel because it had occurred at the very last moment of possible danger, when he was on his way down after the final victory.

Before Annapurna, Jimmy Roberts and Norman Dyhrenfurth, joint leaders of the proposed International Everest Expedition, had invited me to join them as climbing leader of their face party. At first it had seemed too good an opportunity to miss, but on the way back from the mountain I realised, with increasing force, that I could not go through with another major expedition the following spring. Annapurna South Face had drained my reserves of nervous energy. The responsibility and the work involved in the organisation, the leading of the expedition on the mountain, and now the prospect of closing it down and writing the expedition book, had been like a long, unending marathon. I knew instinctively that I needed at least a year to recover my equilibrium and rebuild any enthusiasm for the expedition game. I do not think Ian's death affected my decision. However great the sorrow at the loss of a close friend, I realised that this is the price you must be prepared to pay if you go climbing; you minimise risk where possible, calculate the odds and turn back if the odds seem to be against you. But sometimes, however careful you are, and Ian had been the most careful of climbers, the fact that you have spent long periods exposed to risk can catch up with you.

On our return to Kathmandu, I broke the news to Jimmy Roberts of my withdrawal from the International Everest Expedition; Jimmy runs a trekking business there. He took my decision wonderfully well and was very sympathetic. He had already decided to invite Don Whillans and Dougal Haston to join the expedition, and the three of them began planning the next year's trip, talking with the Japanese climbers who were on their way back from an unsuccessful attempt on the South-West Face of Everest. They had made a reconnaissance in the autumn of 1969, reaching a height of 26,000 feet on the face, just below the rock wall that stretches across it barring the way to the summit rocks. That spring they had failed to reach a point as high as on their autumn reconnaissance. The face had been unusually bare of snow and as a result had been swept by stone-fall. They had had difficulty in finding ledges for their camps and finally had abandoned the attempt in favour of ensuring at least a limited success, by putting the first Japanese on the summit of Everest by the South Col route.

At this point I felt no regrets about my decision to withdraw from the expedition; I just wanted to get home to Wendy, get the book written and close down our own expedition. But by the time I had reached England a few doubts began to crystallise – had I turned down the opportunity of a lifetime? These doubts came to a head when Jimmy Roberts, on a short holiday in England, came to ask my advice about equipment for the expedition. It was too much! Impulsively, I asked him if he would have me back in the team; he accepted immediately and a few days later I had a warm, friendly letter from Norman Dyhrenfurth, welcoming me aboard. But in that period I had taken yet another back flip. My change of mind had been dictated on emotional grounds, of not wanting to be left out – but now, having decided to rejoin the expedition, I began to think again of all that it implied.

The job of climbing leader could be an invidious one. I hadn't chosen the team, wondered what level of loyalty climbers from France, Austria, Germany and the United States would feel to someone they knew only by reputation. I was so involved in getting *Annapurna South Face* written that I could have done little or no work for the expedition in the preparatory stage. I found myself wondering how effectively it would be possible to take over a position of responsibility on the climb itself, having contributed nothing to the preparations, and knowing very little about the equipment which was going to be used. Another very real worry was the financial backing of the expedition. Norman Dyhrenfurth and Jimmy Roberts had taken a very courageous step in launching a massive and very expensive expedition without any kind of sponsor to back them if they failed to raise sufficient funds. On Annapurna I had had none of these worries, since we had been fully backed by the Mount Everest Foundation. As a member of the International Expedition, however, I felt that I would have a financial responsibility towards it, but very little control over whether the expedition went into the red. Obviously, I was going to become heavily involved in fund-raising for the expedition, since Dyhrenfurth, at that stage, was having considerable trouble with the finances.

Perhaps all this sounds a long way from the simple romance of climbing a mountain. I know that it was something which did not worry either Don or Dougal – they simply wanted to go and climb Everest, and were probably fortunate in that no one expected them to become involved in the organisation of the expedition. Because of the experience I had gained in the field of journalism and in expedition organisation, it was inevitable that I should become more heavily involved. The more I examined it, the more frightened I became of that involvement.

Obviously, there were going to be problems in making the team cohesive on the expedition itself. There would be problems in raising the money, in getting the equipment together for a team scattered throughout the world, and I was tired from a year of such exceedingly exacting, nerve-racking work. I rocked back and forth for three days, tossing the conflicting motives and problems from side to side, and then I finally decided – I could not face the prospect of another big, complicated expedition. I resigned yet again.

In the midst of all this indecision I was under heavy pressure, anyway, while writing *Annapurna South Face*. I have no doubt at all that, had I not gone to Annapurna, I would have stayed in the International Everest Expedition, even though I, as did many of the other members, foresaw many of the problems which were likely to arise.

But still I had not escaped from Everest. Some weeks after my withdrawal, the BBC, who had bought television and feature rights in the expedition, approached me to go out as their reporter. There is no doubt that this was a magnificent professional opportunity for me, in my role as photojournalist, yet I felt I could not take it. My reasons, I suspect, were part egotistical, part genuine worry about the structure of the expedition and, over all, a total mental fatigue. Having just finished writing the story of one expedition – how on earth could I summon the fresh enthusiasm needed to write about another?

On the egotistical level, I had known the satisfaction of having the ultimate responsibility; it would have been difficult to have gone back to being an observer and, in the final analysis, it would have been difficult for me to have accepted the role of climbing leader, even though I respected both Jimmy Roberts and Norman Dyhrenfurth.

As the new year of 1971 came in, my own book finished, my batteries of energy recharged, I began to have many doubts about my withdrawal from the expedition. I became insufferable to live with, as I reproached myself over and over again for what seemed a failure to snatch the opportunity which had been offered.

I followed the fortunes of the expedition with mixed emotions, and have to confess I was even almost relieved that my own fears were proved justified. The South-West Face remained unclimbed. By this time I had resolved to try to organise an expedition of my own; the first problem, however, was to gain permission for the climb, and the mountain was fully booked for the next five years. Dr Karl Herrligkoffer, a German climber who had led a series of highly controversial expeditions to Nanga Parbat, had permission to attempt the Face in the spring of 1972. He had already invited Dougal Haston and Don

Whillans to join his expedition. He also invited Jimmy Roberts, who declined the invitation.

It was rumoured that the Japanese had permission to try the Face next, if Herrligkoffer failed, and so that summer of 1971 it seemed very unlikely that I should ever get the chance of going for the South-West Face of Everest. Then, in the autumn of 1971, I received a letter from Dougal. He told me that Herrligkoffer wanted to increase the size of the British team, mainly as a means of tapping more funds, since he was having trouble in raising sufficient money in Germany. Dougal, having suggested my name to Herrligkoffer, asked me if I would like to join them.

At this stage I was trying to organise a small expedition with Joe Brown, Hamish McInnes, Martin Boysen, Paul Nunn and Will Barker, to the Trango Tower, a magnificent granite monolith in the Baltoro Glacier. From photographs it looked like the Old Man of Hoy, but was ten times as big. This would have been a perfect expedition, with magnificent rock-climbing and none of the problems associated with altitude (for it was only 20,000 feet high). With a small party of friends there would have been few worries about personality conflict. Our only problem was in getting permission from the Pakistan Government. When Dougal invited me to join the Herrligkoffer expedition there still seemed to be a chance that we might get permission for the Trango Tower, and so I declined his invitation with very few regrets: Herrligkoffer's expedition seemed to be fraught with even more pitfalls than those of the International Everest Expedition.

But we did not gain permission for the Trango Tower. I was in a vacuum once again and could not resist the temptation of writing to Herrligkoffer to ask whether I could accept his invitation after all. He agreed to my joining as one of the four British members. Don and Dougal were already in the team so that left one more representative from this country to be invited. I phoned Don to find out whom he thought should join us, and was gratified that, in his own mind, he had settled on the same person that I had mentally selected – Doug Scott. Doug was a climber who had always been on the outside of the mainstream British climbing scene but who, in the last few years, had completed a large number of very impressive new routes in north-west Scotland. He was essentially an innovator, having adapted himself to the American style of Big Wall climbing, being one of the Britons to have climbed successfully in Yosemite. He also had behind him a long record of small expeditions to out-of-the-way places. A school teacher by profession, he had devoted himself to climbing to a degree equalled by very few people I know. His powerful physique and big set of lungs are attributes useful for any Everest climber.

Back in the Everest stakes, the more I learned about Herrligkoffer's arrangements the less happy I became. It was now January 1972, but he did not yet appear to have any oxygen equipment at all, seemed to have made few arrangements in Nepal and, above all, was unbelievably secretive about his plans and organisation.

I had resolved that I would avoid getting involved in the preparations for the expedition and therefore went off to Chamonix to climb with Dougal. We were going to attempt a new route on the North Face of the Grandes Jorasses. We spent twelve days on the face – twelve glorious days, when the problems of life were reduced to a few feet of ice in front of our noses, trying to hack a platform for a bivouac in ice that was frozen as hard as the rocks it covered, of trying to survive the fury of a winter storm. We did not get up, but it didn't seem to matter – the experience had been well worthwhile, for we had had twelve days of real climbing, uncluttered by politics and commercial pressures. During this climb, I have a feeling that both of us, separately, without discussing it, had decided to withdraw from the Herrligkoffer expedition. And so, once again I was out of Everest!

I was, nevertheless, still trying to get permission to attempt the South-West Face. It seemed unlikely that Herrligkoffer could possibly succeed. From what I had gathered, his gear was inadequate, he had postponed engaging his Sherpas to the last minute, and there seemed to be all the risks of a bi-national expedition which could be even greater than in an international one. With two clearly divided groups, each loyal to themselves, rather than the concept of the expedition as a whole, there seemed to be small chance of success.

And so I continued to manoeuvre for a chance of going to Everest. I received an immense amount of help from Mike Cheney, Jimmy Roberts' assistant, who kept his ear close to the ground in Kathmandu, and acted as my representative.

At last, a chance began to materialise. An Italian millionaire, Signor Monzino, had permission for an autumn reconnaissance in 1972 to be followed by a spring attempt in 1973. Owing to sickness he gave up his autumn slot. Mike Cheney informed me, and I applied for it immediately. There followed months of waiting – we still did not have permission from the Nepalese authorities – Herrligkoffer might still climb the South-West Face. Even if he failed, I could not help worrying about our prospects for raising, in the seven or eight weeks before our departure, the £60,000 I estimated the expedition would cost, at the same time as assembling all the gear and food.

On top of this were the problems of the autumn season. No expedition had succeeded in climbing Everest during the post-monsoon period, although two have tried and failed, beaten by the appalling winds and the cold which is experienced during the autumn.

The entire prospect seemed too far-fetched, but then I conceived a compromise solution. Why not have a mini-expedition to Everest – just four climbers and a few Sherpas? It was an exciting, refreshing prospect. In addition, it would be comparatively easy to organise and would not demand a vast budget.

I asked Dougal Haston, Mick Burke and Nick Estcourt whether they would like to come along, and they all agreed. It became obvious that we should need some support and so I asked Peter Steele, who had been a member of the International Expedition, to come along as doctor, together with Mike Thompson to be our Base Camp Manager.

The expedition was planned before we learned of the failure of Herrligkoffer's expedition. I heard the news in late May – and then the temptation built up. The South-West Face was still unclimbed!

It is not an aesthetically pleasing problem, hasn't the uncompromising yet tenuous line of ice arête and rock spurs that led to the summit of the South Face of Annapurna, which made that such a fascinating route. The South-West Face seemed a problem of brutal logistics – could you get all the oxygen, food and gear you needed to the foot of the Rock Band at a height of over 27,000 feet – higher than most of the other mountains in the Himalaya. Having got it there, would the climbers be able to keep going – climbing in the autumn cold, on steep ice and rock?

This was a real challenge. It was also one to which, in the last eight years, I suspect I have slowly built up – in climbing, in working as a photojournalist and, finally, in organising and leading the Annapurna South Face Expedition.

I find a fascination in putting an expedition together, in encouraging a group of climbers, all of whom are friends and whose friendship I value, to coalesce into a single team. I am challenged by the struggle with my own personality and its shortcomings. I cannot claim to be the perfect leader; cannot claim to be unselfish; I made mistakes on Annapurna, was perhaps impulsive at times, perhaps allowed myself to be swayed by others at the wrong times. I shall probably make mistakes on Everest, because everyone is fallible. The challenge lies in learning from these mistakes.

In organising a big expedition to Annapurna or to Everest, one sometimes loses the stark simplicity and romanticism of mountaineering, becoming involved in the maze of finance, public relations, commercial exploitation. Yet there is a fascination in this – at least there is to me. This also is a game – to be played as a game. It is serious; it is exacting. There are more pitfalls than on any mountain, but surmounting these pitfalls has its own special thrill and challenge. And in the end you come back to the mountain.

I have written these last few words in the hours before flying to Everest to attempt its South-West Face. We might or might not succeed; this certainly will be the greatest challenge of my life so far. But whatever the outcome, I know that the mountains will always fill a vital part of my life; that my quest will be for the next horizon.

The Paine Expedition: standing L.–R.: Vic Bray, Derek Walker, Chris Bonington, our two cooks loaned by the Chilean Army. sitting L.–R. John Streatley, Barrie Page, Don Whillans, Ian Clough.

Barrie Page looks out of the box shelter which Don Whillans and Vic Bray designed – the prototype of the Whillans Box on Annapurna – the only shelter that could stand up to the high wind in Patagonia.

Our first home in the Lakes at Loughrigg Tarn – one room above a garage.

Woodland Hall Lodge and our trusty Minivan.

Bonington on *Fool's Paradise*, Gowder Crag, Borrowdale – one of the best routes in Borrowdale.

Mick Burke.

Joe Brown near the top of the Old Man of Hoy.

Martin Boysen.

First ascent of *The Medlar*.

Left: Coronation Street: the route.
Photo: John Cleare, Mountain Camera.

Below left: Haston and Harlin after
being trapped by storm in a snow hole.

Below: John Harlin.

Top right: Dougal finds his way
out to the top in the storm.

Below right: Sangay in eruption.

Below: Suave, sartorial Sebastian
before Sangay.

An unusual view of the Old Man of Hoy.

Above: Hoy: Tom Patey climbing the fixed rope up the *Difficult Crack.*

Left: The Huskies sleep while the igloo is being made.

Below: The end of the journey: Blashford-Snell in command with flags flying.

Right: Annapurna from Base Camp: Whillans' box in foreground.

Below: Annapurna: looking across the Difficult Traverse on the
ce ridge.

The Annapurna team.

Chris and Wendy Bonington with Daniel and Rupert.
Photo: Liverpool Echo.

Acknowledgements

I owe a great deal to all the people who appear by name in these pages, in many instances for their forbearance. I owe my special thanks to John Anstey, Editor of the *Daily Telegraph* Magazine, who showed confidence in my ability to produce photographs and to write. He started me on a new stage of my life as adventure journalist; to George Greenfield, my Literary Agent, who has done a great deal more than negotiate contracts, and has been my adviser and friend over the two most important expeditions in my life so far; to Livia Gollancz for her editorial advice and her patience in waiting for a book which was finished literally in the last hours before flying out to Kathmandu, en route for Everest; to Betty Prentice, who typed the manuscript, corrected the spelling and improved my grammar; to my mother, who thought of the title and lastly, and most of all, to Wendy for her love and her courage through these years and, on a more immediate level, for her selection and layout of the pictures.

C.B.

About the author

Born in 1934, Chris Bonington – mountaineer, writer, photographer and lecturer – started climbing at the age of sixteen in 1951. It has been his passion ever since. He made the first British ascent of the North Face of the Eiger and led the expedition that made the first ascent of the South Face of Annapurna, the biggest and most difficult climb in the Himalaya at the time. He went on to lead the expedition that made the first ascent of the South-West Face of Everest in 1975 and then reached the summit of Everest himself in 1985 with a Norwegian expedition. He has written seventeen books, fronted numerous television programmes and has lectured to the public and corporate audiences all over the world. He received a knighthood in 1996 for services to mountaineering, was president of the Council for National Parks for eight years, and is the Non Executive Chairman of Berghaus and a Chancellor of Lancaster University.

Printed in the USA
CPSIA information can be obtained
at www.ICGtesting.com
JSHW012014140824
68134JS00025B/2419